COVID Lockdown Insanity

The COVID Deaths It Prevented,
the Depression and Suicides It Caused,
What We Should Have Done, and
What It Shows We Could Do Now to Address
Real Crises

by Hugh McTavish, Ph.D.

**WEST
FORK
PRESS**

West Fork Press
Published by West Fork Press
7460 Pinehurst Road,
Saint Paul, MN 55115 USA

Print ISBN: 978-1-7373271-1-0

This book is dedicated to the children and young people of the world, who have been hurt the most by the lockdowns, for no benefit to themselves, and, in the case of children, entirely without their consent.

Table of Contents

Introduction:

Our response to COVID has surprised, fascinated, and appalled me from the beginning. It seemed obvious to me from the beginning that we were vastly overreacting to this and doing more harm than good. For a moment in the spring of 2020, I doubted my position, thinking, basically, "Every country in the world is reacting to this with lockdowns. The health departments in almost every country in the world are in favor of lockdowns. What are the odds I am right and practically every other expert in the world is wrong?" But it turns out I was right. And it turns out I was not the only expert who thought at the beginning that this was a vast overreaction; it is just that the media did not present them and allow them to express their point of view, just as the tech giants and the news media would do to me.

I also knew COVID was not trivial and that I and everyone was likely to contract it and that there was a small possibility, maybe 1 in 1,000, that I would die from it at my age. My main fear from that was not that I might die, but that if I did people would laugh at me and mock me because I had been outspoken in saying we had overreacted to COVID.

The heart of this book is an examination of the evidence of, first, how many COVID deaths has the lockdown strategy prevented and, second, how much harm has it done, mostly not in economic terms but in human terms, including increasing suicides, drug overdose deaths, and clinical depression. It is shocking to me that the U.S. Centers for Disease Control and Prevention (CDC) and our government officials have never estimated or made any claims of how many COVID infections and COVID deaths the lockdown strategy has prevented, let alone any estimate of how much harm lockdowns have done. It is treated as if we had no choice: We had to close schools, issue stay-at-home orders, order mask wearing, close restaurants, close churches, etc. And since we had no choice, supposedly, I guess we are supposed to think it is pointless and heartless toward the elderly and the 550,000 who have died of COVID-19 in the U.S. to ask whether and to what extent the lockdown strategy worked, i.e., how many COVID deaths did it prevent? Oh well, call me heartless, but I will ask anyway.

When you have terminal cancer and your doctor gives you the option to take chemotherapy, I think it is perfectly reasonable to ask whether it would do any good and how much additional time of life it will get you. In fact, of course, it would be malpractice for your doctor not to give you an estimate of how much time of life chemotherapy would give you, even if you did not ask. In a like manner, we should ask, and our leaders and experts should have asked also and told us, how many COVID deaths would be prevented by the lockdowns, and now that we are a year into this, how many COVID deaths the lockdowns have prevented.

Likewise, when you have terminal cancer and your doctor suggests the option of chemotherapy, you should ask, and your doctor should tell you, how unpleasant the chemotherapy will be and what the side effects will be. For the lockdowns, we should ask and our leaders and experts should have told us what the harms of the lockdowns would be, and now that we are a year into this, what those harms have been.

Our leaders have not answered those questions, so I will. In this book, I ask, Can we quantify the harms of lockdowns and compare the harms to the benefits of COVID deaths prevented to determine whether the lockdowns were worth it? Did the lockdowns cause more harm than benefit? Seem like reasonable questions to ask.

First, I should say that I have bent over backward in this book and in my writings to lean toward overestimating the lethality of COVID and the benefits of our lockdown strategy and to be conservative in my calculations and leaning toward underestimating the harms of the lockdown strategy. I do not want to leave myself open to criticism that I am exaggerating. I do not need to exaggerate. All the facts and data are on my side.

The first part of this book is a human benefit-harm analysis where I estimate how many COVID deaths the lockdowns may be preventing and how that balances against the harms the lockdowns have caused. This analysis is in human terms, rather than dollar terms; it is in terms of lost happiness and other harms and lost and gained time of life from preventing COVID deaths and causing other deaths.

Then we analyze the economic harm of the lockdown strategy and how that is borne by the poor, middle class, and the rich.

Part 2 calculates the overall risk of death from COVID-19, the risk of death if you are infected with the virus (the infection fatality rate), the age-specific risk of death from COVID-19, and how that compares to the current risk of death from all causes and risk of death from ordinary influenza.

It is shocking and appalling to me that the CDC has never given either an official or even unofficial estimate of the infection fatality rate of COVID-19. What percentage of infected people die of COVID and how does that vary by age and health condition? This allows anyone to evaluate their risk and make an informed decision of whether and how to modify their behavior. It is the first question each of us was asking about this, and the CDC should have answered it.

Part 3 looks at the evidence of how COVID infection is transmitted and the effectiveness of the interventions we have tried, including mask wearing, closing schools, and hand washing, in reducing transmission. Based on that and the harms of our overall lockdown strategy and of each specific strategy, I recommend what we should have done.

Part 4 is miscellaneous observations on various political and public policy issues, including emergency powers of governors, how the courts have treated those emergency powers and the restrictions on our freedoms, how the public has accepted the restrictions, and my surprise at some of that. It looks at how the tech giants and media companies have responded to the lockdowns and their censorship, which I think is not too strong a word, of voices that have criticized the lockdowns. It also looks at who is and is not to blame for the lockdown disaster, and who has behaved well and who has behaved badly. Part 4 also looks at various conspiracy theories (or I should probably say alternative theories since they do not necessarily involve a conspiracy) about COVID and the lockdowns and the evidence for and against some of those conspiracy theories.

Part 5 compares the severity of COVID in deaths and lost time of life to other epidemics of the past, including smallpox, the Black Death, AIDS, and the 1918 flu, and to the current leading causes of death of cancer, heart disease, suicide, and drug overdose, and to Vietnam and 9/11. The purpose is not to say COVID-19 was not bad—it was—but to put it in perspective. I found those calculations and comparisons very interesting.

Part 5 also compares the lost time of life and human damage caused by the lockdowns—not by COVID but by the lockdowns—to the lost time of life and human damage from the Vietnam War, which many would consider the worst public policy disaster of recent times for the

U.S., at least until the lockdowns.

Part 6 has my philosophical musings on what the lockdown response to COVID suggests about humans and our values, particularly our views toward our mortality and toward whether time is precious or not.

Part 7 is perhaps my favorite part. Our societal response to COVID shows we are willing and able to remake society on a dime and bear enormous sacrifices in response to a crisis. That is the one piece of good news to come out of the lockdowns. It expands the horizon of what is politically feasible enormously. So with the optimism that anything is possible, we can brainstorm what we can and should do to address our most pressing problems, especially environmental problems, that are quite a bit more serious than COVID ever was. And part 7 asks, If the goal of our public policy were happiness for the greatest number, instead of preventing death for a few more years for elderly sick people as it seems it is during the lockdowns, or instead of increasing GDP and in particular increasing wealth and income for the richest and most powerful individuals and corporations, as I heretofore thought was the primary goal of the U.S. government, what should we do? In other words, What is the primary goal of life: happiness, money, or a long life? I choose happiness. If that is the goal, what should our policies be?

So you know where I am coming from, I am a scientist—I have a Ph.D. in biochemistry and my latest papers have been in immunology. I invented a drug that boosts the immune system to prevent cold sore outbreaks in people with frequent outbreaks, and started a company around that drug. So I consider myself an immunologist. I like playing with numbers, and in this project I have found I like playing with numbers and statistics even more than I realized. And I am a Democrat and consider myself a liberal, although a lot of my views are not doctrinaire liberal. It is stated that "we are following the science" with the lockdown strategy (although as I will elaborate that is a big lie) and most Democrats support the lockdown strategy. So you might think I am an outlier in my views. In reality, at least among scientists, I am hardly alone in opposing lockdowns. The Great Barrington Declaration, for instance, is a declaration signed by over 14,000 epidemiologists, immunologists, and other scientists, over 42,000 medical practitioners, and almost a million citizens, opposing the lockdowns.

I have had the strange feeling during this time of pandemic and lockdowns of being a stranger in my own country. I have been surprised about so many things in this response and have often felt like the little boy in the "Emperor Has No Clothes" story: The media is saying, and everyone around me seems to believe, that this lockdown response was necessary and beneficial and the Emperor is wearing a beautiful suit as he parades through town. I have been standing there saying, "Huh? He's buck naked!"

Part 1
Quantifying the Benefits and Harms of the Lockdown Strategy

Chapter 1

Comparison to Sweden Suggests COVID Lockdowns Did Not Prevent Any COVID Deaths at All

First, we would like to know how much our societal lockdown response to COVID has reduced COVID deaths. We ordered everyone to stay at home for 51 days in Minnesota and a comparable time in most states. We shut down restaurants, bars, health clubs, and numerous other non-essential businesses for about three months. The governor of Minnesota ordered all churches closed for about three months. We closed the schools and universities for most of a semester, and most schools and universities are still partially or fully closed to in-person instruction and apparently will remain so for all of this school year. We have eliminated handshakes and hugs. We are told to keep 6 feet from one another and wear masks in public even when more than 6 feet from others. That is a lot of sacrifice. How much did it help?

Ideally for a perfect scientific study we would want a comparison of an identical society that simply ignored COVID and then see how much of a difference in COVID deaths there is between the two societies. Of course that is not possible, but there are a few countries that did not employ lockdowns that we could use for comparison, including Japan, South Korea, Taiwan, Singapore, Iceland, and Sweden. The closest comparison in that group is Sweden. It is a Western country like the U.S., with a northern climate, like most of the U.S., and a democracy with a tradition of freedoms that resembles the U.S., and it is less isolated than Iceland and has a much larger population than Iceland, closer to that of the U.S.

Here is a table of our response to COVID compared to Sweden's:

	U.S.	Sweden
Stay-at-home orders	Yes	No
Closed restaurants and bars	Yes	No
Closed churches	Yes	No
Closed health clubs	Yes	Briefly
Closed non-essential businesses	Yes	No
Closed schools	Yes	No
Closed universities	Yes	Briefly
Mandated masks in public	Yes	No
% Urban	83%	88%
COVID deaths per million population (as of Nov. 25, 2020)*	833	671

*Death numbers are from Worldometer.com/coronavirus

Sweden had almost no mandatory restrictions. They did not close schools and did not even allow parents to keep their children out of school. They briefly closed health clubs and universities, but soon reversed those restrictions.

Sweden did not even mandate mask wearing. They just recommended mask wearing and only recommended it if you were in an indoor space where you could not keep 3 feet from others. In the U.S., we have mandated mask wearing indoors and suggested keeping 6 feet, rather than 3 feet, from others even when wearing masks. Some localities have even mandated mask wearing outdoors! Sweden's approach to masks is actually consistent with World Health Organization's (WHO) guidance.

Based on all that, you would assume Sweden has a higher death rate from COVID, right? No, they actually have a lower death rate per million population than the U.S.—671 in Sweden vs. 833 in the U.S. as of November 25, 2020. Sweden's death rate per capita is also lower than that of most of the large countries in Europe, including the U.K., France, Italy, Spain, and Switzerland, but higher than Germany. Now, some might say, "Yes, but Sweden is a rural country; that is why they have a low COVID death rate." Unfortunately for that argument, Sweden is a more urbanized nation than the U.S.

In fairness, Sweden's per capita COVID death rate is also quite a bit higher than its closest Scandinavian neighbors Norway, Finland, and Denmark. But it should also be noted that none of those countries used the full lockdown approach either. Norway closed schools and gyms in the spring of 2020 initially, but reopened schools in April 2020 and has kept them open in the fall of 2020, and Norway never closed restaurants and bars if they could maintain 3 feet of social distance (*Financial Times*). Denmark and Finland took a similar approach. None of them ever issued stay-at-home orders for the entire population, as we did almost everywhere in the U.S.

It should also be noted that Sweden—which again has a lower COVID death rate than the U.S.—has the highest death rate of any nation that did not use the lockdown approach and never closed schools or businesses. Japan, South Korea, Taiwan, Singapore, and Iceland all have COVID death rates that are 10% or less that of the U.S. Sweden is the only one that is even close to the rate in the U.S. or other major Western countries that used the lockdown approach.

So from the comparison to Sweden and the other countries that did not use the lockdown approach of stay-at-home orders and closing schools, restaurants, and businesses to fight COVID, one would conclude that the lockdown approach did not prevent *any* COVID deaths at all and may have increased COVID deaths.

References:

1. *Financial Times*. https://www.ft.com/content/daf20d07-738f-4640-8a4a-d6de3e1e4c37)

Chapter 2

COVID Dead Have Median Life Expectancy Had They Not Contracted COVID of Less Than 1 Year and an Average Life Expectancy of About 4 Years

How much remaining life span do the people dying of COVID have? To know how much good our COVID restrictions have accomplished, we would like to know, not only how many COVID deaths the restrictions have prevented, but also how much longer the COVID dead would have lived if they had not contracted COVID.

I have said in conversations with people about COVID that we are all going to die someday, and often people get offended when I say that. But I do not mean to be offensive and I am not being flippant. We really are all going to die someday, and someday is probably sooner than we like to think. Most great religions and spiritual traditions teach that an awareness of our mortality and the fact we will die is one of the most important, if not *the* most important, lesson we need to learn to live an ethical and happy and grateful life. The Buddhists have a tradition of meditating on your own mortality and imagining yourself as a rotting corpse. Jesus said, "Leave the dead to bury the dead."

So again, how long would the people dying of COVID have lived if they had not contracted COVID?, and when we prevent a COVID death, how many years of life is that saving? The information in the top three rows of this table is relevant to that calculation and the bottom three rows present my conclusions.

Characteristics of Persons Dying of COVID (in Minnesota)

Long term care	70%
Age 80+	60%
Age 60+	92%
Pre-existing conditions	99%

Median life expectancy	< 1 year
Average life expectancy considering health condition and age.	about 4 years
Average life expectancy considering only their age (1)	11.7 years

The COVID dead are not only old and sick relative to the population as a whole, they are actually somewhat older and sicker than people who die as a whole. For the overall dead, 99% do not have a pre-existing serious health condition. For the overall dead in the U.S., only 80% are age 60 and up, whereas 92% of the COVID dead are. I cannot find what percentage of the U.S. who die (from all causes) were living in long-term care facilities when they died, but I'm sure it is not 70%.

From their age alone, a paper in the *Proceedings of the National Academy of Sciences* (USA) (PNAS) calculated the COVID dead have 11.7 years of life expectancy remaining at the time of their deaths, on average (Goldstein et al.). But that did not consider their health, and it is clear that people dying of COVID are in much worse health than average for their age. For one thing, 99% of them have at least one serious pre-existing condition. Secondly, the fact that they died of COVID shows they were in worse health than average for their age, since at every age the large majority of infected people survive COVID and it stands to reason that those who survive COVID were in better health on average, and therefore had a longer actual life expectancy, than those of the same age who die from it. Even in the age 85+ group in the U.S., I will calculate in a later chapter that the COVID infection fatality rate (IFR) is 9%. No one would dispute that the 91% of age 85+ who survive COVID infection were in better health (on average, although not in every case) prior to COVID infection, and therefore had a longer actual life expectancy, than the 9% who die of it. Likewise for every other age group.

In Minnesota, 70% of the COVID dead lived in a long-term care facility. A study in Sweden found that the median life expectancy of the long-term care COVID dead is 5 to 9 months (Stern et al.). The median length of stay in a nursing home in the U.S. is 5 months until death and the average is 13.4 months (Kelly et al.). If the average stay from entry is 13.4 months, the average for a current resident should be about half that or 7 months. It should be noted that the term "long term care facility" is broader than nursing homes; it includes assisted living facilities and hospices as well. The assisted living residents would have a longer life expectancy than nursing home residents, and hospice patients would have a shorter life expectancy. But still, it appears that the long term care residents dying of COVID have a median life expectancy of certainly less than a year and probably about 7 months. The average or mean is longer than the median, but the average for long term care residents who die of COVID is also almost certainly less than a year. (To refresh your memory, "median" is the value where 50% of the numbers are higher and 50% are lower, whereas the average is the sum of all individual values divided by the number of individual values. In this series—1, 2, 3, 4, and 20—the median is 3 but the average is 6.)

The median person dying of COVID in Minnesota is an 84-year-old male living in a long-term care facility with serious preexisting conditions who is sicker than the average 84-year-old man living in a long-term care facility (again, because those who die of COVID are sicker than those of the same age who survive it). So that person has a life expectancy of less than a year in reality, considering his health, whereas the average 84-year old has a life expectancy of 6 years. The actual life expectancy considering his health, therefore, is less than 20% of his age-based life expectancy.

The *PNAS* article (Goldstein et al.) calculates the average age-based life expectancy of the COVID dead as 11.7 years. But their actual life expectancy considering their health is certainly much less than that. It is not possible to precisely calculate that, but when 50% of the COVID dead had a life expectancy of less than a year and the median person dying of COVID had a life expectancy considering his health status that is less than 20% of that considering only his age, I estimate the average life expectancy of the COVID dead, had they not been infected with the SARS-CoV-2 virus (the coronavirus that causes COVID-19), as about 4 years or one-third of their age-based life expectancy.

References

1. Goldstein JR, Lee RD. 2020. Demographic perspectives on the mortality of COVID-19 and other epidemics. *Proc. Natl. Acad. Sci USA* September 8, 2020 117 (36) 22035-22041; first published August 20, 2020; https://doi.org/10.1073/pnas.2006392117

2. Kelly A. et al. 2010. Length of Stay for Older Adults Residing in Nursing Homes at the End of Life. *J. Am. Geriatrics Soc.* 58:1701-1706. https://doi.org/10.1111/j.1532-5415.2010.03005.x

3. Stern C and Klein DB. 2020. *Society.* 2020 Jul 19 : 1–12. https://doi.org/10.1007/s12115-020-00508-0

Chapter 3
....
COVID Policies May Have Averted
200,000 COVID Deaths in U.S.

Based on the comparison to Sweden and other countries that did not use a lockdown strategy to combat COVID, it may be that our lockdown strategy of issuing stay-at-home orders, mandating mask wearing, closing schools, closing churches, and closing restaurants and other businesses did not reduce COVID deaths at all. The lockdown strategy may have been no more effective in reducing COVID deaths than an alternative strategy of

- simply informing people of their risk based on their age and health status,
- informing people of the measures they could take to reduce their own risk, and
- letting them modify their behavior as they see fit, with no mandatory restrictions at all.

But logically the lockdowns must have reduced infections and reduced COVID deaths somewhat. That was presumably the intent of the strategy. So how much might the U.S. strategy have reduced COVID deaths?

First, to estimate how many deaths our strategy might have prevented, we need to know what percentage of the population has been infected and then the infection fatality rate (IFR), or percentage of infected people who die. We know how many people have died of COVID, the numerator of that fraction, but we do not know as accurately how many people have been infected, the denominator.

To determine how many people have been infected, the best method is to conduct a seroprevalence survey, collecting blood from, ideally, a random sample of the population and assaying the blood or plasma for antibodies against the SARS-CoV-2 virus. The assumption is that if anyone has been infected, he or she will have raised antibodies to the virus and the antibodies will be detectable months or years later.

The best COVID seroprevalence study I am aware of in the U.S. involved collecting plasma from dialysis patients nationwide in early July 2020 and testing over 20,000 of them for COVID antibodies (Anand et al.). The result was that 8.0% of the samples were positive for COVID antibodies, and after adjusting from the age, demographics, and zip codes of the patients to the age, demographics, and zip codes of the U.S. as a whole the researchers arrived at a conclusion that 9.3% of the U.S. population had been infected as of early July 2020 (Anand et al.).

It takes about 10 days after infection to develop antibodies, so I consider that to be the infection rate as of July 1. It takes about 2 weeks after infection, on average, for people to die of COVID if they die from it. So to calculate the IFR I am using deaths as of July 15 to compare to the infections as of July 1. On July 15, 2020, we had 140,775 COVID deaths in the U.S., which, if 9.3% of the population of 328 million was infected as of July 1, gives an IFR of 0.46%.

That 0.46% IFR should be viewed as probably an upper estimate of the IFR in the spring wave of COVID because the data from Anand et al. is more likely to underestimate the infected population than overestimate it for two reasons. First, we know many infected people never raise detectable antibodies (Burgess et al.) and, second, one would expect dialysis patients, since they are rather sick, to be more careful to try to avoid COVID infection than most people and therefore to have a lower infection rate than the general population. Also, other researchers have calculated a 0.2% IFR in Los Angeles county (Sood et al.).

We had 140,775 COVID deaths as of July 15, 2020, and we have 574,025 as of April 8, 2021. If the fatality rate per infected person has remained constant in that time at 0.46%, as of April 8, 2021, 37.9% of the U.S. population has been infected (it is a 4.08-fold increase in deaths and if we multiply 9.3% x 4.08 the result is 37.9%).

In fact, we know the fatality rate has been lower in the fall-winter wave than it was in the spring wave of 2020. In New York city in the spring, 27% of hospitalized COVID patients died; now only 3% do. For Minnesota I calculate from the state health department numbers 36.3% of hospitalized COVID patients before July 15 died, and since then it has been 21.9%. Also 3.9% of laboratory-confirmed cases in Minnesota died before July 15 versus 0.93% since then. The reasons COVID is getting less deadly is, first, the medical community is learning what treatments work and what do not, and has some new treatment tools, including serum of recovered patients and monoclonal antibodies, and second, the virus is mutating to forms that are at least slightly less lethal. From an evolutionary standpoint, the virus does not care whether it kills us; it just wants to spread. So it has an evolutionary interest in becoming more contagious but none in becoming more lethal; and we know the mutant forms that are becoming more common are more contagious but at least a little less lethal.

So the IFR was 0.46%, or perhaps a bit less, in the spring 2020 wave and less since then. Overall, 0.40% is a reasonable estimate. Using the 0.46% IFR, in April 2021 we have 37.9% of the U.S. population already infected. If the IFR is 0.40%, it is 43.8% of the population infected as of April 8, 2021.

The percentage of the U.S. population that has been infected by SARS-CoV-2, the virus that causes COVID-19, up to April 2021 is about 40%. The most our strategy could possibly have achieved is prevent the other 60% of the population from being infected. Obviously that is not the case, and if it were it would mean we will have no cases or deaths going forward. In fact, if our strategy were able to stop all infections we would have never had an epidemic. A fairly generous estimate would be that the lockdown strategy has prevented and will prevent about 15% of the population from being infected, almost half as many as have already been infected, which would prevent 200,000 deaths. (15% of the U.S. population is 49 million people. If the infection fatality rate is 0.40%, preventing 49 million infections prevents 197,000 deaths.)

How many COVID deaths is it possible the lockdowns prevented?

Another way of looking at this is to ask, If we were at herd immunity in the U.S., how many COVID deaths would we have? The worst we could have done if we had not done lockdowns is to get to herd immunity.

R is the average number of people an infected person transmits the infection to, for any contagious disease. R_0 is the special case of R at time zero when the population is naïve and every person the infected person encounters is non-immune. For COVID-19 and SARS-CoV-2 infection, R_0 was estimated as 2 to 4. As more people become infected and immune, R drops over time. Also R is dependent on human behavior as well as the biology of the virus, and the point of the lockdowns and physical interventions like masks, hand washing, and social distancing is to reduce R. When R falls below 1.0, meaning the average person infects fewer than one new person, the epidemic dies out (although you can still get some new cases) and you have reached herd immunity. It is estimated for COVID-19 that we need to have 70%, or at most 80%, of the population infected to get to herd immunity. (If R_0 is 4, then in principle if 3 out of 4 people are already immune, then R has fallen by 4-fold from R_0 of 4 to a current R of 1.0. By that calculation, if R_0 for COVID was 4, which was the highest estimate, then you need 3 of 4 or 75% of the population infected to get to herd immunity.) The U.S. population is 328 million; 70% of that would be 230 million and 80% would be 262 million.

I calculated above that the infection fatality rate (IFR), or percent of infected people who die, was 0.46% in the spring wave and somewhat lower than that in the fall-winter wave. Overall it has been about 0.40%.

0.40% of 230 million would be 920,000, and 0.40% of 262 million would be 1,049,000. In other words, if the U.S. were at herd immunity, the epidemic would be over, and we would have about 1.0 million COVID deaths. Instead we are at 574,025 as of April 8, 2021, and the University of Washington Model predicts we will be at 600,000 on June 1, 2021, with almost no deaths after that (and the only deaths past that point being persons who chose to not be vaccinated and accept the risk, as is their right).

So the most COVID deaths the lockdowns could possibly have prevented is 400,000 (the difference between the 1.0 million deaths we would have, were we at herd immunity, and the 600,000 we actually will have before we have vaccinated everyone at risk who wants to be vaccinated).

Yet another way of looking at this is to look at the worst COVID death rates in the world and consider that the worst we could have done in the absence of lockdowns is to be there. Among nations with populations of 1 million or more, the most COVID deaths per million population is Czechia at 2,575. Among U.S. states, the most are New Jersey at 2,790 and New York at 2,631. (As of April 8, 2021.) So no nation or U.S. state will get to 3,000 deaths per million. If the U.S. were at 3,000 deaths per million population, that would be 984,000 COVID deaths, again very close to 1.0 million.

So from two angles we reach the same conclusion that 1.0 million total COVID deaths, or 400,000 more than we will actually get, is the worst we could have possibly done if we had not done lockdowns. Therefore, the most COVID deaths the lockdowns could possibly have prevented in the U.S. is 400,000.

Conclusion:

The most COVID deaths the lockdowns could possibly have prevented in the U.S. is 400,000.

The Sweden comparison suggests the lockdowns may not have actually prevented any COVID deaths at all. (And as we will see in a later chapter, all the evidence indicates that is about right.)

A generous but not unreasonable estimate would be that the lockdowns have prevented 200,000 COVID deaths in the U.S., which also happens to be half as many as the most they could possibly have prevented.

References

1. Anand S. et al. 2020. Prevalence of SARS-CoV-2 antibodies in a large nationwide sample of patients on dialysis in the USA: a cross-sectional study. *The Lancet* 396: 1335-1344. Published: September 25, 2020. https://doi.org/10.1016/S0140-6736(20)32009-2.

2. Burgess S. et al. 2020. Are we underestimating seroprevalence of SARS-CoV-2? *BMJ 2020; 370* (Published 03 September 2020) https://doi.org/10.1136/bmj.m3364

3. Sood N et al. 2020. Seroprevalance of SARS-CoV-2-specific antibodies among adults in Los Angeles County, California in April 10-11, 2020. *JAMA* 2020; 323:2425-27. https://jamanetwork.com/journals/jama/fullarticle/2766367

Chapter 4

....

Time of Life Saved by the Lockdowns.
200,000 COVID Deaths Averted Equals Less Than 1 Day
of Life Span Extension Per Person.
Has Living This Way for a Year Been Worth it to You to
Add 1 Day to Your Life?

The estimate that the lockdowns have prevented 200,000 deaths and prevented infection of 15% of the U.S. population does not fit the data because if our strategy had prevented that many cases and deaths, then our death rate should be about a third less than that of Sweden's instead of being more than Sweden's. But let's say it did.

If we are averting 200,000 COVID deaths, how many person-years of life did that save? I estimated in Chapter 2 that the average life expectancy of the COVID dead, had they not contracted COVID, considering both their age and their health condition, is 4 years. If our strategy has saved 200,000 lives from COVID death, then with an average life expectancy lost of 4 years, saving 200,000 lives would mean 800,0000 person-years of life in the U.S. That is a lot. But with a population of 328 million (dividing 800,000 person-years into 328 million persons) that works out to 0.0024 years of life extended on average, or 0.9 days. And that is not 0.9 days in your 20s; that is 0.9 days at the end of your life in poor health.

If you believe the lockdowns prevented us from getting to herd immunity, then they prevented 400,000 COVID deaths and added 1.8 days to each of our lives on average. Do you want to claim that the average life expectancy lost is 12 years rather than 4 years? OK, that is not true when you consider the pre-existing health status of people who die of COVID, but if it were true, then our strategy has saved 2.7 days of life on average. Do you want to claim both that our strategy prevented us from getting to herd immunity and that the COVID dead were not in worse health than average for their age? Then our strategy has still only saved 5.4 days of life on average.

But the reality is that all the sacrifices we have made have added less than 1 day per person of life expectancy. I calculate 0.9 days even with a generous estimate of how many lives have been saved that is close to a worst case scenario of what might have happened if we had ignored COVID. Does anyone think it has been worth living the way we have lived for more than a year to add 1 day to our lives? I certainly don't. I wouldn't even be willing to give up handshakes and hugs for a year to add one day to my life, let alone all the other sacrifices we have made.

Now, some will say, "Well, you are not making these sacrifices for yourself; you are making them for others, for the elderly who are at risk of death." I would respond, Your life is just as valuable as anyone else's. You are just as worthy of love and consideration as anyone else. The Bible says, "Love your neighbor *as* yourself," not "*instead* of yourself." The proper way to analyze this ethically is to ask, "Would you be willing to make these sacrifices for your own benefit, to extend your own life?"

Second, some will say, "Well, you are hoping to add 1 year, or 4 years, or occasionally 20 years to someone's life by preventing a COVID death." OK, then the question to ask is not "Would you make these sacrifices to add less than 1 day to your life?," but "Would you make these sacrifices for a 1/400 chance of adding 1 year to your life or a 1/1,600 chance of adding 4 years to your life." It is the same calculation and phrasing it that way with probabilities just confuses the issue. The better way to phrase the question is simply: Would you be willing to make these sacrifices, to live the way we have lived for over one year, to add 0.9 days to your life?

Would you? Do you think it has been worth it to live this way for a year to add less than a day to your life?

Note on claims COVID cost us one year of life expectancy:

I'm sure it is a shock to readers to hear that the COVID deaths prevented by the lockdowns represent time of life saved of less than one day per person in the population, or even only 5.4 days if you assume that without the lockdowns we would be at herd immunity by now and you ignore the fact that people dying of COVID are sicker than average for their age. You may have heard estimates that COVID has cost us about a year of life expectancy (Andrasfay et al). How can both those numbers be right?

The answer is in how life expectancy is calculated. Life expectancy is calculated with life tables that give the percentage of people in the population of each age who die in a year. About 0.3% of babies die before their first birthday. Then let's say in 2018, 0.1% of 1-year-olds died, 0.11% of 2-year-olds, etc., up to 15% of 85-year-olds and 30% of 99-year-olds. To calculate life expectancy you multiply a person's likelihood of survival at each year of age of life to get an average age at death. And the quoted life expectancy in the U.S. in 2018 meant life expectancy for a *baby* born in 2018, assuming the then odds of dying each year at a given age in 2018 remained the same for that baby for the next 100 years or so. For 2020, the odds of dying at each age, especially at elderly ages, increased due to COVID. The statistical life expectancy for a baby born in 2020 assumes implicitly that those death rates stay constant for the duration of that baby's life of maybe 100 years. *The calculation assumes we will still have COVID in 80 years and it will kill just as many 80-year-olds 80 years from now as it killed in 2020.* That, of course, is wrong (and would have been wrong even without development of a vaccine). It is statistically true that life expectancy in 2020 decreased by about a year due to COVID, but that does not mean the average person will die one year earlier because of COVID. It only means in the hypothetical world where COVID deaths stay the same forever and being infected with COVID and surviving does not mean you are immune, so that you are likely to be infected again next year and might die from it then, that would reduce your life expectancy by about 1 year. There is nothing dishonest about the calculation, but it is kind of a statistical trick.

The more accurate and meaningful calculation is that COVID killing 600,000 Americans over 2020-2021, with an average life expectancy had they not contracted COVID of 4 years, cost the U.S. population 2.4 million person-years of life (600,000 deaths times 4 years of life lost per death = 2.4 million person-years), which, divided into our population of 328 million persons, is 0.0073 years or 2.7 days of life per person in the population. And if the lockdowns prevented 200,000 COVID deaths, they saved 0.9 days of life on average, as calculated above, or prevented that 2.7 days from being 3.6 days.

The calculations and results of Andrasfay et al. that COVID-19 in 2020 resulted in a decrease in life expectancy at birth of 1.13 years are roughly consistent with my calculations. They estimate without COVID in 2020 the life expectancy at birth would have been 78.61 and with it, 77.48. Again, that change in life expectancy only applies in the hypothetical world where being infected with COVID does not make you immune to it and we never develop a vaccine, so a baby born today would be as likely to die of COVID 80 years from now, if she is still alive, as an 80-year-old was in 2020. So it is a proportional cost. It is paid every year of her life. Spread over 78 years, those 1.13 years (412 days) means they estimate COVID cost 5.28 days of life per person in 2020. It is in the same neighborhood as my estimate above that it cost us 2.7 days over the entire epidemic of 2020-2021 (with 1.6 of those days in 2020 and 0.9 days in 2021). The difference is I considered life expectancy at death of the COVID dead to have been 4 years on average, allowing for their being sicker than average for their age, and Andrasfay et al. did not make that adjustment, considering it to be 12 years.

The idea that COVID-19 in 2020 resulted in a decrease in life expectancy at birth of 1.13 years I think actually proves my point and poses roughly the same question I asked of whether these sacrifices for the past year were worth it to you to gain 0.9 days of life. The 1-year life expectancy loss means if COVID raged every year for the next century at the same toll it exacted in 2020, a baby born in 2020 would have a 77 year life expectancy instead of 78. That does not seem like the end of the world to me. I would rather be born into a nation with a 78 year life expectancy than one with a 77 year life expectancy, but I would hardly consider it a tragedy to be born into the world with a 77 year life expectancy. And that is not the reality of what a baby born in 2020 is born into. She had no chance of dying from COVID in 2020 or 2021 and never will again. But let's say hypothetically that she will face COVID every year of her life and it will cost her 1 year of life expectancy. Do you think it would be worth it to her to live the way we have lived this year for her entire life in a desperate attempt to get back that 1 year of life expectancy—to never attend school in person, never attend church in person, never have a large wedding, not be able to invite friends to her parents' funerals when they die, to wear a mask in public for her entire life, and to spend two months of each year locked in her house and forbidden from going out for nonessential tasks?

References:

1. Andrasfay T, Goldman N. Reductions in 2020. US life expectancy due to COVID-19 and the disproportionate impact on the Black and Latino populations. *Proceedings of the National Academy of Sciences*, 2021; 118 (5): e2014746118. https://doi.org/10.1073/pnas.2014746118

Chapter 5

Do Happiness and Quality of Life Matter?
Depression and the Lockdowns

Our lockdown response to COVID may have prevented a large number of COVID deaths. We all hope it has. But it unquestionably has inflicted enormous harms on us. The biggest harm, in my view, is that it has made us all more unhappy and thrown many of us into clinical depression. How many were thrown into depression? Ettman et al. found these increases in the percentage of the U.S. population with depression symptoms:

Depression category	% of U.S. pre-COVID	% of U.S. during COVID	Increase during COVID
Severe	0.7%	5.1%	4.4%
Moderately Severe	2.1%	7.9%	5.8%
Moderate	5.7%	14.8%	9.1%
Sum of Major Depression	**8.5%**	**27.8%**	**19.3%**
Mild	16.2%	24.6%	8.4%

Summing the severe, moderately severe, and moderate increases, we threw 19.3% of the population into moderate to severe depression because of our response to COVID (not because of COVID, but because of our response to COVID). Moderate to severe depression is classified as major depression. So we threw 19.3% of the U.S. population or 63.3 million people into major depression.

I estimated in Chapter 3 that the lockdown response might have prevented 200,000 COVID deaths. We had in the U.S. in 2020 COVID deaths of 354,380. So we have thrown 178 people into major depression for each COVID death in 2020 and 316 people into major depression for each 1 COVID death our policies may have averted. That is just the depression caused in the spring of 2020. Presumably some different people became depressed later, so this certainly understates the amount of depression caused by the lockdowns. And the estimate of 200,000 COVID deaths prevented by the lockdowns is generous and probably too high, as we will see in Chapter 23, so it is probably an overestimate. Essentially all of that increase in depression is because of our response to COVID, not because of COVID. Grief at the deaths of loved ones, especially when those loved ones are elderly and sick, as the large majority of COVID dead are, is not a major cause of depression. And in any case, deaths have only increased about 10% in 2020, so even if death of loved ones were the sole cause of depression in our society, it would only have caused a 10% increase in depression, not a 327% increase, as has happened.

People become depressed basically because of a lack of social contact—a lack of friends and a lack of feeling connected to others or appreciated and loved by others. Our COVID policy was to *deliberately isolate everyone from each other*: order everyone to stay home, close restaurants, bars, churches, health clubs, schools, and businesses, and for the businesses that remained open order everyone to work from home if possible. And order everyone to wear masks so we cannot see each other's faces. The policy was literally to reduce contact with other human beings as much as possible and, for the contact that cannot be prevented, order people to wear masks so they cannot see each other's faces. If you wanted a policy deliberately designed to make people unhappy, you could not have come up with a better policy. (Note 1.)

It is as if our leaders have no familiarity with human beings and what makes them happy or what makes life valuable! Social connection is the source of nearly all of our happiness.

Again, we threw 316 people into major depression for every 1 person whose COVID death we might have prevented. Was that worth it?

It is comparing apples and oranges so initially we might not be certain whether it is worth it to throw 316 people into major depression to save one life. Certainly we would think it was worth it to make one person unhappy for awhile, or even depressed, in order to save one other person's life. Is there a way we can compare depression to death or lives saved?

Yes, I think there is. Depression can be viewed as a lost time of life. If you could just go to sleep or be temporarily dead while you are depressed and wake up when it is over, you may well take that deal. If a depressed person believes his depression will never lift, he is in fact quite likely to kill himself. He is likely to prefer death to living with depression. Think about it this way: Would you rather now, at whatever age you are now, suffer major depression for the next 12 months or would you rather at the end of your life, whenever that will be, die 12 months earlier than you are otherwise going to die? I think it is not an easy choice, which shows it is fair to consider depression as lost time of life.

I presented this idea of depression as lost time of life to a friend and she said, "No, it is worse than death. Death is oblivion; depression is pain." So again, I think it is fair to consider time spent depressed as lost time of life, which means it can be compared to the time of life extended or saved when we prevent a COVID death.

In Chapters 2 and 3 I estimated that our lockdown response to COVID may be averting as many as 200,000 COVID deaths, and that the people dying of COVID have on average 4 years of life expectancy remaining, if they had not contracted the virus that causes COVID.

- 200,000 COVID deaths averted times 4 years life expectancy = 800,000 person-years of life saved.

The average episode of major depression lasts for 20 weeks or 0.38 years (Solomon et al.).

- 63.3 million people thrown into major depression times 0.38 years = 24 million person-years of life lost = 30 times the person-years of life saved in COVID deaths averted!

It should be noted, the depression number is not an estimate. It is actual measured increase in depression that has already happened and is continuing to happen.* In fact, it is a minimum. It is just the increased

---

* In fact, it is low because it was the depression measured in April 2020. Those people presumably suffered depression for 20 weeks on average. But the lockdowns did not stop causing depression in the spring. More depression was undoubtedly caused by the lockdowns and restrictions throughout the rest of 2020 and in 2021.

Undoubtedly many of the people depressed in the spring of 2020 continued to be depressed in the fall and winter of 2020-2021 as the lockdowns continued, and other people not depressed in the spring became depressed. So conservatively I think we should multiply these depression numbers by one-and-a-half to get 36 million person-years of life lost to major depression caused by the lockdowns in the U.S., which is 45 times the person-years of life saved in COVID deaths averted and 15 times the person-years of life lost to COVID deaths over the entire epidemic.

depression in the spring of 2020. You could add as much as an equal
amount of increased depression in the fall and winter of 2020-2021.

The number of COVID deaths prevented is an estimate, but I think
it is a generous estimate and more likely to be an overestimate than
underestimate. Even if it were a 2-fold underestimate and the COVID
lockdowns prevented 400,000 COVID deaths, which is the most they
possibly could have prevented because that would put us at herd immunity as explained in Chapter 3, we would still be causing a minimum of 15 times as much loss of life in time spent in depression as
person-years of life saved in COVID deaths averted.

Person-years of life lost or saved by our COVID response

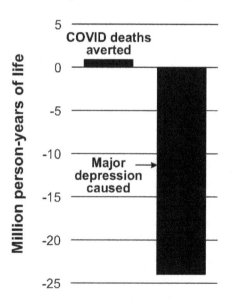

Look at that figure. The debate should be over. Was our COVID
lockdown response worth it? Did it do more good than harm? Of course
it was not worth it! Of course it did more harm than good! It's not even
close. It is not even debatable. The only way you can conclude that our
COVID response was worth it is if you consider depression, happiness,
joy, and quality of life as of absolutely no consequence. The only way is
if you say, "I don't care about quality of life. I don't care about happiness and joy. The only thing that matters is duration of life. The only

thing that matters is how long you live." If that is your attitude, then perhaps you can consider our lockdown response to COVID to have been worth it and good policy. Otherwise, no, you cannot.

Note 1:

Well, a couple of other ideas came to mind when I tried to imagine what else you could do if your goal was to make people as unhappy as possible: You could bar them from owning dogs or other pets and you could bar them from exercising. Aside from being emotionally connected to other people, the other major contributors to happiness are owning a pet, especially a dog (in other words loving and being loved by a person who happens not to be human), and exercising. And we sort of have tried to prevent exercising: We closed the health clubs. Regarding pets, I have seen stories asking whether dogs and cats are carriers of COVID, as though, if they were, we should get rid of them.

It is an interesting thought experiment. Imagine you are an evil dictator whose goal is to maximize unhappiness as much as possible, but you do not want to do anything obviously evil, like kill everyone's first born. What would you do? I think you would do pretty much what we have done with COVID lockdowns. But try the thought experiment yourself.

References

1. Ettman CK et al. 2020. Prevalence of Depression Symptoms in US Adults Before and During the COVID-19 Pandemic. *JAMA Netw Open*. 2020;3(9):e2019686. https://doi.org/10.1001/jamanetworkopen.2020.19686.

   Similar results were found by the Colorado School of Public Health: https://www.cpr.org/2020/05/05/colorado-survey-finds-heightened-rates-of-depression-anxiety-and-stress-during-pandemic/

2. Solomon DA et al. Predicting recovery from episodes of major depression. 2008. *J Affect Disord*. 107(1-3): 285–291. https://doi.org/10.1016/j.jad.2007.09.001

Chapter 6

Do Suicides Matter or Only COVID Deaths? Suicides and Deaths of Despair Caused by the Lockdowns

Even if happiness and quality of life do not matter to you and all you care about is duration of life, COVID policies have probably caused loss of more than three times as many person-years of life in increased suicides and other deaths of despair (drug and alcohol deaths) as they are saving in averted COVID deaths.

Our lockdown response to COVID-19 has produced unprecedented social isolation and loneliness, unprecedented levels of clinical depression, and unemployment for 16% of U.S. workers. Those factors all lead to deaths of despair, defined as deaths due to suicides and drug and alcohol misuse. By our COVID response we are trying to reduce deaths due to COVID, but we knew, or should have known, that the response would cause other deaths. In other words, to be blunt, we decided to kill some people by driving them to suicide and drug and alcohol overdose in order to try to save others from COVID death. Was it worth it? Are we killing fewer people than we are saving?

The Well Being Trust, a nonprofit devoted to promoting mental, social, and spiritual health, estimated that our response to COVID will cause 27,644 to 154,000 excess deaths of despair, with a midpoint estimate of 68,000 (Reference 1). This was based solely on the unemployment from our COVID response, because there was good previous research showing that a 1% increase in unemployment causes a certain number of increased suicides and deaths of despair. The estimate of 68,000 did not include the effect of the unprecedented social isolation from closing churches, restaurants, bars, and health clubs and mandated mask wearing that makes it harder to meet and emotionally connect with others. My guess would be those factors would cause more deaths of despair than the unemployment alone, so it is very likely the 68,000 estimate is an underestimate.

We have to use estimates since we do not know how many people have died from suicides or drug or alcohol overdoses during the pandemic because the CDC and the state health departments, although they tell us literally every day how many people died of COVID in the previous day, have not told us yet how many died of suicide even for 2019. You can make of that what you will. It suggests to me that they consider deaths from COVID to be of much greater consequence than deaths from suicide.

For 2018 though, there were 67,386 drug overdose deaths, 48,344 suicides, and over 95,000 alcohol-caused deaths, of which over 40,000 were classified as "100% alcohol attributable" (References 2, 3, 4). That is a total of 210,000 deaths of despair per year, or 155,000 if you exclude indirect alcohol-related deaths such as liver cancer and cirrhosis of the liver. Taking the lower 155,000 figure, an increase of 68,000 would require an increase of only 22% per year for two years. I find it hard to believe that we will not have at least a 22% increase in suicides and other deaths of despair for 2 years because of our COVID response.

The CDC has not released total numbers of suicides or other deaths of despair for 2019 or 2020, but they did put out a press release saying that for the 12-months ending at the end of May 2020 there were 81,000 drug overdose deaths and this was an 18.2% increase over the prior 12 month period, which had been a 4% decline from the year before that (Reference 5). Since drug overdoses had been declining, my guess would be that the 18% annual increase for the 12 months ending in May 2020 occurred entirely in the three months of March-May 2020, during the COVID lockdowns after the unemployment and social isolation hit. If so, then it was a 72% increase during those 3 months. This again suggests to me that we will have at least a 22% increase in deaths of despair for two years and indeed have at least 68,000 excess suicides and other deaths of despair as a result of our COVID lockdown response.

The median age of a person dying by suicide is about age 42 (Reference 6). A person aged 42 has about 38 years of life expectancy remaining in the U.S. So 68,000 excess deaths of despair x 38 years life expectancy = 2.58 million person-years of life lost from excess deaths of despair caused by our COVID lockdown response. That is more than 3 times the 800,000 person-years of life I estimated in Chapter 4 our lockdown response is saving in averted COVID deaths.

So it is almost certain that the lockdowns are causing more lost person-years of life due to driving people to suicides, drug overdoses, and alcohol deaths, than they are saving in prevented COVID deaths.

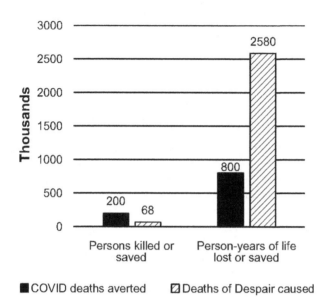

Deaths of Despair Caused vs. COVID Deaths Averted

■ COVID deaths averted   ▨ Deaths of Despair caused

These findings are summarized in the figure above. While it is true that I am estimating that our COVID lockdown response is killing fewer people by driving them to suicide or *de facto* suicide by drug or alcohol abuse than we are saving by preventing COVID deaths, the deaths of despair we are causing are in far younger people with far more years of life remaining than those whose lives we are saving by preventing COVID deaths, so we wind up causing more than 3 times more person-years of life lost due to deaths of despair than we are saving in prevented COVID deaths.

In the previous chapter I said that because we are causing 30 times more person-years of life lost in time spent with depression than we are saving in prevented COVID deaths that the only way you can say that our societal lockdown response to COVID has been worth it is if you say, "I don't care about quality of life. I don't care about happiness and joy. The only thing that matters is duration of life. The only thing that matters is how long you live." Actually, now we see that even then you cannot say the COVID restrictions have been worth it, because they have caused and will cause more actual loss of life in person-years of life lost to suicides and other deaths of despair than they are saving in prevented COVID deaths.

It should be pointed out again that the deaths of despair are probably underestimated since they are based just on unemployment and not the unprecedented social isolation and depression, and the COVID deaths averted are probably overestimated. So I think it is a certainty that the person-years of life lost to deaths of despair caused by our COVID response will exceed those saved in prevented COVID deaths.

The Well Being Trust in their report said the excess deaths of despair are caused by COVID. That is not correct. They are caused by our response to COVID. If we had simply ignored COVID and gone on with life as before, we would have had more COVID deaths, but we would have had no, or almost no, increase in unemployment, social isolation, or depression, and therefore no increase in deaths of despair. The increased deaths of despair are caused by our *lockdown response* to COVID, not by COVID itself. And these excess deaths of despair were entirely predictable, in fact they were predicted by the Well Being Trust among others. We knew by our societal lockdown response to COVID that we would drive a certain number of people to suicide and drug and alcohol overdoses. We decided to do it anyway. We decided as a society that it was worth it to kill, conservatively, 68,000 mostly young and middle-aged people with 38 years of life expectancy remaining by driving them to suicide or *de facto* suicide in order to prevent death by a natural cause of 200,000 of the oldest and sickest people in society with 4 years of life expectancy remaining on average. Do you think that was worth it? Do you think that was a moral thing to do?

References:

1. Well Being Trust. https://wellbeingtrust.org/areas-of-focus/pol-icy-and-advocacy/reports/projected-deaths-of-despair-during-covid-19/

2. U.S. Centers for Disease Control and Prevention. https://www.cdc.gov/drugoverdose/data/statedeaths.html#:~:text=In%20 2018%2C%2067%2C367%20drug%20overdose,2018%20(20.7%20 per%20100%2C000).

3. American Foundation for Suicide Prevention. https://afsp.org/sui-cide-statistics/

4. U.S. Centers for Disease Control and Prevention. https://nccd.
   cdc.gov/DPH_ARDI/Default/Report.aspx?t=AAM&P=1A04A664-
   0244-42C1-91DE-316F3AF6B447&R=B885BD06-13DF-45CD-
   8DD8-AA6B178C4ECE&M=32B5FFE7-81D2-43C5-A892-9B9B3C-
   4246C7&F=&D=

5. U.S. Centers for Disease Control and Prevention. https://www.cdc.
   gov/media/releases/2020/p1218-overdose-deaths-covid-19.html

6. Wikipedia. https://en.wikipedia.org/wiki/Suicide_in_the_United_
   States

Chapter 7

Unemployment Caused by the Lockdowns

COVID lockdown policies threw 127 people out of work for each 1 COVID death averted.

The U.S. number of employed persons decreased by 16.0% from pre-COVID to the trough of COVID and is still down 7.1% as of October 2020 (Reference 1). This was not caused by COVID; it was caused by our societal response to COVID. It was caused by ordering everyone to stay at home, closing non-essential businesses, closing restaurants and bars, banning or discouraging travel, banning live music and live professional sporting events, etc. This massive unemployment was predicted in the news media, so everyone knew it was coming, including the politicians, but we decided to do it anyway.

The fact this was caused by the lockdowns and not by COVID itself or even by our spontaneous fear of COVID and voluntary changes in our behavior is shown by a comparison to Sweden. Sweden did not employ the lockdown strategy and their number of employed persons only went down 1.4% after COVID, and as of October 2020 was 1.4% higher than it was pre-COVID (Reference 1). Sweden chose a different path and as a consequence suffered almost no unemployment.

Again, if we had chosen to simply ignore COVID, or chosen the Sweden strategy of no mandatory restrictions at all, just inform people of their risks and what they can do to mitigate those risks and let them make their own decisions, we presumably would have had more people die of COVID (I estimated in Chapter 4 200,000 more COVID deaths), but we would have had no or almost no increase in unemployment. We decided it was worth it to throw a large number of people out of work in order to extend the lives of others by preventing their infection and death from COVID.

What is the ratio of the numbers? Employed persons in the U.S. decreased from 158.76 million in February 2020 to 133.40 million in April 2020 at the trough of the COVID recession, which is loss of work for 25.36 million persons and 16.0% of the U.S. workforce. Divided by 200,000 averted COVID deaths that is 127 persons thrown out of work for each COVID death averted by our strategy, and divided by the 354,380 COVID deaths in the U.S. in 2020 it is 72 people thrown out of work per 1 person who died of COVID in 2020.

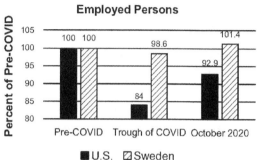

Employed Persons

U.S.   Sweden

* 25.36 million people thrown into unemployment in U.S. because our COVID response.

* 127 persons thrown into unemployment by our response per 1 COVID death averted.

Here we are really comparing apples to oranges, unlike with the suicides where we were comparing deaths to deaths and person-years of life of the persons we decided to kill (by driving them to suicide) to the person-years of life of those we decided to save (by preventing their COVID death). If unemployment were the only harm of our COVID response, you might think it is worth it to throw 127 people out of work to prevent 1 COVID death. Personally, I disagree, but it would not be unarguably wrong to think it is worth it. The important thing is we have to be adults about this and recognize we made a choice to harm some people by throwing them out of work in order to save others by reducing COVID infections and preventing COVID deaths.

References

1. Statistics from TradingEconomics.com, which cited government statistics.

Chapter 8

COVID Policies Have Increased Deaths From Cancer and Heart Disease

In response to COVID, hospitals and health systems suspended elective procedures, sometimes by order of governors and sometimes at their own decision, and have switched from in-person visits to telemedicine visits.* In other words, we have basically discouraged everyone from going to the doctor for anything other than COVID, and when people insist on seeing a doctor anyway, we shunt them to telemedicine where they are less likely to be treated or diagnosed properly and certainly less likely to feel that their doctor cares about them.

There have been many reports that cancer diagnoses are down in the U.S. That is not because fewer people are getting cancer; it is because fewer people with cancer are being diagnosed. That will ultimately lead to more cancer deaths. Fewer people with heart disease or other serious and life threatening illnesses are being diagnosed or treated also.

A study estimated that in Great Britain there will be about 3,400 additional deaths for the four most common cancers over a 5 year period due to excess missed diagnoses during COVID (Maringe et al.). Projected to the U.S. population size, that would be 17,000 additional deaths in the U.S. That is just the four most common cancers—adding missed diagnoses of other cancers, heart disease, and other life-threatening conditions, the number of excess deaths would certainly ex-

---

* Psychiatrists and psychotherapists have also mostly switched to counseling by video, which seems particularly unwise and unkind to me because most of their clients need counseling *because* of the loss of face-to-face contact with other humans because of our COVID restrictions. The primary thing the patients need is face-to-face interaction with a caring human being, which is the primary mission of psychological counseling— yet most counselors are refusing to give them that, either because their health systems will not let them or because the counselors are afraid (I think more than they should be) of contracting COVID.

ceed 20,000 and probably exceed 30,000. Relative to my estimate of 200,000 COVID deaths averted by our lockdown response to COVID, that would be 10 to 15 total excess deaths caused by missed diagnoses and forestalled treatment of cancer and other serious illnesses per 100 COVID deaths averted. In response to these facts, the health systems say, "It is the patients' fault." They say the patients are choosing not to go to the doctor because they are afraid of contracting COVID in the hospitals or clinics, and in some cases have even had heart attacks and do not go to the emergency room. There is certainly truth to that and it is undoubtedly true that most of the missed diagnoses are because patients voluntarily have reduced their visits to the doctor, but the health care systems bear blame for this too. They have suspended elective procedures and discouraged in-person medical visits and tried to shunt patients to telemedicine. They have also gone along with promoting fear of COVID instead of educating people about their actual risk of COVID death, which is less than most people think it is, and promoting calm.

References

1. Maringe C et al. 2020. The impact of the COVID-19 pandemic on cancer deaths due to delays in diagnosis in England, UK: a national, population-based, modelling study. *The Lancet* 21:1023-1034. July 20, 2020. https://doi.org/10.1016/S1470-2045(20)30388-0

Chapter 9

Lockdowns Have Increased Domestic Abuse and Child Abuse

There have been many reports in the media of increased domestic violence against both adults and children during COVID. I spoke to a psychologist who serves on a child abuse board who told me they had a large increase in reports of child abuse and calls for help with child abuse. In a cursory search I did not find any peer-reviewed literature that seemed to give good data on that, but it makes sense that there would be increased domestic abuse and child abuse. By the lockdown policies, we made people more depressed and irritable (19.3% increase in major depression), and we confined families together at home more by closing schools, increasing unemployment, closing restaurants, bars, churches, health clubs and every place people gather outside of the home, and, for those still working, increased working from home. More depressed and irritable family members involuntarily spending more time together at home is a recipe for increased domestic abuse and child abuse. That was entirely predictable and was predicted by many when we began our COVID lockdown response, but we decided as a society that this was another harm that was worth it to reduce COVID deaths.

I am not really going to try to quantify how much increased child abuse and domestic abuse has occurred because of our societal COVID restrictions because we do not have good data on that. But we do have good data on the incidence of child abuse in 2018 pre-COVID. According to the U.S. government, there were 678,000 children (unique individuals) who were victims of abuse in 2018 in the U.S. and 1,770 were killed (references 1 and 2). Thirty-nine percent or 264,000 of these were victims of physical or sexual abuse and the rest were victims of neglect only. If the COVID restrictions have increased abuse only 10%, and it seems like a certainty to me that abuse would have increased at least 10%, then our COVID restrictions are responsible for causing an additional 68,000 children to suffer abuse and 177 to be killed. If the restrictions have doubled child abuse, which seems possible, then they have caused 678,000 children to suffer abuse and 1,770 to be killed. That compares to the 200,000 COVID deaths I am estimating the restrictions prevented.

References:

1. National Children's Alliance. https://www.nationalchildrensalliance.org/media-room/national-statistics-on-child-abuse/#:~:text=Nearly%20700%2C000%20children%20are%20abused,which%20there%20is%20national%20data.

2. U.S. Centers for Disease Control and Prevention. https://www.acf.hhs.gov/cb/data-research/child-maltreatment

Chapter 10

Closing Schools and Colleges and Universities. Should a Society Sacrifice the Interests of all of Its Children and Young People to Prolong the Lives of a Portion of the Oldest and Sickest?

COVID policies have caused lost or impaired education for 350 children and young people for each 1 COVID death averted.

Should a society sacrifice the interests of all of its children and young people to prolong the lives of a portion of the oldest and sickest?

In the U.S. we closed almost all schools for the spring of 2020 and many or perhaps most have been closed to in-person instruction for most or all of the 2020-2021 school year.

Children are at almost no risk of dying from COVID. They are at much less risk of dying from COVID than from ordinary influenza each year, as elaborated in Chapter 13.* Adults in their 20s are also at less or equivalent risk of dying from COVID than influenza (Chapter 13), so college students are also at essentially no risk of dying from COVID and at no greater risk than they are every year of dying from influenza. We closed their schools anyway, and prevented students from playing sports or engaging in choir or other extracurricular activities. Since they were at lower risk from COVID than they are every year from influenza, this was clearly not done for their benefit. We required this sacrifice from children for the sole benefit of those at significant risk of dying from COVID—their grandparents and great grandparents. We sacrificed the interests of children—and not trivial interests but their interest in getting an education like every previous generation got, in normal social development from meeting with and socializing with their peers at school, and in fun and enjoying their lives by social-

---

* 47 children age 5-14 have died from COVID in the U.S. up to Dec. 12, 2020, according to the CDC, whereas in the 2017-2018 flu season 528 children age 5-17 died from influenza, also according to the CDC.

izing with other kids at school and playing with other kids and playing sports or engaging in other extracurricular activities—for the benefit of the oldest and sickest people in society, with very few years of life expectancy remaining. We have a moral obligation toward our children. They are 100% dependent on us to do what is right for them. They have a right to get an education, to socialize with their peers, to be allowed normal social development, and to play and have fun. We have violated those rights and we have abandoned our responsibilities to them.

And why did we abandon our duties to all of our children and violate those supreme moral duties? Because we were scared by a strain of the flu going around that is 3-1/2 times deadlier than ordinary influenza and shortens the lives of 0.2% of the population by 4 years on average (see Chapters 2, 3, and 13).

This bogles my mind. I cannot fathom how anyone, let alone teachers and parents and apparently the majority of society, could believe this was morally justified, let alone a good idea.

We should also note that closing the schools to in-person instruction will worsen the black/white and rich/poor educational achievement gaps. Students who are motivated to learn, have educated parents who can teach them, and have two parents with some money so one can stay home with the child will be less harmed by closing the schools than children without some or all of those advantages.

I have never seen any official even deign to articulate the reasons why schools needed to be closed. It is just stated that "it was necessary" or "this is for safety." Safety of whom? Not the children. As I have stated, they are at lower risk from COVID than they are from ordinary influenza.

At the least if officials are going to inflict this harm on every child and college student in America, they can do us the courtesy of explaining very clearly, with actual data, facts, and articulated reasoning, why they believe this is necessary and why the benefits of this step exceed the harms and justify us abandoning our moral duty to children in our care.

How do the numbers work out? There are 62 million Americans age 5 to 19. For age 6 to 18 it is about 53 million. There are about 19 million college students in the U.S. So altogether about 70 million students in K-12 and colleges and universities. Seventy million divided by 200,000 COVID deaths averted is 350 students whose schooling and social development and enjoyment of childhood or young adulthood has been severely impaired per one COVID death averted.*

---

* This is not to say that keeping 350 students out of school prevented one COVID death. It did not. My estimate of 200,000 COVID deaths averted is based on *all* of the restrictions, including closing workplaces, bars, restaurants, health clubs, and mandatory mask wearing, as well as closing schools. It is not clear that closing schools contributed significantly or at all to reducing the spread of COVID. In fact, the evidence, discussed in Chapter 20, indicates closing schools did not prevent *any* COVID deaths.

Chapter 11

The Trolley Dilemma: Do We Switch the Train From Track 1 to Track 2?

Philosophers have a thought experiment known as "The Trolley Dilemma" that is illustrated by this diagram.

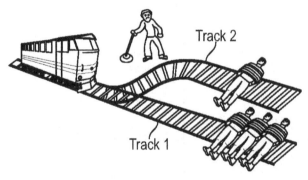

Imagine there is a trolley or train coming down the track and below it on the track, in this diagram, three people are tied to the track who will be killed by the train. But between the train and where the three people are tied to Track 1, the lower track in this diagram, there is a fork in the tracks and a switch, and you are standing at the switch and you could pull the switch to divert the train to Track 2, the upper track in this diagram, to avoid having the train run over the three people tied to Track 1 and save their lives. Unfortunately, however, there is a different person tied to Track 2 who will be killed if you pull the switch, who would not have been killed if you did not intervene. So you would be responsible for that person's death, whereas you could argue you would not be responsible for the deaths of the three people on Track 1. Do you pull the switch?

This is figuratively what we have done with COVID. The train of

COVID was coming down the tracks and it was going to kill some people from COVID if we did nothing. So we decided to intervene with our lockdown response to divert the train to Track 2 to avoid those COVID deaths. But we forgot, or more accurately, refused to acknowledge, that there were people tied to Track 2 who were harmed, and in some cases killed, by that decision.

The tables below show the choices we had, and still had throughout the year+ of lockdowns, between Track 1 and Track 2, as I have calculated them in Chapters 2-9. The numbers between Track 1 and Track 2 are normalized to one person on Track 1 whose COVID death our policies averted from the 200,000 COVID deaths (or zero to a maximum of 400,000 deaths) I estimated in Chapter 3 may be averted by the lockdowns. (So in the table for Track 2 we have fractional people; if you do not like to think of fractional people you could multiply the numbers in both tables by 10 or 100 or 1,000.)

Track 1 versus Track 2: The Choices We Had

Track 1 (If we had done nothing and let COVID take its course).			Track 2 (The lockdown approach we took of stay at home orders, school and church and business closings, mandatory mask wearing, etc.		
	Persons Harmed	Person-years of life lost		Persons Harmed	Person-years of life lost
Additional COVID dead	1 (0-2)	4 (0-8)	Suicides and other deaths of despair	0.34	12.9
			Major depression	>316	>120
			Cancer and heart disease deaths	0.1	0.5
			Loss of work	127	
			Loss of education and schooling	350	
			Children and adults victims of domestic abuse	?	
			Slightly lonelier and less happy	1,640	

Which track do you think involved more harm? Did we cause more harm than we prevented by switching the train from Track 1 to Track 2? If Track 2 involved more harm, was it ethical to pull that switch and have the train run over the people tied to Track 2, instead of allowing it to run over the one person tied to Track 1? Now that we know what these numbers are, and once we knew these numbers by about the summer of 2020, is it and was it ethical to continue to pull that switch and continue to pursue the lockdown approach and continue to run over the people tied to Track 2?

It is important to emphasize again that none of these bad outcomes on Track 2 were caused by COVID—they were caused by <u>our response</u> to COVID. They were caused by the lockdowns. We did not have to take the approach we took. We could have educated people about their actual risk of death if they become infected with SARS-Cov-2, and then let them make their own decisions about whether they want to isolate themselves to reduce their risk of being infected, wear a mask, etc. That is the approach Sweden took, and they had fewer deaths per capita than us (Chapter 1) and had almost none of the other collateral damage we suffered of increased unemployment, depression, suicides, and general unhappiness.

My moral code says it cannot be justified to cause 19.3% of the population to become clinically depressed in order to extend life by 1 day on average. It should also be noted that the people we have imposed the sacrifices on are not the people at risk of dying from COVID. So we ordered some people to sacrifice to benefit others.

In fact, we <u>decided</u> to kill some people, almost all of them young or middle aged, by driving them to suicide or drug or alcohol deaths, in order to extend the lives of other people, almost all of them old and in poor health and with little life expectancy left. All of the costs listed were entirely predictable and were in fact predicted, so we <u>decided</u> as a society to inflict those harms in order to save the lives of other persons from COVID.

One of the worst parts is that when the people we have killed or harmed who were tied to Track 2 object to the decision to harm them to try to save the lives of some elderly people from death by COVID, we self-righteously scream at them that they are selfish. When people have lost their jobs or their businesses because their restaurants were ordered closed, they are shouted down that they have no right to complain when others are dying of COVID. The same happens when parents or university students complain that schools are closed and they or their children are being denied an education and the right to simply live their lives. The millions we have driven into major depression mostly don't object or complain because they are too beaten down at this point to object and afraid that if they object people will like them even less than they do now. The people who have killed themselves, of course, are no longer around to object, and those contemplating killing themselves are too beaten down to object.

I am here to say that the people tied to Track 2 that we decided to run over by diverting the train from Track 1 have every right to object. Their lives are every bit as valuable as the elderly who are dying, like all of us will die, from, in this case, pneumonia caused by a natural virus

I would not have pulled that train switch. I think it was immoral to do so. Knowing what we know now, I would not continue to keep that switch pulled. I think even more clearly it is immoral to continue to keep that switch pulled.

Why we might have chosen lockdowns

Looking at this table it seems pretty obvious to me that the outcomes on Track 2 are worse than those on Track 1. And these harms were predictable. We knew the lockdowns would cause massive unemployment. We knew the social isolation we were mandating and the unemployment would lead to massive increases in depression and suicides. We obviously knew we were impairing education and harming young people by closing their schools and universities. And the experts, although perhaps not the public, knew at the very beginning of this that the infection fatality rate was less than 1% and probably less than 0.5%, so the number of deaths we have had is not much of a surprise, and even if we thought the restrictions would nip COVID in the bud and we would have almost no COVID deaths, the number of deaths prevented would only have been about five times the 200,000 I am estimating here, and therefore the harms of our policy would still have exceeded the benefits. And very soon into the spring lockdowns it was very clear the policies were not going to eliminate COVID deaths, so at that point the most you could hope for is maybe the restrictions would prevent 600,000 COVID deaths or three times the number in Track 1. Again, it should have been obvious at that point that the harms would have vastly exceeded the benefits of preventing those deaths. So why did we persist in our lockdown approach and persist in pulling the switch and running over the people tied to Track 2?

I think the answer is human psychology. We were faced here with two bad choices. People would die from COVID or people would die from suicide and have their lives ruined for a period of time with clinical depression. We were faced with a choice between bad and worse, not bad and good. We are not good at facing that. We have all been raised on movies where the good guy beats astronomical odds to escape and save the day. We hoped against hope that somehow that would happen here, and we have kept hoping even to this day, when the evidence is very clear that it has not happened and will not happen and that our approach has been a disaster and caused vastly more harm than it has prevented.

We need, and needed, to be adults and realize that sometimes bad things happen and the best thing to do then is move on and try not to make things worse.

Chapter 12

Economic Cost of Lockdowns

As we all know, the economy took a large hit in 2020. It is often said that was because of the pandemic. That, of course, is not true. It was because of the lockdown response, because of the COVID restrictions, not because of the disease itself. Our governments, not only in the U.S. but around the world, knew the lockdowns would produce large economic damage, but decided it was worth it to try to reduce COVID deaths. Was it worth it? Let's see how large the economic damage was.

Most of us have been surprised the damage was not worse than it was. The U.S. stock market now, as of March 2021, is above where it started 2020. Total wages and salaries, in nominal dollar terms though not in inflation-adjusted dollar terms, were slightly higher in the 4th quarter (Q4) of 2020 than they had been in Q1 of 2020. So in those senses, we have recovered completely, but we are well below where we would have been without lockdowns, and in Q2 and Q3 of 2020 we were certainly far below where we would have been without lockdowns. Millions of people lost their jobs. Millions more saw their wages decline. Millions more lost retirement savings in the stock market and sold stocks at the wrong time during the trough. And millions of small business owners saw their businesses decline or fail.

The table below shows the raw data on gross domestic product (GDP) and salaries and wages used to make my calculations here. (Source, U.S. Bureau of Economic Analysis (1)).

Gross domestic product (GDP) and wages and salaries in U.S. 2018-2020							
			Seasonally adjusted at annual rates				
	2018	2019	2020	2019	2020		
				Q4	Q1	Q2	Q3	Q4
Gross do- mestic prod- uct (GDP)	20,611.9	21,433.2	20,934.9	21,747.4	21,561.1	19,520.1	21,170.3	21,487.9
Wages and sala- ries	8,894.2	9,309.3	9,331.9	9,422.5	9,526.1	8,908.8	9,343.3	9,549.4

The numbers in the table above are in nominal dollars, not inflation adjusted.

From this table, GDP had increased by 3.98% from 2018 to 2019. That is right in line with the 4.00% average annual increase for 2009 to 2019. So this was an average annual increase and it is fair to project the same increase to 2020 if we had not had lockdowns. If GDP had risen again by 3.98% in 2020, we would have had a GDP of $22,286.24 billion in 2020. Instead we had a GDP of $20,934.9 billion in 2020, a deficit of $1,351 billion. I think nearly everyone would agree that entire deficit is due to the lockdowns, so the lockdowns cost the U.S. $1,351 billion in economic production in 2020, plus a little more for the first two quarters of 2021 that I will not include here.

$1,351 billion divided by 328 million persons in the U.S. is an economic cost of $4,119 per person.

Wages and salaries are another way to look at this. This is pay to employees. It does not include profit for business owners or corporate profits or government assistance payments or dividends or capital gains for individuals. This increased by 4.67% from 2018 to 2019. If it had increased by the same 4.67% in 2020, we would have had wages and salaries of $9,743.8 billion in 2020, instead of the $9,331.9 billion we had, so workers lost the difference of $411.87 billion in 2020.

There were about 159 million full and part-time employees in the U.S. in the February 2020 before a fall to about 133 million in April and a recovery to 150 million by January 2021. If we use the 159 million workers immediately pre-lockdowns, the average annual wage in

2019 was $58,547. The median wage was $35,977 in 2019 (Reference 2). Again, to refresh your memory, the average is the total of all wages divided by the number of workers, while the median is the figure at which 50% of workers made more and 50% made less.

The lost total wages and earnings in 2020 of $411.87 billion due to the lockdowns in 2020, divided by 159 million workers pre-lockdown, is a loss of $2,590 per worker. This was disproportionately borne by the lower wage workers, those making less than $35,977, as shown by the fact that 26 million workers lost their jobs due to the lockdowns (Chapter 7 and Reference 3). So for those, their wages went to zero, at least for part of 2020. The $2,590 average lost wage would be 7.2% of the median wage or 4.4% of the average wage.

I have estimated here that the lockdowns may have prevented 200,000 COVID deaths, and at most prevented 400,000 COVID deaths because we would have been at herd immunity with 400,000 more COVID deaths. With the GDP loss of $1,351 billion, divided by 200,000 COVID deaths averted, it was $6.75 million of GDP loss per person saved from COVID or, with an average life expectancy remaining of 4 years, $1.69 million per person-year of life saved.

Economic cost of lockdowns

GDP loss per person	$4,119
Wage and salary loss per worker	$2,590
Cost per COVID death averted	$6.75 million
Cost per person-year of life saved in COVID deaths averted.	$1.69 million

By these calculations, with the lockdown strategy we spent $1.69 million to save one person-year of life from COVID death. But it should be remembered that it is actually much worse than that. We spent $1.69 million in order to save one person-year of life by preventing a COVID death *and* in order to lose three person-years of life by causing a suicide or drug overdose. So it is a lose-lose proposition. We lost the money, and the money went toward the cause of killing people on balance, not saving them.

But let's pretend the lockdowns did not cause any suicides and assume they prevented 200,000 COVID deaths in the U.S., as we have assumed. Is it worth $6.75 million to save one life? If it's your own life and you have $6.75 million to spare, yes, of course. If it is anyone else's life and you have exactly $6.75 million in your bank account, probably not. If it is anyone else's life and you have $100 million in your bank account, yes, it would be nice if you were willing to pay $6.75 million to save that life (although I don't think you would be doing it two or three times). The U.S. government for its cost-benefit analysis uses a figure of $10 million as the value of saving one life. So by that metric $6.75 million is worth it to save one life. But that $10 million is for a generic life, not any particular age. The COVID dead die with on average 4 years of life expectancy remaining had they not contracted COVID. I would say we do not believe it is worth $1.69 million for one person-year of life. The median person dying of COVID is 84 years old. If your 84-year old father or mother dies due to medical malpractice or in a car accident or other wrongful death, and you sue for wrongful death, you are not going to get an award of $6.75 million. You probably would not get that if your teenage child dies due to negligence or medical malpractice.

In Minnesota we have had four well publicized cases of police wrongfully killing civilians in recent years. Those four cases and two others from elsewhere and the dollar amounts awarded for each of those deaths were these:

• Justine Damond. 40-year-old white woman. Shot by a policeman from the driver seat of his squad car because she banged on his hood for attention and startled him after she had phoned for police help because she had heard a woman scream. $20 million.
• Breonna Taylor. Black woman, 26-year-old medical technician. Shot 6 times by police in Louisville, KY, in her bed in a wrongful drug raid. (She had nothing to do with drugs and had done nothing wrong.) $12 million.
• Philando Castile. Black man, 32 years old. Pulled over in a traffic stop and shot and killed by the officer because the officer panicked after Castile politely and calmly told the officer that he had a permit to carry a gun and had a gun in the car. $3 million to his family and $0.8 million in a separate settlement to his girlfriend.
• Jamar Clark. Unarmed 24-year-old black man killed by Minneapolis police when they stopped him for questioning for domestic abuse. The alleged abuse victim had not reported domestic abuse. She called 911 and said she had hurt her ankle and asked for an ambulance. The 911 operator argued with her that she was the victim of domestic abuse instead

of an accident and sent police, which the purported victim did not request. Jamar Clark was unarmed. In the video it appears a first officer attacked him without provocation and wrestled Clark to the ground, and Clark defended himself by wrestling back, before the first officer's partner standing nearby shot and killed Clark. $200,000.

- George Floyd. 46-year-old black man. Stopped as a suspect for allegedly passing a counterfeit $20 bill at a grocery store. The police took him to the ground and kneeled on his neck for over 9 minutes until he died by suffocation, despite his telling the officers he could not breathe and many onlookers screaming at the officers that they were killing him. $27 million.

- Eric Garner. 43-year-old black man. Killed by police in New York during a stop for suspicion of illegally selling cigarettes on the sidewalk. He was choked to death by an officer after telling him and other officers that he could not breathe. $5.9 million.

None of families of the young black men in these examples got $6.75 million except for George Floyd, and his family only got it because his death triggered such national outrage, and they were all a lot younger than 84. The two women got more, and the white woman received the most except for George Floyd. Our society obviously values white lives more than black lives. Perhaps less obviously, it can also be argued that it values women's lives more than men's.

I asked a plaintiff's attorney in Minnesota what a typical award might be in a case of clear-cut wrongful death due to medical malpractice or a traffic accident, and she said that for a victim in his 80s the award would rarely reach $1 million. Surprisingly to me, she also said that $1 million would be almost as rare for a teenage victim. She said there was a case recently of three teenagers killed in a train accident where each family got $6 million from the railroad, but there was an element of punitive damages included in that to punish the railroad, rather than merely to compensate for the deaths, and that is the largest recent award she is aware of. The same element of punitive damages applies to the settlements for police killings listed above. Each of those settlements includes money as punishment for wrongdoing or negligence by the cities involved, so the actual value of the lives lost can be deemed to be less than the award size.

Another, I think, interesting way to think about the monetary value of a person-year of life is to imagine that you are middle aged and the only child of your parents, and your father has passed away. Your mother is still alive and in her 80's, and you love your mother and she loves you. You have almost no retirement savings. Would you rather have your mother live one year longer and have nothing to leave you in inheritance or have her die one year earlier than she otherwise will die, whenever that will be, and leave you $1.69 million? Don't worry; you don't have to answer out loud. If you were the mother in that scenario, would you volunteer to die a year earlier if it meant you could leave $1.69 million to your child instead of zero?

We do not as a society behave like we think a person's life is worth $6.75 million and certainly not like we think one person-year of life is worth $1.69 million. And I agree with that assessment. Just the financial cost of the lockdowns was not worth it to save the relatively small number of lives, almost all of them elderly with little time left to live, that the lockdowns have saved in prevented COVID deaths, even if the lockdowns had not caused suicides and depression and the other human costs discussed in this book, and even if the economic cost had been borne mostly by the well off, instead of being borne mostly by poor people and middle class people, as it was.

It should be remembered that this economic cost was borne mostly by the poor and middle class, not the rich. First, as mentioned above, total U.S. wages and salaries in Q4 2020 were narrowly above what they had been in Q4 2019 and Q1 2020. So in that sense wages had recovered. But 26 million Americans lost their jobs in the lockdowns, and as of January 2021 there were still about 6 million fewer workers than there had been in February 2020, and those unemployed were disproportionately low-wage workers, so clearly the lowest paid suffered the most and the highest paid may have actually profited from the lockdowns. Billionaires as a group actually *did* profit from the lockdowns. The total net worth of billionaires in the U.S. was $3.0 trillion in February 2020 and now in February 2021 it has grown to $4.3 trillion, an increase of a stunning 43% (Reference 4). So this $6.75 million per COVID death averted was not paid *by* billionaires; it was paid *to* billionaires. And it was paid mostly by the poor and middle class.

References

1. U.S. Bureau of Economic Statistics. https://www.bea.gov/data/gdp/gross-domestic-product

2. Wikipedia. https://en.wikipedia.org/wiki/Personal_income_in_the_United_States#:~:text=The%20Bureau%20of%20Labor%20Statistics,a%20base%20year%20of%202019.

3. TradingEconomics.com. https://tradingeconomics.com/united-states/employed-persons, from statistics from the U.S. Bureau of Labor Statistics.

4. Inequality.org, citing statistics from *Forbes*. https://inequality.org/great-divide/updates-billionaire-pandemic/

Part 2
What is the Fatality Rate of COVID-19 and How Does It Compare to the Flu?

Chapter 13

Death Risk from COVID-19 – Overall, by Age, and Compared to the Flu.

CONCLUSIONS

- Overall Infection Fatality Rate (IFR) for COVID, which is the percentage of people infected who die, was 0.46% in the spring wave of 2020. That should be viewed as an upper estimate; it may have been half that in the spring wave, and is almost certainly at least a little less in the second wave occurring in the fall-winter 2020-2021.
- The IFR varies greatly by age. It is less than 0.01% for age <25, about 9% for age 85 and over.
- Overall, the IFR is about 3.5 times higher for COVID than ordinary influenza in recent years, with widespread flu vaccine usage.
- The IFR of COVID is 1.7 times higher than the IFR of influenza in unvaccinated persons.
- COVID is actually much less deadly than ordinary influenza for children under age 18.
- For the year 2020, COVID produced about 6 times more deaths than a typical flu year of recent years.
- 2020 was the deadliest year for influenza and pneumonia deaths since the 1918-1919 "Spanish flu" but had only about 2 times more than the typical number of flu deaths per million population of 1950-1970.
- The 1918-1919 flu produced about 3.5 times as many deaths relative to population as COVID and killed the young at as high or a higher rate than it killed the old, so it produced at least 15 times the person-years of life lost relative to population compared to COVID.

COVID is much closer in its damage to ordinary influenza than to the 1918-1919 flu.

Your risk of death from COVID

You may want to know what your chances are of dying from COVID if you contract it. I do not think the government or media have done a very good job of answering that question, so I will try to answer it here. To answer that question, first we want to know the infection fatality rate—number of deaths divided by number of infected persons. For that, we need to know, in addition to how many people have died of COVID, how many people have been infected. As elaborated in Chapter 3, based on the data of Anand et al. (Reference 1), 9.3% of the U.S. population of 328 million was infected as of early July 2020, which means 30,504,000 had been infected by July 1, 2020. The number of U.S. COVID deaths was 140,775 as of July 15, 2020. Dividing the 140,775 deaths into the 30,504,000 infections gives an infection fatality rate (IFR) of 0.46% in the U.S. in the spring 2020 wave of COVID up to July 15, 2020.

But that is the overall rate. The actual risk of dying is much higher for the elderly and much lower for children, and it is higher for sick people and lower for healthy people. What you probably want to know is what your personal risk is, or the risk of your loved ones, given your age or their age. Based on the age distribution of COVID deaths reported by the CDC as of December 12, 2020 (Reference 2), and based on the percentage of persons of different ages infected reported by Anand et al., I calculate the following age-specific infection fatality rates for COVID, defined as the percentage of infected people who die. (Appendix 1 shows how I calculated these numbers and the sources.)

Table 1

Age	COVID infection fatality rate, %	overall fatality rate for the age (chance of dying from all causes), %	COVID infection fatality rate/overall fatality rate	% chance of having died from COVID in 2020 up to Dec. 12.
0 to 4	0.0013%	0.148%	0.01	0.000%
5 to 14	0.0006%	0.014%	0.04	0.000%
15 to 24	0.0056%	0.106%	0.05	0.001%
25 to 34	0.022%	0.184%	0.12	0.004%

35 to 44	0.064%	0.249%	0.26	0.012%
45 to 54	0.178%	0.489%	0.36	0.033%
55 to 64	0.421%	0.977%	0.43	0.079%
65 to 74	1.150%	1.796%	0.64	0.188%
75 to 84	3.031%	4.487%	0.68	0.471%
85 and over	9.076%	14.300%	0.63	1.320%
Overall	0.46%	1.020%	0.451	0.084%

It is interesting that even in the age 85+ group, about 91% of the infected persons survive COVID.

In fact, these numbers for the infection fatality rate should be viewed as an upper estimate for the spring wave. Jay Bhattacharya of Stanford writes that the median infection fatality rate from seroprevalence surveys around the world is 0.2% (Sood et al.). Moreover, there is reason to believe the seroprevalence tests are underestimating the number of people who have been infected by missing people who had mild or asymptomatic disease because they produce low levels of IgG antibodies, the type being tested, and those levels may fade over time (Burgess et al. and Bajema et al.). (See Appendix 2.) Also, the estimate of 0.46% is based on Anand's study of dialysis patients, and that is a sick group of people that you would expect would take more precautions than normal to try to prevent being infected, so it is a group I would expect to have a lower seroprevalence than the population as a whole.

So the true infection fatality rate in the spring wave of 2020 may be half the 0.46% I have estimated. In that case, each of the age-specific infection fatality rates should be cut in half. And in the second wave of fall-winter 2020-2021, it seems certain that the infection fatality rate is lower than it was in the spring wave. It is lower because: (1) We have new treatments and have learned which treatments work, and (2) the virus has mutated to forms that are more contagious but less deadly. This is discussed in more detail in Chapter 3. Data discussed in Chapter 3 suggests at least a third fewer infected people are dying in the fall-winter 2020-2021 wave than in the initial spring 2020 wave. So in the fall and winter wave I think it is likely that the infection fatality rate is about 0.30% or two-thirds of the 0.46% I used for the spring wave, and your chance of dying in the fall-winter of 2020-2021 if you were infected was probably about two-thirds of the number in Table 1.

The 4th column is the percentage of people of each age who actually have died of COVID in 2020 up to about December 12, according to the CDC.

The 3rd column I think is a useful way to think about your COVID risk. It is the ratio of your risk of dying from COVID *if you are infected* to your risk of dying from any cause this year or in 2019 before COVID hit. We all have an intuitive sense of how likely we are to die in the coming year (although we probably don't think about it much and probably underestimate the possibility). For age 65 and up, their risk of dying from COVID if they are infected is about 65% of what their risk of dying was this year if COVID had not happened. For persons under age 25, their risk of dying from COVID if they are infected is negligible—5% or less of their risk of dying from all causes—and most people under age 25 do not spend a lot of time worrying about their risk of dying this year from any other cause. For adults aged 25 to 64, their risk of dying from COVID if they are infected is between 12 and 43% of their risk of dying from any cause. So if you are age 65 and up, you should be almost as worried about dying of COVID if you are infected as you were of dying this year before COVID hit. If you are less than 65, you should be less worried about dying from COVID, even if you are infected, than you were about dying this year before COVID hit. And if you are a child or adult under age 25, you really should not be worried about dying of COVID at all.

Comparison to Influenza

How do COVID deaths compare to flu deaths, and how does the infection fatality rate for COVID compare to the infection fatality rate of the flu or influenza?

I think the best way to answer that is just to look at raw deaths. In the U.S. we had 59,120 deaths in 2018 due to "influenza or pneumonia" according to the CDC (Reference 6), which in most years is about the 8th leading cause of death. That was a pretty normal year for the past decade. According to Worldometer, we had 362,664 COVID deaths in the U.S. in 2020. So by that measure it was about six times worse than a normal year for flu deaths.

That 6x figure represents a combination both of how contagious it is and how lethal it is once a person is infected by the virus. COVID is, or was in the spring 2020 wave, 3.5x more lethal (by IFR or percent of infected people who die, as calculated above) and therefore to achieve 6x higher deaths must be almost 2 times more contagious than influenza. That makes sense because other strains of coronavirus cause the common cold, and the common cold infects about 50% of the population in a given year, while influenza infects about 15% typically. The evidence suggests that SARS-CoV-2, the virus that causes COVID-19, is almost 2x more contagious that influenza and about equally as or slightly less contagious than coronaviruses or other viruses that cause the common cold.

Let's look just at lethality compared to influenza—how lethal the virus is among infected people. The most recent complete data from the CDC for influenza is "Estimated influenza illnesses, medical visits, hospitalizations, and deaths in the United States – 2017-2018 influenza season." (Reference 7.) It estimates 61,099 deaths and 44,802,629 symptomatic illnesses. That is a 0.136% infection fatality rate. I have calculated the COVID infection fatality rate as 0.46% or 3.4-fold higher than influenza. The CDC report breaks down illnesses and deaths by age, allowing me to calculate the following numbers by age.

Table 2

Age	COVID IFR %	Influenza IFR %	COVID IFR/Influenza IFR
0 to 4	0.0016	0.0031	0.52
5 to 17	0.0000	0.0070	0.00
18 to 49	0.0243	0.0194	1.25
50 to 64	0.2062	0.0510	4.04
65 +	3.0198	0.8561	3.53
All ages	0.46%	0.136%	3.38

In Table 2 I used Minnesota numbers to calculate the COVID IFR because Minnesota has finer age breakdowns that allow more precise comparison to the age breakdowns used for influenza.

One interesting finding here is that COVID is much less deadly than influenza for children. Of course, influenza is not very deadly for children either, but COVID almost never causes death in children. The same result would be the case if I had used U.S. numbers. Also interesting to find that among 18 to 49 year-olds, COVID and ordinary influenza are about equally deadly in terms of infection fatality rate.

Overall, the COVID IFR is 3.38 times as high as the influenza IFR. But really it is less than that, because we have not had a vaccine against COVID until the spring of 2021, and the COVID IFR was calculated from the spring of 2020 before any vaccine was available, whereas about two-thirds of persons over age 65, among whom nearly all COVID and flu deaths occur, receive the flu vaccine (Reference 8), and receiving the flu vaccine reduces the risk of Intensive Care Unit (ICU) admittance by 80% (Thompson et al. (Reference 9)). If two-thirds of the elderly receive the flu vaccine and among that group it cuts flu deaths by 80%, overall the vaccine cuts flu deaths by a bit more than half. So you could cut that ratio of IFR in half and say unvaccinated COVID is not 3.4-fold, but rather 1.7-fold, more lethal than unvaccinated influenza. This fits with the fact that COVID deaths in 2020 relative to the population were about twice the ordinary year's influenza deaths from 1950-1970, before widespread use of flu vaccines, as is discussed below.

COVID-19 produced six times as many pneumonia/influenza deaths as an ordinary year in 2020. Going into the six-fold increase in deaths is both greater lethality or likelihood of dying if you are infected than the flu, and greater contagiousness or greater likelihood of being infected than the flu. We determined the lethality or IFR is 3.4-fold higher than influenza. Contagiousness, therefore, must be 1.8-fold higher than the flu.

6 *times greater deaths than flu* = 3.4 times more lethal x 1.8 times more contagious

And going into the 3.4-fold greater lethality is both inherent lethality of COVID and flu and the fact that flu's lethality is cut by use of the flu vaccine. So the overall equation is

6 *times greater deaths than flu* = 1.7-fold *greater lethality than unvaccinated flu x* 2-fold *cut in deaths by the flu vaccine x* 1.8-fold *more contagious.*

1918 Flu and other flu seasons
How does COVID compare to the 1918-1919 "Spanish" flu and to other flu seasons of the past? Here is a table of deaths in the U.S. per million population calculated from CDC statistics.

Table 3

	Deaths per million population
COVID in 2020	1,106
COVID for entire epidemic 2020-2021 (600,000 deaths projected)	1,829
Influenza	
2018	149
2015	152
2010	151
2000	237
1990	368
1980	314
1970	417
1960	537
1950	481
1968	500
1957-58 flu season	674
1918-1919 Spanish flu	6,555

Influenza and pneumonia deaths per capita in the U.S. have gone down quite a bit just since 1990. In the 1950s and 60s, influenza deaths were usually about 500 per million population, which is half of the current COVID epidemic.

COVID is also often compared to the 1918-1919 Spanish flu. It should not be. The Spanish flu killed about 6 times as many people relative to the population in one year and 3.5 times as many over the course of the epidemic as COVID killed, and equally importantly killed the young at perhaps a higher rate than it killed the old. According to the CDC, the 1918 flu had high mortality in persons under age 5 and age 20-40, as well as age 65 and up (Reference 10). Stories on it often say the young died at a higher rate than the old. (It should be noted that data is not great on the 1918 flu. The total number dead is an estimate, and while it is clear soldiers and other young people died of the flu at very high rates, the exact age breakdown of deaths is not precisely known.) So on top of the 3.5x greater deaths, the lost life expectancy per death was probably 4 to 8 times greater. Altogether, it should be considered 15 to 30 times worse in terms of lost person-years of life per capita than COVID. COVID is much closer in its death toll to ordinary influenza than it is to the 1918 flu.

Commentary

You may or may not find these numbers to be a high risk of COVID death for yourself or others. If you are under age 50, you certainly should not for yourself. Children are at a far lower risk of dying from COVID than of ordinary influenza, and are at less than 0.001% chance of dying from COVID. Adults younger than 50 are at about the same risk of dying from COVID as from ordinary influenza and had less than a 0.04% chance of dying from COVID in 2020.

Likely you find all of those numbers to be lower than you thought they were. But the experts knew from the very beginning of this outbreak, before it had really reached the U.S., that the infection fatality rate was certainly less than 1% and probably less than 0.5%. That was not well conveyed to the public and has still not been well conveyed to the public.

I am pretty sure you have never seen a story in the media that said that children are at much less risk of dying from COVID than they are from the flu. Or that young and early middle aged adults are at about the same risk of dying from COVID as of dying from ordinary influenza.

Although the infection fatality rate of 9% for persons 85 and older is three to four times that of influenza, most people are probably under the impression that infection with COVID is almost a death sentence for the elderly and that at least one-third of the 85-and-overs who are infected die. Even I thought that would be the result when I did these calculations. That is not correct. About 9% do.

COVID deaths in 2020 are about 6 times ordinary influenza deaths in a year. Some might think that is high, and the media, health officials, and most politicians seem to think it is self-evident that if you have 6x the normal number of flu deaths, you must shut down schools and businesses even at the cost of causing 16% unemployment, causing tens of thousands of suicides, and throwing 19% of the population into clinical depression. It is not self-evident to me. The way I think about it is, How worried were you on January 1, 2020, that you would die of the flu this year? Multiply that number by 6 and that is how worried you should have been of dying from COVID. For me, I had zero worry I would die from the flu in 2019 or 2020. Six times zero is still zero.

And COVID is less than twice as lethal, in terms of infection fatality rate, as ordinary influenza if you have not been vaccinated against either disease. If you chose not to get the flu vaccine in 2020 or any recent year and then you become infected with COVID, at that point you should be not quite twice as worried about dying from it as you would have been about dying from the flu if you had been infected with the flu. Your fear of COVID death should be less than 2x your fear of flu death, which was probably zero if you chose not to get a flu vaccine. Again, two times zero is zero.

While COVID has produced six times the number of recent influenza deaths in a year, it is only twice the number in an ordinary year as recently as the 1960s before we had widespread use of the flu vaccine. We did not think in the 1960s that our biggest problem was influenza deaths.

These numbers have not been well conveyed to the public.

The key question for the public is "What is my chance of dying of COVID if I am infected?," shortly followed by "What is my child's chance? and What is the chance of the elderly in our society?" That is what we needed to know and be told in order to make our own informed decisions about how seriously to take this and what precautions to take and what precautions it makes sense for society as a whole to take. The CDC and state health officials, the media, and politicians have never informed us of that. They acted as if the infection fatality rate were the number of deaths divided by the number of verifiable symptomatic infections. But most infected people never bother to get tested, because most infected people have mild symptoms, and we had a shortage of tests until recently. So that greatly overstated the lethality of the virus, giving numbers like 7%, when the actual infection fatality rate is 0.46%. They have also allowed a misunderstanding to persist that everyone is at high risk of dying from this disease, when the reality is that anyone under age 50 is at very low risk of dying even if the they are infected, and is at the same, or for children much less, risk of dying as they are of ordinary influenza. Even for people 85 and over, they are at about a 9% risk of dying if infected, or a 91% chance of surviving COVID if infected, which I do not think is so terrible considering they are at a 15% chance of dying from all causes and an 85% chance of surviving one more year. And of course, like all of us, they are ultimately at a 100% chance of dying, period.

1.7-fold. COVID-19 is 1.7-fold more lethal than ordinary influenza, meaning, if infected with the COVID virus, you are 1.7 times more likely to die from it than you would be if you contracted the flu if you have not had the vaccine for either virus. Not 10-fold, not 20-fold, not even 6-fold. 1.7-fold. Did you ever hear that from the media or from the CDC? Perhaps you don't believe me, but the number of COVID deaths is constantly publicized and it was 6-fold higher than the typical number of flu deaths in 2020. We are also told COVID is much more contagious than the flu. Deaths are a function of both how likely you are to be infected and how likely you are to die if infected, so if COVID is more contagious than the flu, which it is, that means you are more likely to be infected, and that means the likelihood of dying once infected must be less than 6-fold higher. And certainly no one would deny that the flu vaccine cuts flu deaths. It is simple math. The 6-fold number includes the product of how much more lethal COVID is than the flu (1.7-fold) times how much more contagious it is (1.8-fold) times how much the flu vaccine cuts flu deaths (2-fold).

I feel the CDC and health officials, the media, and politicians have failed us. They should not have allowed these misunderstandings to persist. They should have tried to calm us, not to make us more afraid.

In fact, I would express it more strongly than that. With all the fear of COVID, the primary responsibility of the CDC and the media should have been to tell us what the infection fatality rate of COVID is, that is, your chance of dying if you are infected, and how that varies by age and health condition. It is ridiculous that I have to calculate those numbers because the CDC never did.

Appendix 1.

I calculated the numbers in Table 1 from the information in the table below.

Age	Number of COVID fatalities	Percent of COVID fatalities	population millions	percent of population	COVID infection percentage	COVID infection fatality rate (IFR), %!	overall fatality rate (OFR)for the age, %	IFR/ OFR	% chance of dying from COVID in 2020
0 to 4	48	0.017391	19.6	5.97	9.8	0.0013	0.148	0.009	0.0002
5 to 14	47	0.017029	40.99	12.49	9.8	0.0006	0.014	0.043	0.0001
15 to 24	458	0.165942	42.69	13.01	9.8	0.0056	0.106	0.053	0.0011

25 to 34	1969	0.713406	45.93	13.99	9.8	0.0223	0.184	0.121	0.0043
35 to 44	5101	1.848188	41.65	12.69	9.8	0.064	0.249	0.255	0.0122
45 to 54	13580	4.92029	40.88	12.45	9.5	0.178	0.489	0.364	0.0332
55 to 64	33378	12.09348	42.44	12.93	9.5	0.421	0.977	0.431	0.0786
65 to 74	59056	21.3971	31.49	9.59	8.3	1.150	1.796	0.640	0.1875
75 to 84	75165	27.2337	15.97	4.87	7.9	3.031	4.487	0.675	0.4707
85 and over	87259	31.61558	6.61	2.01	7.4	9.076	14.300	0.635	1.3201
Total	276061		328.25		9.3		0.84%		0.084%

Number of COVID fatalities was from Reference 2, with numbers up to December 12, 2020. Percent of COVID fatalities is the number in a given age group as a percentage of the 276,061 total COVID fatalities. Population in each age group is from statistica.com. The COVID infection percentage is the percentage of each age group infected from the data of Anand et al. (1), as of early July 2020. The COVID infection fatality % is calculated as: (percentage of COVID deaths/percentage of the population)*(the average infection percentage of 9.3/the infection percentage of the given age group)*0.46%, where 0.46% is the overall COVID infection fatality rate I have calculated from Anand et al.. The 0.46% infection fatality rate was calculated from number of deaths as of July 15, 2020, divided by number infected, which was calculated from 9.3% overall seropositivity as of early July times 328 million population of U.S. The overall fatality rate for each age group is from Reference 6.

Appendix 2:
Others have found that antibody tests underestimate seroprevalence, and, confirming that, one article that reported conducting seroprevalence surveys in various jurisdictions in the U.S. on three occasions found that in most places the seroprevalence went *down* over time (Bajema et al.). That can only happen if antibody titers are decreasing over time so that a person tests positive at one point and negative later, even though they have been infected (Burgess et al.). If that is the case, it means many people who are infected are not raising IgG antibodies or their IgG antibody levels fade over time. Also, it was reported that many people with mild infections test negative by the IgG antibody

tests but are raising T cells against COVID. That confirms much other evidence that a T cell response is more effective in controlling COVID than an antibody response. Immune response broadly comes in two types—cellular, meaning T cells, or humoral, meaning antibodies. T cells are the cells depleted in AIDS. We know that T cells and a cellular immune response are generally more effective in controlling viral infections than an antibody response, and evidence suggests that is true also of controlling COVID. So the people who mount the best immune response to COVID, and therefore have mild or no symptoms, are those who produce T cells and not antibodies, and are therefore likely to test negative for prior infection with SARS-CoV-2 by antibody tests, even though they have been infected and even though they have long-lasting immunity.

References:

1. Anand, S. et al. 2020. Prevalence of SARS-CoV-2 antibodies in a large nationwide sample of patients on dialysis in the USA: a cross-sectional study. *The Lancet* 396: 1335-1344. Published: September 25, 2020. https://doi.org/10.1016/S0140-6736(20)32009-2

2. U.S. Centers for Disease Control and Prevention. CDC weekly provisional COVID death counts. https://www.cdc.gov/nchs/nvss/vsrr/covid19/index.htm

3. Sood, N et al. 2020. Seroprevalance of SARS-CoV-2-specific antibodies among adults in Los Angeles County, California in April 10-11, 2020. *JAMA* 2020; 323:2425-27.

4. Burgess, S. et al. 2020. Are we underestimating seroprevalence of SARS-CoV-2? *BMJ 2020; 370:m3364.* https://doi.org/10.1136/bmj.m3364 (Published 03 September 2020)

5. Bajema, KL et al. 2020. Estimated SARS-CoV-2 Seroprevalence in the US as of September 2020. *JAMA Intern Med.* Published online November 24, 2020. https://doi.org/10.1001/jamainternmed.2020.7976

6. National vital statistics reports, Vol. 68, No. 7, June 24, 2019, United States Life Tables 2017.

7. U.S. Centers for Disease Control and Prevention. "Estimated influenza illnesses, medical visits, hospitalizations, and deaths in the United States – 2017-2018 influenza season." https://www.cdc.gov/flu/about/burden/2017-2018.htm

8. U.S. Centers for Disease Control and Prevention. https://www.cdc.gov/flu/fluvaxview/coverage-1920estimates.htm

9. Thompson MG, Pierse N, et al. 2018. Influenza vaccine effectiveness in preventing influenza-associated intensive care admissions and attenuating severe disease among adults in New Zealand 2012–2015. *Vaccine* 36: 5916-5925. https://doi.org/10.1016/j.vaccine.2018.07.028

10. U.S. Centers for Disease Control and Prevention. https://www.cdc.gov/flu/pandemic-resources/1918-pandemic-h1n1.html

Part 3

Review of the Effectiveness of Specific Strategies to Slow or Stop the Spread of COVID-19

Chapter 14

How Transmission of Upper Respiratory Tract
Infections Happens

Before we get into the evidence for and against the effectiveness of specific strategies to slow the epidemic, it is best to look at how respiratory virus illness generally is spread from person to person. That gives us a lens through which to look at the evidence on effectiveness of the strategies and allows us to predict which strategies are likely to be effective.

The evidence suggests that nearly all upper respiratory tract viral infections—colds, flu, and COVID-19—pass by contact with hands and then touching your hands to yourself at or near a mucous membrane of the face (the mouth, nose, or eyes). The best data is on common cold caused by rhinovirus, but everything we know about influenza and COVID-19, particularly the data on what works to reduce transmission, suggests they are transmitted the same way.

The best evidence on this is from Gwaltney et al. In their experiments, they deliberately infected volunteers with rhinovirus that causes the common cold by spraying virus-containing solution into the nose. Of 11 persons infected, the six that became sickest were used as donors to other volunteers to test whether the recipients could become infected by hand-to-hand contact, large particles, or small particle aerosols. Each donor was contacted with recipient volunteers by all three transmission routes, in most cases with two or three test recipients for each transmission route. Each recipient was exposed to only one donor and by only one transmission route. The recipients were in contact with the donors on every day of days 3 to 5 after infection of the donor.

To test hand-to-hand transmission, the donors blew their nose directly into their hands and then stroked hands with the recipient for 10 seconds. The recipient then went to another location and deliberately placed their fingers on their nasal mucosa and conjunctiva mucosa (the borders of the eyes). This was apparently done once each day on days 3-5.

For large particle aerosol exposure, one donor and two to four recipients sat around a circular 70 cm (2 feet) diameter table and the donor was encouraged to talk loudly, sing, cough, and sneeze during the 15-minute exposure. For the small particle aerosol exposure, donors and recipients were housed in the same large closed room for 72 hours straight, with no outside air entering, separated from each other by a wire mesh to prevent direct contact and minimize or prevent large aerosol contact.

The results: By hand-to-hand contact 11 of 15 recipients became infected versus 1 of 12 by large particle contact and 0 of 10 by small particle aerosol contact. Those differences were highly significant. This supports the idea that nearly all transmission of rhinovirus colds is by transmission from the recipient's hands to his or her own face. In the real world, the hands may become contaminated with virus by shaking hands, as in this experiment, or by touching a contaminated surface such as a drinking glass or a railing, that was sneezed on or touched by someone with a cold.

Table. Gwaltney et al. results of testing rhinovirus common cold transmission routes*

Transmission route	Infected recipients / test recipients exposed (P value vs. hand-to-hand)
Hand-to-hand	11/15
Large particle aerosol	1/12 (P=0.001)
Small particle aerosol	0/10 (P=0.001)

That was the best data I found on the subject, and it indicates that most, and possibly nearly all upper respiratory tract infection transmission is by hand, and it indicates no or almost no transmission occurs by small particle aerosols. For large particle aerosols, the one

---

* This table has P values. P values are used to measure statistical significance. They measure how likely it is that an experimental difference between two groups is due to chance and is not a real difference. The first two lines of the table show 11 of 15 received a cold by hand-to-hand transmission and 1 of 12 by large particle aerosols. The P value of 0.001 means there is a 1 in 1,000 possibility that difference is due to random chance. Conversely, there is a 999 in 1,000 likelihood it is not due to random chance and that it really is easier to transmit a common cold by direct contact than by the large particle aerosol route. By convention, if a P value is less than 0.05, the result is considered statistically significant.

recipient apparently infected by that route was living with another recipient who was infected by hand-to-hand. So she could have actually been infected hand-to-hand at home. But probably she was infected by large particles. In the real world, large particle transmission is really a combination of large particle and contact transmission, probably. A person sneezes or talks and droplets containing viruses either fall on a surface, such as a railing, that another person later touches, or fall on the chest of the second person and that second person later touches their chest, so the virus gets on the second persons hand, and then the second person touches a mucous membrane of his face to infect himself. It is much less likely the droplet actually directly hits the eye, mouth, or nasal membranes of the second person.

I find the small-particle data really remarkable. Ten persons each spent 72 hours straight in a small room with no air circulation with a person with an active symptomatic cold. Not one of the ten experimental recipients caught a cold! The experimenters did everything possible to force infection by that route, and they could not make it happen.

References:

1 Gwaltney Jr. JM, Moskalsik PB, Hendley JO. Hand-to-hand transmission of rhinovirus colds. *Annals of Internal Medicine* 1978. 88:363-367. https://doi.org/10.7326/0003-4819-88-4-463

Chapter 15

Effectiveness of Masks

The available evidence indicates that mask wearing makes "little or no difference" to reducing the spread of influenza-like illness and "little or no difference" to reducing the spread of laboratory-confirmed influenza. Jefferson et al. 2020. Physical interventions to interrupt or reduce the spread of respiratory viruses. *Cochrane Database Systematic Reviews of Medicine*, 2020 (Reference 5).

Cochrane Reviews is the gold standard for assessing the weight of evidence for evidence-based medicine. They are the judges. They represent consensus expert opinion on the evidence for and against the effectiveness of medical procedures and interventions. During COVID, their review on physical interventions to reduce the spread of respiratory illness—and they explicitly include COVID-19 in that purview in the article—concluded that mask wearing makes "little or no difference." "Huh?!," you say. "That is sure not what Anthony Fauci tells me." No, it is not.

I went into my review of the data on the effectiveness of mask wearing to reduce upper respiratory tract infections assuming the evidence must indicate it is effective, at least modestly. I was surprised to find that it is really not supported by the evidence, on the whole, although in theory if worn perfectly masks might modestly slow the spread of respiratory viral diseases, including COVID-19.

My conclusions after reviewing the data, and the conclusions of most researchers, are these:
Do mask mandates reduce rate of spread of COVID? Not significantly and probably not at all.

In theory, if everyone always wore their mask perfectly and changed masks several times per day, and we had 100% compliance with that, would that reduce the rate of spread of COVID? Somewhat, but not enough to end the epidemic. It would just flatten the curve and delay the spread. And anyway, that is not the real world.

If you want to reduce your own risk of infection, would it make a difference to wear a mask if you are diligent and wear it perfectly, preferably with an N95 mask, and change masks frequently, always have it cover your nose and mouth, and have it fit perfectly? Yes, that would significantly reduce your risk of getting COVID, but not by 100%.

By far the best data on the real world effect of mask wearing for prevention of COVID is a randomized clinical trial in Denmark conducted in the spring, before widespread mask wearing in that country and before any governmental recommendation to the public to wear masks (Bundgaard et al.). Volunteers who spent at least 3 hours per day outside of the home (6,000 persons) were randomized with instructions to wear a 3-layer surgical mask or not, followed for 1 month, and then tested for antibodies against SARS-CoV-2 that would indicate whether they had been infected with the virus. At the end of the one month, 2.1% of the non-mask wearing control group were infected versus 1.8% of the mask wears. That difference was not significant. The relative risk ratio was 0.82, meaning the mask wearers were 82% as likely to be infected as the non-mask wearers; and the 95% confidence interval was 0.54-1.23, meaning we can be 95% certain that if this experiment were conducted on an infinite number of people, mask wearers would be somewhere between 54% and 123% as likely to be infected as the non-mask wearers. In other words, this study proved that mask wearing does not reduce the likelihood of infection by more than 46% and could actually increase risk of infection by as much as 23%. (Bundgaard et al.)

The mask wearers were 18% less likely to be infected, and the P value was 0.38. A P value of less than 0.05 is considered statistically significant, but with a P value of 0.38, which is less than 0.5, one can say it is more likely than not that the slightly lower risk of infection in the mask wearers is real and not due to random chance.

In this clinical trial the mask wearers did an excellent job of complying with the instructions. Of the study participants, 93% wore their masks predominantly or always as recommended. The participants went through an average of 1.7 masks per day. That is much better than in the real world outside of a clinical trial. In the real world in the U.S. most people probably never change their mask and many wear it below their nose or with little or no attempt to have it fit their face. Despite that good adherence to protocol in the trial, mask wearers were not significantly less likely to be infected than the non-mask wearers. The authors of this study should be commended for analyzing their results honestly and publishing them. It was undoubtedly not good for the researchers' careers to publish this, and they certainly hoped at the outset that their study would show masks were effective.

There was some pushback in the public debate that this paper should not have been published because, supposedly, we do not want people to believe that masks make no difference, even though that is what the data showed. In other words, "You can't handle the truth." It's a condescending view of the public. Fortunately for those that have that condescending view of the public, the media barely covered this paper and its publication had no effect on CDC recommendations and state mandates to continue wearing masks, despite the fact that they make no significant difference.

Some have objected that this only shows mask are ineffective to protect the wearer but it is still possible they protect others from being infected by the wearer. But masks block particle flow both ways. If they do not prevent virus flowing in to the wearer, then they do not prevent virus flowing out to others either. Now admittedly, the study did show an 18% reduction in infections, so if there is also an 18% reduction in infecting others, then everyone wearing masks might reduce the rate of spread of the virus by 36%. But that would not be much and it is based on better compliance with the mask wearing by these motivated clinical trial volunteers than is likely in the general public.

That study actually appears to be the best randomized clinical trial ever done to assess the efficacy of mask wearing in preventing any respiratory infection, not just COVID-19.

To return to the Cochrane Review (Jefferson et al.) again, it concluded "There is low certainty evidence from nine trials (3507 participants) that wearing a mask may make little or no difference to the outcome of influenza-like illness (ILI) compared to not wearing a mask (risk ratio (RR) 0.99, 95% confidence interval (CI) 0.82 to 1.18."

"Low certainty evidence" means the evidence is not certain, but latter part of the sentence means that the evidence (which involves nine clinical trials and 3507 participants, which is not bad) gives a result that wearing a mask results in relative risk of 0.99 or 99% of the risk of contracting influenza-like illness of not wearing a mask, or a 1% reduction in risk, and the range of uncertainty with 95% confidence is 0.82 to 1.18 or anywhere from an 18% reduction in risk to an 18% increase in risk. In other words, masks don't make any difference.

The previous two paragraphs pertain to influenza-like illness in studies where that was judged by symptoms, as distinct from studies where studies where patients were tested by swabs for laboratory confirmation of influenza. In those studies, the Jefferson et al. Cochrane Review stated, "There is moderate certainty evidence that wearing a mask probably makes little or no difference to the outcome of laboratory-confirmed influenza compared to not wearing a mask (RR 0.91, 95% CI 0.66 to 1.26; 6 trials; 3005 participants)" (Jefferson et al.). "Moderate certainty" means the authors considered the evidence pretty good. The latter part of the sentence means that in six different clinical studies involving 3005 patients they calculate a relative risk ratio of 0.91, meaning those wearing a mask had 91% of the risk of contracting influenza of those not wearing a mask, and the confidence interval of 0.66 to 1.26 means we can say with 95% confidence from these studies that wearing a mask results in between at 34% decrease and 26% increase in your risk of contracting influenza.

In other words, going into COVID, the evidence pretty clearly showed mask wearing made little or no difference in risk of contracting influenza or other respiratory infection. The data on COVID-19, specifically the Bundgaard et al. paper, has only confirmed that.

The CDC was basically correct in the spring of 2020 when their recommendation to the public was to not wear masks because they are not effective. They were basically wrong when they changed that recommendation to wear masks. And importantly, there was no new evidence that prompted that change.

In theory, would masks reduce the spread of the virus if everyone always wore an effective mask and wore it with perfect fit and 100% of the time? Yes, but not completely.

The best data on this is a study in hamsters (Chan et al.). A group of hamsters infected with SARS-CoV-2 was placed in one cage and uninfected hamsters were placed in an adjacent cage. A fan blew air from the infected cage to the uninfected cage. Between the two cages was either no filter or barrier (the control group) or a 2-layer surgical mask material through which all air had to pass. After 5-7 days the hamsters in the test cage were tested for SARS-CoV-2 infection. All together, 10 of 15 animals (66.7%) in the cage not protected by a mask became infected versus 6 of 24 (25%) with the mask separating the cages. The difference was significant (p=0.016). So this says that under ideal conditions, worn perfectly, masks can significantly reduce the rate of transmission of the virus, but not totally prevent transmission.

Another paper used mechanical mannequins to test the effect of N95 masks and surgical masks in preventing coughing out of influenza virus and influx of them (Noti et al.).

"Tightly sealing a [surgical] mask to the face blocked entry of 94.5% of total virus and 94.8% of infectious virus (n = 3). A tightly sealed respirator [N95] blocked 99.8% of total virus and 99.6% of infectious virus (n = 3). A poorly fitted respirator [N95] blocked 64.5% of total virus and 66.5% of infectious virus (n = 3). A mask documented to be loosely fitting by a PortaCount fit tester, to simulate how masks are worn by healthcare workers, blocked entry of 68.5% of total virus and 56.6% of infectious virus (n = 2)."

In other words, N95 masks are better than surgical masks if worn properly, but neither is 100% effective, and if not fitted properly an N95 mask is no better than a surgical mask.

On whether N95 masks work better than surgical masks, the Jefferson et al. Cochrane Review concludes a summary of studies conducted mostly among health care workers, "There is uncertainty over the effects of N95/P2 respirators when compared with medical/surgical masks on the outcomes of clinical respiratory illness (RR 0.70, 95% CI 0.45 to 1.10; very low-certainty evidence; 3 trials; 7779 participants) and ILI (RR 0.82, 95% CI 0.66 to 1.03; low-certainty evidence; 5 trials; 8407 participants)."

Here the first part of the sentence says N95 masks reduce the rate of clinical respiratory illness by 30% compared to surgical masks (RR or relative risk of 0.70), with a confidence interval of 0.45 to 1.10 or a range of 55% reduction to 10% increase in risk compared to surgical masks. The second part of the sentence says for ILI or influenza-like illness instead of clinical respiratory illness, N95s had a relative risk ratio of 0.82 compared to surgical masks, or gave an 18% reduction in risk, with a 95% confidence interval of 0.66 to 1.03 or between a 34% reduction to 3% increase in risk of influenza-like illness. In other words, in health care workers, where N95s are likely to be used properly, wearing an N95 mask appears to probably moderately reduce risk of influenza-like illness, by about one-third, compared to a surgical mask, and a surgical mask probably does not reduce risk at all, as noted above. But the article notes, N95s are uncomfortable, which means there are problems with health care workers wearing them properly, and probably no chance the public at large would wear them properly in most cases.

To convince you I am not selectively quoting the Cochrane Review (Jefferson et al.), here is the full quote of the relevant sections on masks of the abstract:

Medical/surgical masks compared to no masks
We included nine trials (of which eight were cluster-RCTs) comparing medical/surgical masks versus no masks to prevent the spread of viral respiratory illness (two trials with healthcare workers and seven in the community). There is low certainty evidence from nine trials (3507 participants) that wearing a mask may make little or no difference to the outcome of influenza-like illness (ILI) compared to not wearing a mask (risk ratio (RR) 0.99, 95% confidence interval (CI) 0.82 to 1.18. There is moderate certainty evidence that wearing a mask probably makes little or no difference to the outcome of laboratory-confirmed influenza compared to not wearing a mask (RR 0.91, 95% CI 0.66 to 1.26; 6 trials; 3005 participants). Harms were rarely measured and poorly reported. Two studies during COVID-19 plan to recruit a total of 72,000 people. One evaluates medical/surgical masks (N = 6000) (published Annals of Internal Medicine, 18 Nov 2020), and one evaluates cloth masks (N = 66,000).

N95/P2 respirators compared to medical/surgical masks
We pooled trials comparing N95/P2 respirators with medical/surgical masks (four in healthcare settings and one in a household setting). There is uncertainty over the effects of N95/P2 respirators when compared with medical/surgical masks on the outcomes of clinical respiratory illness (RR 0.70, 95% CI 0.45 to 1.10; very low-certainty evidence; 3 trials; 7779 participants) and ILI (RR 0.82, 95% CI 0.66 to 1.03; low-certainty evidence; 5 trials; 8407 participants). The evidence is limited by imprecision and heterogeneity for these subjective outcomes. The use of a N95/P2 respirator compared to a medical/surgical mask probably makes little or no difference for the objective and more precise outcome of laboratory-confirmed influenza infection (RR 1.10, 95% CI 0.90 to 1.34; moderate-certainty evidence; 5 trials; 8407 participants). Restricting the pooling to healthcare workers made no difference to the overall findings. Harms were poorly measured and reported, but discomfort wearing medical/surgical masks or N95/P2 respirators was mentioned in several studies. One ongoing study recruiting

576 people compares N95/P2 respirators with medical surgical masks for healthcare workers during COVID-19.

In conclusion, mandating mask wearing does not significantly—and probably does not at all—reduce the spread of COVID. In theory, if worn perfectly by all persons all the time, mask wearing might modestly reduce the spread of COVID or other respiratory illnesses, but in the real world a mask mandate does nothing to slow the spread of COVID or other respiratory illness.

But worn perfectly and consistently a mask could modestly, but not completely, reduce a person's risk of contracting COVID or other respiratory illness. So if you are worried about your own risk of contracting COVID, it is not irrational to wear a mask, preferably an N95 mask. Other people wearing masks or not has no effect on you, so don't worry about their behavior.

The mask mandate or mask recommendations are often justified under the rubric of "the precautionary principle" that, basically, we cannot know for sure that masks make no difference and they may have a modest benefit, so we should require their wearing. The implication is that there is no harm to mask wearing or to mandating mask wearing, and there is a possible benefit, so we might as well mandate it. This is a perversion of the precautionary principle. The definition of the precautionary principle in the Oxford English Dictionary is "the principle that the introduction of a new product or process whose ultimate effects are disputed or unknown should be resisted. It has mainly been used to prohibit the importation of genetically modified organisms and food."

The precautionary principle therefore would mean that introducing a new mandate, mask wearing in this case, should not be done unless we are relatively certain that the benefits exceed the harms. For mask wearing we know, really for a fact, that the harms vastly exceed the benefits. At the outset of COVID the harms of a mask mandate were known and certain. The benefit was not only uncertain but all available evidence, with a fairly high degree of certainty, indicated there was little or no benefit to mandating mask wearing.

The benefit of mandating mask wearing:

- Probably none. Maybe a 10% reduction in the rate of spread of COVID (i.e., slightly slowing the spread of the virus but not ultimately preventing infection or ending the epidemic). More likely no benefit at all.

But there were known harms to mask wearing.

- It is uncomfortable.
- It at least modestly increases the carbon dioxide and decreases the oxygen that the mask wearer breathes, and we know that that decreases IQ and mood.
- It makes it difficult or impossible to read a person's facial expression.
- It makes it harder to recognize other individuals.
- It makes it harder to talk and communicate with others.
- It contributes to dividing us from each other socially so as to decrease happiness and increase clinical depression,
- That increased depression, in turn, leads to increased suicides and alcohol and drug abuse.

As I have shown elsewhere, as a result of all of our interventions put together, the person-years of life lost to depression are at least 30 times the persons years of life saved in prevented COVID deaths (Chapter 5), and the suicides and deaths of despair caused by the interventions are conservatively estimated at 3 times the person-years of life lost compared to the person-years of life saved in prevented COVID deaths (Chapter 6). So for all of the COVID interventions together, the harm-benefit balance is not close. The harms vastly exceed the benefits. The same is certainly true of the mask mandates. The weight of evidence is that they have not reduced COVID deaths at all. But they have significantly contributed to the social isolation and unhappiness, which in turn also causes suicides and drug and alcohol abuse and deaths. So there is no doubt that the harms from the mask mandates vastly exceed the benefits.

The mask mandates and the public health messaging that falsely claims that mask wearing reduces the spread of COVID significantly is also wrong-headed in that it really encourages turning on each other and fearing others and blaming them for your COVID if you contract it. The public health authorities have focused on your "duty" to protect others from contracting COVID from you by wearing your mask. Several comments on that:

(1) If that is a duty, then we have all always had a duty to protect others from contracting influenza from us by always wearing masks in public, even when we have no flu symptoms or it is not flu season, because of the minute risk that, even though we are asymptomatic, we could be carrying influenza and could infect another person and they could die from it.

That really is a fair comparison. Asymptomatic people do not spread COVID any more than they spread influenza. (See Chapter 18). The lethality of COVID is comparable to influenza—about three-and-a-half times higher, and less than two times higher than influenza if you have not been vaccinated (Chapter 13). So the death risk if you contract COVID is not really that different from the death risk if you contract influenza. If it is a moral duty to always wear a mask to prevent infecting others with COVID, even when you are asymptomatic and even outside of cold and flu season, then it should also be a moral duty to always wear a mask to prevent infecting others with influenza.

(2) Bizarrely, we went from *prosecuting* Muslim women in at least one western country (France) for wearing masks in public, because this covered their faces and made them hard to identify, to *mandating* that *everyone* must always wear a mask. Because there is a strain of flu going around that is three-and-a-half times deadlier than usual.

(3) This only serves to divide us and only serves to give a license to hate others for the crime of merely wanting to show their face in public and live their lives as they have always lived them. The better, and more accurate and truthful, message would be:

Your own mask wearing might reduce your risk of being infected with COVID. If you are worried about COVID for yourself, feel free to wear a mask. Others wearing masks has no effect on your risk of contracting COVID, so do not demand that they wear masks or hate them for not wearing masks. Take responsibility for your own health; you do not depend on others.

This would not only give at least as good COVID outcomes, it would unite us, instead of dividing us, and would be a message of personal empowerment, instead of victimization. The current message, in contrast, is a message of victimization. It says:

You are helpless. Wearing a mask does not protect you. You need everyone else in society to wear a mask to avoid infecting you. If you see anyone not wearing a mask, that is a terrible person and you are permitted to hate her. She's trying to kill you.

Confronting and Evaluating the Data that the Centers for Disease Control and Prevention Cites as Evidence that Masks Reduce Transmission

The CDC and state health authorities have pushed masks strongly. In the spring of 2020 they initially said only people sick with COVID should wear masks and the general public should not, in part in order to save masks for health care workers. The U.S. Surgeon General put the mask guidance bluntly in late February when he emphatically tweeted: "Seriously people- STOP BUYING MASKS!"

Later in the spring of 2020 the CDC changed the direction of their advice 180 degrees: Now everyone must wear a mask in public, and masks, not social distancing or hand washing, seemed to be the primary intervention the CDC advocated. This change was not prompted by new data. No data came out that showed masks were effective, or at least no convincing data.

Since my conclusions that masks make little or no difference in rates of transmission of COVID contrast with the recommendation of the CDC, I should confront and discus the evidence the CDC cites that masks work. The CDC citation of evidence is at reference (8).

The top reference they cite is Hendrix et al. (4), which is a CDC report, not a refereed journal article. It recounts that a hair stylist in Springfield, MO, worked while symptomatic with COVID (not knowing it was COVID) and wore a mask with clients but did not wear a mask in the break room when with other stylists. One other stylist became infected, presumably from the first stylist. Together the two stylists saw 139 clients and during all of those interactions both the stylists and the clients were wearing masks. The clients were contacted later to ask whether they contracted COVID and to be offered testing for COVID. The majority (72 of 139) of the clients refused to participate in the survey and answer whether they had COVID symptoms or submit to testing, so we do not know whether they were infected. Sixty-eight (68) of the clients submitted to COVID testing and none of them had become infected. So this is trumpeted as proving that masks work because there was one, yes one, transmission of COVID between people presumably not wearing masks; and among those wearing masks who answered the question, none of 68 people became infected; and among 72 other people wearing masks, we do not know whether they became infected or not.

This is the best they've got! First, the paper does not say how many stylists worked there or were exposed to stylists A and B without masks. So mathematically we have a numerator of 1 transmission and a denominator of ? who knows?—we are not told how large this salon was or how many other stylists or family members contacted these two stylists without masks and for how long. Then on the other side of the equation we have zero transmissions to the 68 people we know about and an unknown number of transmissions to the 72 people we do not know about. So mathematically, this could be expressed as

$$\frac{1}{X} > \frac{0}{68} + \frac{Y}{72}$$

where X and Y are both unknown. That is not a valid mathematical equation. We do not even know the fraction on the left is greater than the sum of the fractions on the right, let alone that it is statistically significantly greater. So I think I am not exaggerating in saying that this report has literally no evidentiary basis. It does not provide any evidence at all that masks prevent COVID transmission. It is an anecdote, not data. And the CDC apparently considers that to be the single best piece of evidence they have that masks prevent COVID transmission.

A second paper the CDC cites to support mask wearing is Duong-Ngern et al. (3). Analysis of this paper shows its data actually shows mask wearing *increases* risk of contracting COVID, contrary to what the CDC cites it for.

Duong-Ngern et al. is a refereed journal article giving a report from Thailand that involved contact tracing of three large COVID-19 clusters in nightclubs, boxing stadiums, and a state enterprise office in Thailand. Eighteen (18) primary index COVID-positive persons were the original infected people (index persons). Contacts (1706 persons) who were originally asymptomatic but were known to be in close contact with the index persons were identified. Of the 1706 contacts, 666 were excluded from the analysis and 1050 were analyzed, of whom 211 became infected with COVID within 2 weeks (cases) and 839 did not (controls). The paper compares the characteristics of the cases who became infected to the controls who did not become infected, particularly their mask wearing and other behaviors. The abstract of the paper states that:

> Wearing masks all the time during contact was independently associated with lower risk for SARS-CoV-2 infection compared with not wearing masks; wearing a mask sometimes during contact did not lower infection risk. We found the type of mask worn was not independently associated with infection and that contacts who always wore masks were more likely to practice social distancing. Maintaining >1 m distance from a person with COVID-19, having close contact for <15 minutes, and frequent handwashing were independently associated with lower risk for infection. Our findings support consistent wearing of masks, handwashing, and social distancing to pro-

tect against COVID-19.

From my analysis of their data, I would disagree with the conclusion that mask wearing was associated with lower risk of COVID infection. Not making physical contact with the index case starkly reduced risk of infection; hand washing significantly reduced risk of infection; but mask wearing actually *increased* risk of infection. Their statement "Wearing masks all the time during contact was independently associated with lower risk for SARS-CoV-2 infection compared with not wearing masks; wearing a mask sometimes during contact did not lower infection risk" is technically true, but highly, *highly* misleading. What their data actually shows is that wearing a mask all the time gave a slightly lower risk of COVID infection than never wearing a mask, but the difference was not significant; while wearing a mask sometimes not only "did not lower infection risk," it very significantly *increased* risk of infection. And if you pool together the groups wearing a mask sometimes or always, the data shows wearing a mask sometimes or always significantly *increased* risk of infection compared to never wearing a mask. The sentence in the abstract should actually have said, "Wearing masks all the time during contact slightly reduced risk of infection, but the difference was not significant; wearing a mask sometimes during contact significantly *increased* risk of infection."

Here's the data they present for distance of contact from the index person.

Table 1. Distance of contact

Shortest distance of contact	Cases (infected)	Controls (uninfected)	Infected as a percent of total and p value
Physical contact	132	292	31.2%
≤1 meter, without contact	61	335	15.4%, P<0.0001 versus physical contact
> 1 meter	4	182	2.1%, P<0.0001 versus <1 meter, without contact

Not making physical contact with the index person cut risk of infection in half if you were within 1 meter and to almost nothing if you were more than 1 meter away from the index person. So this is a huge factor.

Table 2. Hand washing

Handwashing behavior	Cases (infected)	Controls (uninfected)	Infected as a percent of total and p value
None	44	121	26.6%
Sometimes	114	333	25.5%, P=0.76
Often	52	372	12.2%, P<0.0001

From this, frequent handwashing significantly decreased risk of infection, as is shown by other studies discussed in Chapter 16.

Table 3. Mask wearing

Mask wearing behavior	Cases (infected)	Controls (uninfected)	Infected as a percent of total and p value versus not wearing a mask
None	102	500	16.9%
Sometimes	79	125	38.7%, P<0.0001, higher risk
Always	29	198	12.7%, P=0.17, lower risk
Always or sometimes	108	323	25.1%, P=0.002, higher risk

What the mask data actually says is that "sometimes" wearing a mask results in highly significantly greater risk of contracting COVID. Always wearing a mask results in slightly lower risk of contracting COVID compared to not wearing a mask, but the difference was not statistically significant (P=0.17, or 17% probability the difference is due to random chance). Pooling those who always and sometimes wore a mask, they had a significantly greater risk of contracting COVID than those who never wore a mask.

This is data the CDC cites to supposedly show that mask wearing reduces the risk of contracting COVID, when it actually shows mask wearing significantly *increases* the risk of contracting COVID. You may be objecting, "How is it possible that mask wearing could increase your risk of contracting COVID?" The answer is it could lead to touching your face more often, and touching your face with virus on your hands is likely the most important risk for contracting COVID, as shown by the risk of physical contact with the index case and the reduced risk with frequent hand washing, and as described in Chapter 14.

The next reference the CDC cites to support the proposition that mask wearing reduces COVID transmission is Wang et al. (9). This reports "a retrospective cohort study of 335 people in 124 families and with at least one laboratory confirmed COVID-19 case was conducted from 28 February to 27 March 2020, in Beijing, China. The outcome of interest was secondary transmission of severe acute respiratory syndrome coronavirus 2 (SARS-CoV-2) within the family." This reports that families that reported mask wearing before the index cases became symptomatic were less likely to have transmission from the index case than families that were not wearing masks before the index person became sick. So mask wearing by the other people in the household before the index case became symptomatic was a factor associated with reduced secondary COVID transmission risk. But so was frequent house cleaning and frequent surface disinfection in the household. Undoubtedly, all these factors were associated with each other, and undoubtedly hand washing was as well. That is, households that wore masks in the household even before anyone became symptomatic with COVID (and who wears masks inside their own house when no one is sick?!) are also households that clean frequently and wash their hands frequently. So you cannot say whether it was the mask wearing or the surface disinfection or hand washing, or all of the above, that cut COVID risk. So I do not find this convincing at all that mask wearing independently cuts infection risk. Moreover, the same study found that mask wearing after the index case became symptomatic did not cut secondary infection risk. That is, households that began mask wearing only when the first person became symptomatic were just as likely to have secondary transmission as households that never wore masks in the house. That cuts against the idea that mask wearing reduces risk. If masks make a difference, they should make a difference after symptoms develop as well as before; in fact they should make a greater difference after symptoms develop because we know that is when most or nearly all transmission of infection happens (Chapter 18).

The last reference with real data cited by the CDC is Payne et al. (7). This was a survey of 382 U.S. Navy sailors aboard an aircraft carrier experiencing a COVID-19 outbreak. The sailors were tested for COVID antibodies in April 2020, and 60% had reactive antibodies. All 382 completed a questionnaire about their behavior including mask wearing and social distancing (i.e., trying to keep more distance from others). It reported that mask wearing, avoiding common areas, and increasing distance from others were all associated with lower likelihood of a positive COVID antibody test. But again, as with Wang et al., those traits were undoubtedly associated with each other and with more frequent hand washing and generally making more effort to avoid being infected. So it is really not possible to say from this that mask wearing independently reduced infection rates.

In summary, the data the CDC cites to prove that mask wearing reduces risk of COVID infection are:

- An anecdote that one hair stylist infected one other, probably when they were not wearing masks.
- A study from Thailand that actually shows that mask wearing significantly *increased* risk of COVID infection.
- A study from China that states that mask wearing within a household before anyone in the household was symptomatic with COVID was associated with reduced secondary transmission in the household, as was disinfectant use in the household. This just shows that cleanliness in general, probably including hand washing, reduces risk of COVID. It could easily be, and probably is, the hand washing or the surface disinfection that really reduced COVID risk. Also, the study reported that mask wearing after the primary infected person became symptomatic was not associated with reduced secondary transmission of COVID. That suggests the mask wearing had no effect because we know symptomatic people are much more infectious than asymptomatic people are (see Chapter 18), so if mask wearing reduced transmission, it should affect it more so after symptoms develop than before.
- A study on a U.S. Navy carrier that, like the China study, reported that mask wearing was associated with reduced risk of COVID infection on the ship. But again this could be explained by other behaviors such as hand washing.

None of these are controlled clinical trials. None of them independently analyzed mask wearing separately from other factors such as hand washing, except the Thailand study, which actually showed mask wearing very significantly *increased* risk of COVID infection.

The data the CDC cites do not actually provide any real evidence that mask wearing reduces COVID transmission risk. I would say the CDC-cited data tend to show that mask wearing *increases* transmission risk, which is entirely possible because it tends to lead to touching your face more often.

References:

1. Bundgaard H, Bundgaard JS, et al. 2020. Effectiveness of Adding a Mask Recommendation to Other Public Health Measures to Prevent SARS-CoV-2 Infection in Danish Mask Wearers : A Randomized Controlled Trial. *Ann Intern Med*. 2020 Nov 18;M20-6817. PMID: 33205991 PMCID: PMC7707213. https://doi.org/10.7326/M20-6817

2. Chan JF-W, Yuan S, Zhang AJ, Poon V K-M, et al. 2020. Surgical Mask Partition Reduces the Risk of Noncontact Transmission in a Golden Syrian Hamster Model for Coronavirus Disease 2019 (COVID-19). *Clinical Infectious Diseases*, 71:2139-2149. 15 October 2020. https://doi.org/10.1093/cid/ciaa644

3. Doung-Ngern P, Suphanchaimat R, Panjangampatthana A, et al. Case-Control Study of Use of Personal Protective Measures and Risk for Severe Acute Respiratory Syndrome Coronavirus 2 Infection, *Thailand*. *Emerg Infect Dis*. 2020;26(11). https://doi.org/10.3201/eid2611.203003 https://www.ncbi.nlm.nih.gov/pubmed/32931726

4. Hendrix MJ, Walde C, Findley K, Trotman R. 2020. Absence of Apparent Transmission of SARS-CoV-2 from Two Stylists After Exposure at a Hair Salon with a Universal Face Covering Policy – Springfield, Missouri, May 2020. *MMWR Morb Mortal Wkly Rep*. 2020;69(28):930-932. https://doi.org/10.15585/mmwr.mm6928e2 https://www.ncbi.nlm.nih.gov/pubmed/32673300

5. Jefferson T, Del Mar CB, Dooley L, et al. 2020. Physical interventions to interrupt or reduce the spread of respiratory viruses. *Cochrane Database Syst Rev*. 2020 Nov 20;11:CD006207. PMID: 33215698. https://doi.org/10.1002/14651858.CD006207.pub5

6. Noti JD, Lindsley WG, Blachere FM, et al. 2012. Detection of infectious influenza virus in cough aerosols generated in a simulated patient examination room. *Clin Infect Dis* 54(11):1569-77. PMID: 22460981 PMCID: PMC4680957 https://doi.org/10.1093/cid/cis237

7. Payne DC, Smith-Jeffcoat SE, Nowak G, et al. SARS-CoV-2 Infections and Serologic Responses from a Sample of U.S. Navy Service Members – USS Theodore Roosevelt, April 2020. *MMWR Morb Mortal Wkly Rep*. 2020;69(23):714-721. https://www.ncbi.nlm.nih.gov/pubmed/32525850 https://doi.org/10.15585/mmwr.mm6923e4

8. U.S. Centers for Disease Control and Prevention. https://www.cdc.gov/coronavirus/2019-ncov/more/masking-science-sars-cov2.html

9. Wang Y, Tian H, Zhang L, et al. Reduction of secondary transmission of SARS-CoV-2 in households by face mask use, disinfection and social distancing: a cohort study in Beijing, China. *BMJ Glob Health*. 2020;5(5). https://www.ncbi.nlm.nih.gov/pubmed/32467353 https://doi.org/10.1136/bmjgh-2020-002794

Chapter 16

....

Hand Washing and Hand Sanitizer

There is good evidence that hand washing and use of hand sanitizers reduce the risk and spread of the common cold and influenza and COVID-19.

The following are four of the best studies that I find very convincing.

White, Koble et al. (4), studied the effect of hand sanitizing in college students on upper-respiratory tract infection.

Methods: This study involved a total of 430 students recruited from 4 residence halls during the fall semester at the University of Colorado at the Boulder campus. Dormitories were paired into control and product groups. In the product groups, alcohol gel hand-sanitizer dispensers were installed in every room, bathroom, and dining hall. The data were statistically analyzed for the differences between product and control groups in reported symptoms, illness rates, and absenteeism from classes.

Results: The overall increase in hand-hygiene behavior and reduction in symptoms, illness rates, and absenteeism between the product group and control group was statistically significant. Reductions in upper respiratory-illness symptoms ranged from 14.8% to 39.9%. Total improvement in illness rate was 20%. The product group had 43% less missed school/work days.

Conclusion: Hand-hygiene practices were improved with increased frequency of handwashing through increasing awareness of the importance of hand hygiene, and the use of alcohol gel hand sanitizer in university dormitories. This resulted in fewer upper respiratory-illness symptoms, lower illness rates, and lower absenteeism.

The following study is impressive because it is double-blind placebo-controlled and tests hand sanitizer versus soap alone (White, Shinder et al. (5)). Soap alone kills virus, so I would ordinarily not have expected the addition of hand sanitizer to make much difference. But in this case the researchers used a non-ionic soap or surfactant (no positive or negative charge to the soap molecule), which does not kill virus, whereas most ordinary soap is negatively charged and kills bacteria and virus. So the surfactant or soap helped clean the hands and remove virus from the hands, but it would not have killed the virus that remained on the hands. The hand sanitizer molecule would have killed the virus that remained on the hands after washing. The sanitizer used was not alcohol and had no odor, so the participants could not tell whether they were using just soap or soap + sanitizer, allowing the study to be double blind.

The purpose of this double-blind, placebo-controlled study was to assess whether an alcohol-free, instant hand sanitizer containing surfactants, allantoin, and benzalkonium chloride could reduce illness absenteeism in a population of 769 elementary school children and serve as an effective alternative when regular soap and water hand washing was not readily available. Prior to the study, students were educated about proper hand washing technique, the importance of hand washing to prevent transmission of germs, and the relationship between germs and illnesses. Children in kindergarten through the 6th grade (ages 5-12) were assigned to the active or placebo hand-sanitizer product and instructed to use the product at scheduled times during the day and as needed after coughing or sneezing. Data on illness absenteeism were tracked. After 5 weeks, students using the active product were 33% less likely to have been absent because of illness when compared with the placebo group.

Another study along the same lines assessed the effectiveness of the use of an alcohol gel hand sanitizer in the classroom to help decrease the illness-related absentee rate for elementary school students (Hammond et al. (3)).

Methods: This study involved 5 individual school districts, 16 individual schools, and more than 6000 students in Delaware, Ohio, Tennessee, and California. Individual schools in each district were paired into product and control groups. In the product group schools, an alcohol gel hand sanitizer was used by the students and staff when entering and leaving the classroom. Absenteeism due to infection was recorded, and the data were statistically analyzed.

Results: The overall reduction in absenteeism due to infection in the schools included in this study was 19.8% for schools that used an alcohol gel hand sanitizer compared with the control schools (P <.05). Data from the school system with the largest teacher population (n = 246) showed that teacher absenteeism decreased 10.1% (trend) in the schools where sanitizer was used.

Conclusion: Elementary school absenteeism due to infection is significantly reduced when an alcohol gel hand sanitizer is used in the classroom as part of a hand hygiene program.

The paper showing the effectiveness of hand washing that I found most impressive is Cowling et al. (1). This pertained to influenza specifically and was done in Hong Kong.

Patients with newly diagnosed PCR-diagnosed influenza at urgent care clinics who lived in households with at least two other persons were recruited. Clinicians went to their household as soon as possible after the "index" person's diagnosis with influenza and got informed consent from the household members. Each household was given one of three interventions. The same instructions were given to every member of the household, both the influenza-infected primary person and the so-far uninfected other members of the household. The three groups and the instructions given to each group were as follows:

1. Control group. Just education on healthy diet and lifestyle.

2. Instructed to wash hands and alcohol rub frequently (after washroom visit, after sneezing and coughing, when hands are soiled, and after first returning home, and after touching surfaces they think may be contaminated).

3. Hand washing as in group 2, plus wear surgical facemasks inside the house.

The study recruited 407 people presenting to outpatient clinics with influenza-like illness who were positive for influenza A or B virus by rapid testing (index patients) and 794 household members (contacts) in 259 households.

Household members were followed for 7 days to determine if they contracted influenza.

Among the those contacted by home visit for intervention within 36 hours of diagnosis (the differences were less in homes contacted more than 36 hours after the initial diagnosis), the results were these:

Table 1. Number of household contacts contracting influenza by intervention group. (P value vs. control group)

Type of diagnosis	Control group (n=183)	Hand hygiene alone (n=130)	Facemask plus hand hygiene (n=149)	Both hand hygiene groups (n=279)
PCR-confirmed influenza	22 (12%)	7 (5%) (P=0.049)	6 (4%) (P=0.040)	13 (4%) (P=0.006)
PCR-confirmed or clinical symptomatic influenza	48 (26%)	17 (13%) (P=0.005)	28 (19%) (P=0.12)	45 (16%) (P=0.009)

PCR-confirmed influenza means that influenza virus could be detected in a nasal swab from the person. The other infected persons in the bottom row include persons who were diagnosed with influenza by symptoms but in whom virus was not detected. So 22 of 183 contacts (12%) in the control group became infected with PCR confirmation during the 7 days versus 7 of 130 (5%) in the hand washing alone group and 6 of 149 (4%) in the hand washing plus facemask group. Those ratios in the handwashing groups are both statistically significantly different from the control group, with a P value less than 0.05, meaning there is less than a 5% possibility that the differences would occur by random chance. For the two handwashing groups pooled together 13 of 279 (5%) were infected versus 22 of 183 (12%) in the control group, and that difference is highly significant, with a P value of 0.006, meaning less than a 1% possibility the difference could be due to chance.

For both PCR-confirmed and symptomatic influenza, which seems to me to be the better comparison, both the handwashing alone group and the two pooled handwashing groups had fewer infections at a highly significant difference level (less than 1% possibility the difference was due to chance) versus the controls, but the handwashing plus mask wearing group did less well (19% infected) than the handwashing alone group (13% infected). The P value comparing the handwashing alone group (17 of 130 infected, 13%) versus the handwashing plus masks group (28 of 149 infected, 19%) is 0.25, meaning there is a 25%

possibility that the difference is due to chance. That is not statistically significant, but it means more likely than not the difference is real and not due to chance. I suspect the difference is real and mask wearing actually increases the likelihood of infection. The reason would be that people are more likely to touch their faces if they are wearing a mask, in order to reposition the mask or fit it, and touching your face, specifically the mouth, nostrils, or eyes, with hands that have virus on them, the evidence indicates, is the primary means of becoming infected, as shown in Chapter 14.

One of the impressive things about the Cowling paper (1) is they report that if researchers did not reach the households within 36 hours of the initial influenza diagnosis of the index person, then the hand washing intervention did not make any difference, but if they did, it cut infections of other people in the household about in half. That suggests if the household members had been washing their hands more from the moment the index person became symptomatic, it would have cut infections even more than in half. The data of Gwaltney discussed in Chapter 14 suggests that nearly all transmission of viral upper respiratory tract infection is by the virus getting on our hands and then us touching a mucous membrane of our face (the eyes, nose, or mouth). If that is so, it means that if you are really religious about constantly washing your hands and can train yourself not to touch your face unless you just washed your hands, you can almost eliminate your risk of COVID infection. And if everyone did that, we could have stopped the epidemic, with no other interventions.

(Admittedly, the not touching your face part is very difficult and maybe not realistic. We all touch our faces constantly. Retraining ourselves would be hard. Someone I discussed this with suggested that the CDC, instead of mandating mask wearing, should have mandated we all walk around with clear plastic cones, like we put on our dogs to keep them from scratching themselves, that would be narrow on our necks and expand over our heads to prevent us from touching our faces.)

For COVID-19 specifically, the evidence also shows that hand washing dramatically cuts the rate of transmission.

Doung-Ngern et al. (2), discussed in Chapter 15, was cited by the FDA for data allegedly supporting mask wearing, but, as discussed in Chapter 13, its data, in fact, does not support mask wearing. However, its data does show hand washing is effective.

Doung-Ngern et al., again, is a study from Thailand that involved contact tracing of three large COVID-19 clusters in nightclubs, boxing stadiums, and a state enterprise office in Thailand. Eighteen (18) primary index COVID-positive persons were the original infected people (index persons). Contacts (1706 persons) who were originally asymptomatic but were known to be in close contact with the index persons were identified. Of the 1706 contacts, 666 were excluded from the analysis and 1050 were analyzed, of whom 211 became infected with COVID within 2 weeks (cases) and 839 did not (controls). The paper compares the characteristics of the cases who became infected to the controls who did not become infected, particularly their mask wearing and other behaviors.

Table 2. Hand washing data of Doung-Ngern (2).

Handwashing behavior	Cases (infected)	Controls (uninfected)	Infected as a percent of total and p value vs. "none" group.
None	44	121	26.6%
Sometimes	114	333	25.5%, P=0.76
Often	52	372	12.2%, P<0.0001

This shows frequent hand washing cut infection risk in half and the difference was highly significant.

The evidence is quite convincing that hand washing and use of hand sanitizers decreases upper respiratory tract infections, and the available data shows the same is true for COVID-19. Hand washing is a more effective intervention than mask wearing. Mask wearing, as is shown in Chapter 15, has little or no effect on reducing upper respiratory tract infections or COVID-19 infections.

Our health and government officials have clearly oversold mask wearing, but I think they have actually *underemphasized* the much more effective intervention of hand washing and use of hand sanitizers.

A personal story on hand washing: I had cancer in 2002 and underwent chemotherapy. I was worried about contracting a cold or flu while I was immunocompromised from the chemotherapy and dying from the infection, and I asked my oncologist about that. He said, "Don't worry about it. If you wash your hands religiously and use hand sanitizer and remember not to touch your eyes, nose, or mouth unless you just washed your hands, you can pretty much eliminate your risk of catching a cold or the flu. So wash your hands a lot and use hand sanitizer." That was a great message, and it turns out it was accurate also. It put my fate in my own hands. It was an empowering message: I could control my risk of infection by just washing my hands.

Note he did not tell me, "Yep, you are doomed unless we can convince everyone else in society to wear a mask constantly," which is essentially the message we get from the health officials and government officials about COVID. In addition to being wrong, that message is also very depressing and disempowering. It constitutes telling us we are all victims and dependent on everyone else to protect us.

References:

1. Cowling BJ, Chan K-H, Fang VJ et al. 2009. Facemasks and Hand Hygiene to Prevent Influenza Transmission in Households, A Cluster Randomized Trial. *Annals of Internal Medicine* 151:437-446. https://doi.org/10.7326/0003-4819-151-7-200910060-00142

2. Doung-Ngern P, Suphanchaimat R, Panjangampatthana A, et al. 2020. Case-Control Study of Use of Personal Protective Measures and Risk for Severe Acute Respiratory Syndrome Coronavirus 2 Infection, *Thailand. Emerg Infect Dis.* 26(11). https://www.ncbi.nlm.nih.gov/pubmed/32931726 https://doi.org/10.3201/eid2611.203003

3. Hammond B, Ali Y et al. 2000. Effect of hand sanitizer use on elementary school absenteeism. *Am J Infect Control* 28(5):340-6. PMID: 11029132 https://doi.org/10.1067/mic.2000.107276

4. White C, Kolble R, et al. 2003. The effect of hand hygiene on illness rate among students in university residence halls. *Am J Infect Control.* 31(6):364-70. PMID: 14608304 https://doi.org/10.1016/s0196-6553(03)00041-5

5. White CG, Shinder FS, et al. 2001. Reduction of illness absenteeism in elementary schools using an alcohol-free instant hand sanitizer. *J Sch Nurs* 17(5):258-65. PMID: 11885342

Chapter 17

Social Distancing

Does social distancing—people standing further from each other in public than we typically do—reduce transmission of COVID or other respiratory diseases?

There have not been any controlled clinical trials on the efficacy of social distancing to reduce spread of upper respiratory tract viruses. The best way to do such a trial would probably be in a school to have one elementary or high school where students stagger their desks to sit at least 6 feet from each other and where students are instructed to keep 3 feet or 6 feet from each other in the hallways and lunchrooms at all times, and a comparable school where it is business as usual, and compare the rates of student absences and sicknesses in the two schools. You would want to compare whole schools rather than classrooms because if students from different classrooms mix in the hallways and at lunch, you would not have a pure comparison between students who always socially distance and students who never do. The two groups would have the same behavior in the hallways and at lunch. No one has ever done a clinical trial either by school or by classroom or with any other design to test social distancing as a strategy.

The evidence suggests that nearly all upper respiratory tract infections pass by contact with hands and then touching your hands to yourself at or near a mucous membrane of the face (the mouth, nose, or eyes) (Chapter 14). The study of Gwaltney discussed in Chapter 14 reached that conclusion. And the fact that hand washing cuts transmission of colds, flu, and COVID at least in half (Chapter 16) and mask wearing has little if any effect (Chapter 15) is consistent with that and supports that conclusion.

Social distancing, therefore, would cut infections by reducing transmission via large droplets (that drop to the ground by gravity within a few feet from the infected person). It could do that in part by preventing the droplets from going directly from the infected person's mouth to your own mouth, nose, or eyes. But more likely, its effect would be to reduce droplets that strike somewhere else on your body, which you then wipe and get virus on your hands and you then touch a mucous membrane of your face to infect yourself.

The effect social distancing would have would be to prevent droplets getting on your body before the droplets can drop to the ground. How far away do you need to be to avoid that? We have probably all had the experience of accidentally "spraying it, not saying it," i.e. accidentally emitting spittle because we are laughing or talking excitedly, and then noticing that spittle hit our conversation partner. How far away from others do you need to be to avoid that? I would say 3 feet or one meter is probably enough to prevent 90% of that, and 6 feet would prevent the remaining 10%. So I would say 3 feet is really enough.

The surface area of a sphere is proportional to the square of the radius. So the likelihood of a droplet emitted from another person's mouth striking your face, or any other target on your body, is inversely proportional to the distance squared (meaning raised to the 2nd power). So at 3 feet you would be $1/3^2$ or 1/9th as likely to be hit by that droplet as at 1 foot from the other person. Going to 6 feet instead of 3 feet would only make another 1/4-fold difference and you would be 1/36th as likely to be hit by the droplet compared to a 1-foot distance.

The World Health Organization recommends social distancing of 1 meter or 3 feet. The U.S. CDC recommends 6 feet. I cannot help but suspect that the reason the U.S. authorities expanded that to 6 feet is because our standard social distance in the U.S.—the distance you stand from others when talking to them—is about 3 feet, maybe 2 feet at the shortest. So if the CDC recommended a distance of 3 feet, it would not be a perceptible change for us. We already stand 3 feet from others if it is at all possible because we are socially uncomfortable standing closer than that. The purpose, then, of the 6 foot recommendation was not to reduce COVID transmission, but to remind us we are in a "catastrophic" epidemic and must change our behavior to fight it. It was to provide a reminder—as if the masks were not enough—that we are in a pandemic and this is the worst year of our lives, and to provide another reason to divide us from each other and hate each other: "If someone stands less than 6 feet from you, she is a terrible person and is trying to kill you."

As I said, no controlled clinical trial or experiments have been done on social distancing. The best data I know of is Duoug-Ngren et al. (1), cited and discussed for mask wearing and hand washing in Chapters 15 and 16.

Duong-Ngern et al., again, is a study from Thailand that involved contact tracing of three large COVID-19 clusters in nightclubs, boxing stadiums, and a state enterprise office in Thailand. Eighteen (18) primary index COVID-positive persons were the original infected people (index persons). Contacts (1706 persons) who were originally asymptomatic but were known to be in close contact with the index persons were identified. Of the 1706 contacts, 666 were excluded from the analysis and 1050 were analyzed, of whom 211 became infected with COVID within 2 weeks (cases) and 839 did not (controls). The paper compares the characteristics of the cases who became infected to the controls who did not become infected, particularly their mask wearing and other behaviors.

Here's the data they present for distance of contact from the index person.

Table 1. Distance of contact

Shortest distance of contact	Cases (infected)	Controls (uninfected)	Infected as a percent of total and p value
Physical contact	132	292	31.2%
<1 meter, without contact	61	335	15.4%, P<0.0001 versus physical contact
> 1 meter	4	182	2.1%, P<0.0001 versus <1 meter, without contact

Not making physical contact with the index person cut risk of infection in half if you were within 1 meter and to almost nothing if you were more than 1 meter away from the index person. So this is a huge factor. But 1 meter, or 3 feet, is enough.

In conclusion, the Duong-Ngern et al. data indicates there is definitely an advantage to not touching infected people and a further advantage to keeping three feet from them. There is no evidence that keeping 6 feet instead of 3 feet from an infected person has any advantage, and the math of the area of a sphere, which controls how likely you are to be hit with droplets, suggests there is little advantage in going from 3 feet to 6 feet.

The reason distance from an infected person makes transmission of COVID or colds or flu less likely is probably not that it makes it less likely virus will pass directly from their mouth or nose into your mouth or nose, but rather that it makes it less likely virus they breathe out in droplets will land on your body, where you will subsequently touch yourself to put the virus on your hands and then touch your mouth, nose, or eyes to infect yourself. So to the extent you are within 3 feet of an infected person for some length of time, you can probably still prevent or dramatically reduce your risk of being infected by washing your hands and not touching your face.

Most importantly, any small advantage to keeping 6 feet instead of 3 feet away only applies with *infected* people, and probably only *symptomatic* infected people, as we will see in Chapter 18. Keeping 6 feet from *all* people, nearly all of whom are not currently infected with COVID or any other viral respiratory disease, serves no purpose except to divide us from each other and send the message "I am afraid of you."

References:

1. Doung-Ngern P, Suphanchaimat R, Panjangampatthana A, et al. 2020. Case-Control Study of Use of Personal Protective Measures and Risk for Severe Acute Respiratory Syndrome Coronavirus 2 Infection, *Thailand. Emerg Infect Dis.* 26(11). https://www.ncbi.nlm.nih.gov/pubmed/32931726 https://doi.org/10.3201/eid2611.203003

Chapter 18

Follow the Science: Asymptomatic People Do Not Transmit COVID

Throughout the COVID lockdown we have been hearing a lot of horror stories that "we know asymptomatic people transmit COVID" or at least "asymptomatic people may transmit COVID" and therefore all the restrictions are justified and necessary. That assumption turns out to be incorrect, and the statements that "we *know* asymptomatic people transmit COVID" were simply false. We never *knew* that because it is not true.

CDC authors published a paper on January 7, 2021 (Johannsen et al.) cited as evidence that asymptomatic persons transmit COVID. The press trumpeted it with the headline "Over half of COVID-19 cases are spread by asymptomatic carriers, CDC study finds" (https://www. news-medical.net/news/20210111/Over-half-of-COVID-19-cases-are-spread-by-asymptomatic-carriers-CDC-study-finds.aspx). But in fact, what the authors reported was not data at all. It was a *model* that used the *assumption* that asymptomatic infected people transmit COVID as input for the model and then trumpeted the output for the model as a finding that—surprise, surprise—asymptomatic people transmit COVID. It put the following sentence as a result: "The baseline <u>assumptions</u> for the <u>model</u> were that peak infectiousness occurred at the median of symptom onset and that 30% of individuals with infection never develop symptoms and are 75% as infectious as those who do develop symptoms." That is not a result; that is an assumption.

That assumption was based on cited studies that allegedly showed that viral loads found in sputum and nasal samples peak about the day of symptom onset and are relatively high for at least 2 days before symptom onset. The only study I have found that has direct evidence (and the only study they cited that has direct evidence) suggesting that viral loads peak at symptom onset is He et al., and that data is very, very unconvincing. It is based on rt-PCR testing (a way of detecting virus) of nasal and throat swabs in a Chinese hospital. There were far fewer samples taken in days 0, 1, or 2 after symptom onset, since obviously people with no symptoms do not go to the hospital and it usually takes at least a couple of days after symptoms begin to feel sick enough to go to the hospital. So it appears to me and others (Slifka et al.) that there was little or no basis for the claim that viral loads were higher at the time of symptom onset than several days later, and certainly no basis for the claim that viral loads were higher before symptom onset, since there was no data at all on viral loads before symptom onset or in asymptomatic persons known to be infected.

Even if it is true that viral loads are high on the day of symptom onset or are high in asymptomatic people, it would not mean that asymptomatic people transmit SARS-CoV-2 infection. It would also be possible that despite virus present in their throats and noses, asymptomatic people do not transmit the disease, perhaps because they do not cough or sneeze or wipe fluids from their nose onto their hands. What you want is direct evidence of whether asymptomatic people transmit SARS-CoV-2 infection, not an assumption that they do.

Those studies looking for direct evidence of asymptomatic transmission have been done, and the data clearly shows that infected asymptomatic people transmit COVID at significantly lower rates than symptomatic people, if they transmit it at all. A metaanalysis (Madewell et al.) of other studies looked at household transmission of COVID from asymptomatic and symptomatic infected persons. Household transmission is the best way to investigate the question because it is really only within households that you can have any reasonable confidence that people were exposed to an infected person and that if they become infected after another person in the household was known to be infected, they were probably infected by their household member. The authors calculated a secondary infection rate of 18.0% (95% confidence interval 14.2%-22.1%) from symptomatic individuals and 0.7% (95% confidence interval 0.0%-4.9%) from asymptomatic individuals. Again, <u>18.0% from symptomatic individuals versus 0.7% from asymptomatic individuals</u>. That is a big difference and highly significant. That was based on four studies that compared household transmission of asymptomatic and symptomatic infected individuals. The four studies (References 5-8) found 2/45, 1/23, 0/2, and 0/15 household contacts of the asymptomatic patients became infected. I would add that it is possible that the 3 cases attributed as from contact with an asymptomatic householder could have come from contact with someone outside the household. So we can conclude with certainty that asymptomatic infected individuals transmit COVID significantly less than symptomatic individuals. The best estimate is they transmit it at 4% of the rate of symptomatic individuals and the 95% confidence interval includes 0.0% transmission from asymptomatic individuals.

Transmission from asymptomatic individuals is low enough that it is not worth worrying about. R is the average number of persons an infected person transmits a virus to in a population. R_0 is the special case of R in a naïve population. The R_0 of SARS-CoV-2 was estimated at 1.4 to 4. (https://www.the-scientist.com/features/why-r0-is-problematic-for-predicting-covid-19-spread-67690). In order to maintain the epidemic, R has to stay above 1.0. If it falls below 1.0, that means the average infected person infects fewer than 1 new person and the epidemic therefore wilts away. Fewer and fewer people are infected over time. If asymptomatic people transmit COVID at less than 5% of the rate of symptomatic people, as the data appears to show, or even if they transmitted at less than 25% of the rate of symptomatic people, then asymptomatic people on their own cannot maintain the infection in society. The R from them is less than 1. You, therefore, only need to worry about transmission from symptomatic people.

References:

1. He X, Lau EHY, Wu P, et al. 2020. Temporal dynamics in viral shedding and transmissibility of COVID-19. *Nat Med.* 26(5):672-675. https://doi.org/10.1038/s41591-020-0869-5

2. Johansson, MA et al. 2021. SARS-CoV-2 Transmission From People Without COVID-19 Symptoms. *JAMA Netw Open.* 4(1):e2035057. https://doi.org/10.1001/jamanetworkopen.2020.35057

3. Madewell, ZJ et al. 2020. Household Transmission of SARS-CoV-2A Systematic Review and Meta-analysis. *JAMA Netw Open.* 3(12):e2031756. https://doi.org/10.1001/jamanetworkopen.2020.31756

4. Slifka MK, Gao L. 2020. Is presymptomatic spread a major contributor to COVID-19 transmission? *Nat Med* 26:1531–1533. https://doi.org/10.1038/s41591-020-1046-6

5. Chaw L, Koh WC, Jamaludin SA, Naing L, Alikhan MF, Wong J. 2020. SARS-CoV-2 transmission in different settings: analysis of cases and close contacts from the Tablighi cluster in Brunei Darussalam. *Emerg Infect Dis.* 26(11):2598-2606. https://doi.org/10.3201/eid2611.202263

6. Lee M, Eun Y, Park K, Heo J, Son H. 2020. Follow-up investigation of asymptomatic COVID-19 cases at diagnosis in Busan, Korea. *Epidemiol Health.* 42:e2020046. https://doi.org/10.4178/epih. e2020046

7. Lewis NM, Chu VT, Ye D, et al. 2020. Household transmission of SARS-CoV-2 in the United States. *Clin Infect Dis.* Published online August 16, 2020. https://doi.org/10.1093/cid/ciaa1166

8. Park SY, Kim Y-M, Yi S, et al. 2020. Coronavirus disease outbreak in call center, South Korea. *Emerg Infect Dis.* 26(8):1666-1670. https://doi.org/10.3201/eid2608.201274

Chapter 19

Quarantine

Quarantining can work to limit the spread of an infectious disease, at least in principle, if the quarantined person really has no contact with others until he or she is no longer contagious. "No contact" would have to mean also no indirect contact, such as touching a food plate that is later passed to another without first washing the plate. So no contact can be difficult to achieve in practice, even if the quarantined person is cooperating. If the quarantined person does not know he is infected or does not want you to know because he does not want to go into quarantine, then it is even more difficult to achieve successful quarantine.

We tried stay-at-home orders in many states in the U.S., which basically constitutes quarantining the entire population, and that had no apparent effect on COVID spread (Chapter 21).

In my view, the best evidence that quarantines can work is the examples of the countries that have been almost untouched by COVID. The table below shows the industrial countries with fewer than 150 COVID deaths per million population as of March 1, 2021 (for perspective, the U.S. is at 1,597 deaths per million on that date).

Nation	COVID deaths per million population as of March 1, 2021
Norway	114
India	113
Philippines	112
Iceland	85
Japan	63
Australia	35

South Korea	31
Hong Kong	27
Singapore	5
New Zealand	5

Source: worldometers.info/coronavirus

I have omitted China because I am not sure whether to trust their numbers, but China reports 3 deaths per million. India and the Philippines are hard to explain. The others all had strong policies of quarantining visitors for some time after arriving and made strong efforts to contact trace COVID cases and quarantine known COVID cases and in most cases quarantine their contacts as well. None of these countries ever issued nationwide stay-at-home orders. None closed their schools for more than a month. It seems to me the quarantine policies are probably the best explanation for their success.

This is not to say quarantines are worthwhile or that their benefit in reduced COVID deaths necessarily exceeds their harms to the economy and in inducing depression and causing suicides and other harms. That is a separate question. But it appears they can reduce COVID deaths.

The data shows stay-at-home orders, or quarantining the entire population, has had no apparent effect on the course of the epidemic anywhere they have been tried (Chapter 21). So quarantining needs to be targeted at visitors to the nation, which only makes sense when COVID is still quite rare in the nation, and targeted at symptomatic COVID patients.

We have seen that the data shows asymptomatic people either do not infect others with COVID or are much less infectious than symptomatic people. Reference (1) below studied quarantining in the 2003 SARS epidemic in China, involving the SARS-CoV-1 virus, similar to the SARS-CoV-2 virus that causes COVID-19. People were quarantined there after they had contact with a known SARS case, whether the index case was asymptomatic or symptomatic. They found that 24 of 383 (6.3%) of contacts with an index patient during the symptomatic phase of the index patient became infected. But 0 of 167 (0.0%) of contacts with asymptomatic or presymtomatic index patients became infected. The difference is extremely significant, p=0.0002. This means again that asymptomatic and presymptomatic infected people are not contagious, or at the least are much less contagious than symptomatic people. Resources and inconvenience should be focused where they make a difference; that means quarantine symptomatic people and not asymptomatic people, even if they are known to be infected with the virus. The authors of that paper, which came from the CDC incidentally, agreed with a focused strategy, saying: "Quarantine should be limited to persons who have contact with an actively ill SARS patient in the home or hospital," in other words, do not quarantine contacts who merely work with the index case but only those who live with the index patient or provided medical care to the index patient, and only contacts with an index patient during the time the index patient had symptoms.

That is actually broader than what I am proposing. They are proposing quarantining some people who are asymptomatic, but only those who had very close contact with a symptomatic person. I am saying only quarantine the symptomatic person.

In principle, that should be enough to stop the epidemic before it spreads. R is the average number of people an infected person infects. R_0 is R at time 0, meaning at the beginning of the outbreak in a naïve population that has not seen the virus before and therefore has no immunity. For COVID, R_0 is estimated at 1.4-4 (Chapter 18). R depends on behavior, including quarantines and hand washing, so it can be reduced. If R falls below 1, then the number of newly infected persons in a following time period is fewer than the number in the previous time period and the number of infected people declines and ultimately falls to zero, at least in theory. If the R_0 of COVID is 4, the upper limit of the estimates, in the absence of interventions, then if we can cut R by a factor of 4 we can get it below 1 and the epidemic can die out. We saw in the chapter on asymptomatic transmission (Chapter 18) that asymptomatic people are probably less than 5% or 1/20th as contagious as symptomatic people. In other words, their R is at most 0.2 or well below 1. This means we only need to worry about symptomatic people and we need only quarantine symptomatic people.

How long would symptomatic people need to quarantine for quarantines to be effective? Cheng et al. (2) was a study of 100 infected COVID index patients and 2761 close contacts. Of those secondary contacts, 22 became infected. Eighteen (18) of 1818 persons who contacted the index case within 5 days after symptom onset in the index case became infected versus 0 of 852 with contact only after 5 days. That difference was highly significant (P=0.002). This says that you really only need to quarantine people for five days—from the first day of symptom onset to 5 days after symptom onset. After 5 days of symptoms, the infected person is much less contagious.

I would say quarantine during symptoms or for just 5 days, maybe

7 days, after the first day of symptoms and no more, even if the person is still symptomatic then. That should be enough to get the R below 1. And we would be a lot more likely to get compliance if we told people, "Just quarantine yourself if you have symptoms, and then only for 7 days," than if we tell people *"Everyone* stay home and quarantine yourself for the next 7 *weeks,"* as we did with stay-at-home orders.

References:

1. U.S. Centers for Disease Control and Prevention (CDC). 2003. Efficiency of quarantine during an epidemic of severe acute respiratory syndrome--Beijing, China, 2003. *MMWR Morb Mortal Wkly Rep.* 2003 Oct 31;52(43):1037-40. PMID: 14586295.

2. Cheng H, Jian S, Liu D, et al. 2020. Contact Tracing Assessment of COVID-19 Transmission Dynamics in Taiwan and Risk at Different Exposure Periods Before and After Symptom Onset. *JAMA Intern Med.* 180(9):1156–1163. https://doi.org/10.1001/jamainternmed.2020.2020

Chapter 20

Follow the Science: Open the Schools Because Doing So Does Not Increase COVID Infections

CDC authors have published a peer-reviewed paper in the *Journal of the American Medical Association* (JAMA) in January of 2021 (Honein et al. (1)) saying:

> A case-control study of exposures among children aged 0 through 18 years with (n=154) and without (n=243) SARS-CoV-2 infection in Mississippi found that having attended gatherings and social functions outside the home as well as having had visitors in the home was associated with increased risk of infection; however, in-person school attendance during the 14 days prior to diagnosis was not. In the fall of 2020, 11 school districts in North Carolina with more than 90 000 students and staff were open for in-person education for 9 weeks. During this time, within-school transmissions were very rare (32 infections acquired in schools; 773 community-acquired infections) and there were no cases of student-to-staff transmission. Similarly, in a report released by CDC on January 26, 2021, with data from 17 K-12 schools in rural Wisconsin . . . (4876 students and 654 staff), COVID-19 incidence was lower in schools than in the community. During 13 weeks in the fall of 2020, there were 191 COVID-19 cases in staff and students, with only 7 of these cases determined to result from in-school transmission.

In other words, transmission of COVID is 20 times lower in schools than in the community, and opening schools has no effect on increasing transmission of COVID either in students or in the community.

Perhaps now we can open the schools since the CDC itself now says closing schools has no benefit for reducing COVID cases or deaths.

But no, as it turns out we cannot, because these are just CDC researchers, not the CDC leadership. Anthony Fauci and the CDC leadership, even after this paper came out, continued to resist opening schools.

It was known from published data at least by the summer of 2020 that closing schools had no effect—*none*—on reducing COVID cases.

The Public Health Agency of Sweden released a report in July 2020 (Reference 2) summarizing data available in Finland and Sweden at that time that all showed no significant COVID transmission in schools. Sweden never closed day cares or primary schools (age 2 to 15) but Finland did from March 18 to May 13. Despite that, there was no difference in the number of infections per capita in that age group between the two countries. In fact, Sweden's was somewhat lower, despite Sweden having more infections per capita in adults and more deaths per capita in adults. There were no deaths of children in either country. Moreover, Finland's infections in children did not increase when they reopened schools on May 14. In addition, the study found teachers and day care workers in Sweden had no elevated risk of COVID infection compared to persons in other occupations.

A study in France of a town with high rates of COVID infection in the spring of 2020, before the national lockdown and before closing schools there, found, "Prior to school closure on February 14, three SARS-CoV-2 infected pupils attended three separate schools with no secondary cases in the following 14 days among pupils, teachers and non-teaching staff of the same schools" (Fontanet et al. (3)). There was high clustering of infection among family members but, in view of the non-transmission from infected children in schools, the researchers concluded that the familial clustering involved transmission from parents to children and not vice versa. The researchers concluded, "There was no evidence of onwards transmission from children in the school setting." That was published June 29, 2020.

Similarly, reference (4), published on April 26, 2020, found no transmission from infected students in schools either to other students or to adult staff. Eighteen individuals (9 students and 9 staff) from 15 schools were confirmed as COVID-19 cases; all of these individuals had an opportunity to transmit the COVID-19 virus (SARS-CoV-2) to others in their schools. 735 students and 128 staff were close contacts of these initial 18 cases. No teacher or staff member contracted COVID-19 from any of the initial school cases. One child from a primary school and one child from a high school may have contracted COVID-19 from the initial cases at their schools.

Similarly, reference (5) found that early in the outbreak "an infected child did not transmit the disease despite close interactions within schools." And reference (6), published on May 28, 2020, found "no evidence of secondary transmission of COVID-19 from children attending school in Ireland."

There was never any evidence that children were a significant carrier of COVID-19 and never any evidence that closing schools would reduce COVID-19 infections of adults. That was just a hypothesis. By the summer of 2020 there was consistent and convincing evidence that children were *not* significant transmitters of COVID-19 and that closing schools contributed nothing, literally nothing, to reducing COVID transmission to adults. At the very beginning of this outbreak the evidence from China showed conclusively that children were at essentially no risk of death from COVID, and we now know they are at significantly lower risk of death from COVID than they are from ordinary influenza (Chapter 13). So we knew conclusively by the summer of 2020 that there was literally no benefit at all to closing schools. CDC researchers have now stated that as well in January 2021, but we knew that by the summer of 2020 and had a good idea that was the case in April 2020.

Somehow that data had no effect on recommendations from the CDC or state health authorities. This is not the way science or rational policy should work. Follow the data. The data is clear and it was clear by the summer of 2020: Closing schools has no benefit whatsoever in reducing COVID transmission because, although children can be infected, they rarely become ill at all, almost never die, rarely infect others, and are far less likely to infect others than adults are. *It is scandalous that any school was ever closed in the 2020-21 school year!*

I would add that, contrary to current CDC recommendations, there is no reason children should wear masks or socially distance in school, and plenty of reasons they should not. Again, they are at no risk from COVID and essentially do not transmit it to others, with or without masks. Forcing them to wear masks just impairs their enjoyment of life and school, impairs their learning, impairs their breathing, and contributes to depression and suicides—for no benefit whatsoever. There is also no net benefit to them socially distancing.

Teachers also should not be wearing masks. The school experience should be as normal as possible for children and little if anything is gained from teachers wearing masks. The teachers do not contract COVID from children and children are at no risk from the disease if they contract it from teachers. Teachers wearing masks just makes it harder for them to teach and impairs the education of the children.

It also serves to scare the children as a reminder that we are going through this "crisis" where supposedly everyone, including the children, is at terrible risk of death.

References:

1. Honein MA, Barrios LC, Brooks JT. Data and Policy to Guide Opening Schools Safely to Limit the Spread of SARS-CoV-2 Infection. *JAMA*. Published online January 26, 2021. https://doi.org/10.1001/jama.2021.0374

2. COVID-19 in schoolchildren: a comparison between Finland and Sweden. The Public Health Agency of Sweden. Article number 20108-1 from: https://www.folkhalsomyndigheten.se/publicer-at-material/

3. Fontanet, A et al. SARS-CoV-2 infection in primary schools in northern France: A retrospective cohort study in an area of high transmission. June 29, 2020. https://doi.org/10.1101/2020.06.25.20140178

4. NCfIRAS. COVID-19 in schools – the experience in NSW. Sydney: NSW Government, 2020. http://ncirs.org.au/sites/default/files/2020-04/NCIRS%20NSW%20Schools%20COVID_Summary_FINAL%20public_26%20April%202020.pdf

5. Danis K, Epaulard O, Bénet T, et al. Cluster of Coronavirus Disease 2019 (COVID-19) in the French Alps, February 2020. *Clin Infect Dis*. 2020;71(15):825-832. https://doi.org/10.1093/cid/ciaa424

6. Heavey L, Casey G, Kelly C, Kelly D, McDarby G. No evidence of secondary transmission of COVID-19 from children attending school in Ireland, 2020. *Euro Surveill*. 2020;25(21):pii=2000903. https://doi.org/10.2807/1560-7917.ES.2020.25.21.2000903

Chapter 21

Stay-at-Home Orders

Logically, one would think stay-at-home orders would reduce COVID spread. If no one ever left their home, if you had 100% compliance, how could they spread the disease to each other? But of course, people have to leave their homes for "essential" business. Many workers work in jobs classified as essential, so they had to go to work. Everyone at least needed to go to the grocery store occasionally to get food, unless you ordered every meal by delivery or had groceries delivered, in which case you still interacted with the delivery person. So it is impossible to literally lock everyone at home for over a month. Plus, even if that were theoretically possible, people did not always comply in the real world.

In any case, the data provides no evidence that the stay-at-home orders had any effect on COVID spread.

In my home state of Minnesota, a state-wide stay-at-home order was imposed on March 27 and lifted May 18. Here are charts of COVID deaths and hospitalization and COVID cases over that time period. The arrows show the time of imposing and lifting the stay-at-home orders. If stay-at-home orders worked as intended, one would expect when they were imposed deaths would decrease (after a week or two delay) and when they were lifted deaths would increase (again after a week or two delay). That is not what happened. Looking at the charts, it does not appear the stay-at-home order had any effect.

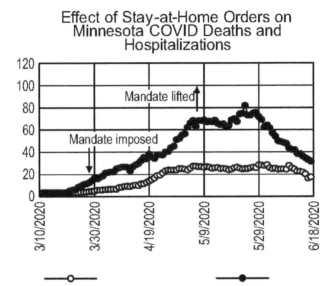

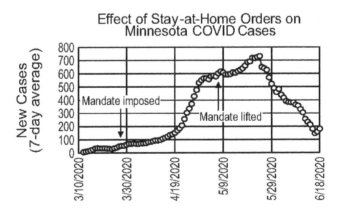

Below are the charts for deaths and cases in California, where a state-wide stay-at-home order was imposed on March 19 and lifted on May 7, 2020. Again, it does not appear the stay-at-home order had any effect on COVID transmission.

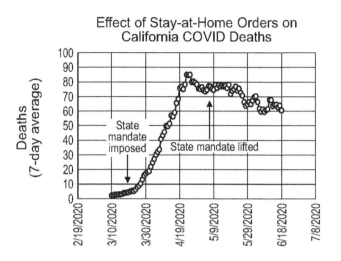

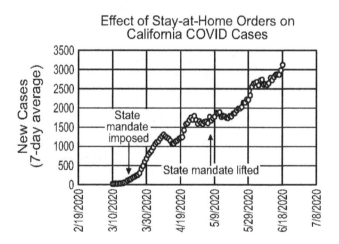

Below are the charts for New York state, where a state-wide stay-at-home order was imposed on March 22 and lifted on May 15, with the order continued in New York City until June 8. I see no hint in these charts, either, that the stay-at-home orders had any effect on COVID transmission.

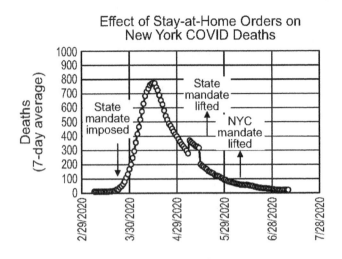

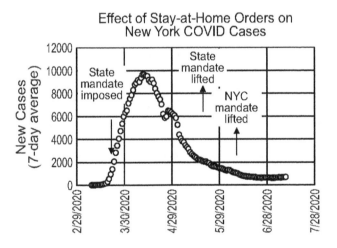

I did not cherry pick these states. It would not matter which state you used. There is no evidence that stay-at-home orders have had any effect on COVID transmission.

Stay-at-home orders as an infringement on liberty

People were remarkably compliant with stay-at-home orders. There were not many organized protests and the majority of people complied, as judged by the decrease in road traffic during stay-at-home orders in Minnesota. It surprises me because this is really a very extreme infringement on personal liberty.

A stay-at-home order is quite similar to a judicial sentence of home confinement as a sentence for a crime. In Minnesota the stay-at-home order was March 27 to May 18, 2020, which is 52 days. To receive a judicial sentence of 52 days of home confinement you need to commit a pretty serious crime. A second or third drunk driving conviction might do it. A first drunk driving offender would not be punished that severely. The sentence for gross misdemeanor assault would be in that range, according to a criminal attorney I talked to.

Two cases I noticed in the news recently shed light on the type of crime you have to commit to receive 52 days of home confinement. Tony LaRussa, a major league baseball manager, was arrested and pleaded guilty to his third drunk driving offense. He received one day of home confinement—yes, one day. Malik Beaseley, an NBA basketball player for the Minnesota Timberwolves, pleaded guilty to threatening a pregnant woman, her husband, and their child with a rifle. He received a sentence of 120 days of home confinement and was allowed to serve the sentence at a time more convenient for him, after the basketball season.

The Governor of Minnesota, merely by executive decree, sentenced every person in the state to 52 days of home confinement—with no due process and with the citizens having committed no crime and with no statute passed by the legislature—which is a judicial sentence roughly commensurate with the crime of a third drunk driving conviction or gross misdemeanor assault. Except that criminals who receive that sentence receive due process.

Chapter 22

....

Harming the Immune System as a Strategy to Reduce COVID Spread and COVID Deaths (?)

Our lockdown strategy included reducing or preventing face-to-face human interaction as much as possible by closing schools, houses of worship, health clubs, restaurants, and bars, and isolating the vulnerable elderly in long-term care facilities from one another and from their loved ones by banning visits from their children and loved ones, forcing them to eat alone in their rooms instead of communally with their fellow residents, and banning them from leaving the facilities to visit their children and outside friends. To the extent we could not prevent face-to-face human interaction, we ordered people to wear masks so they could not see whether they were smiling at each other.

The predictable result of that was to more than triple clinical depression and make everyone less happy. One side effect of being less happy and having less social interaction is that you have a weaker immune system and are more vulnerable to colds and flu and other upper respiratory infections, such as COVID-19, and have a higher death rate from all causes. That is well known. We've all seen articles in the media reporting the latest medical studies showing that people with two or three close friends that they can confide in have lower death rates than those with no close friends. Married people have lower death rates and stronger immune systems than single people, especially married people who report they are happy in their marriages. Every doctor knows or should know that being happier and having a stronger social support system improves your health and reduces your death risk from all causes.

It may not have been the intent of those who designed and advocated for the lockdown strategy to weaken our immune systems, but it might as well have been. That was a certain outcome of the strategy that anyone could have foreseen if you had thought about it at all. That factor undoubtedly has tended to increase COVID deaths, as well as deaths from all other causes. The lockdown strategy included closing health clubs. Insanity. We know that exercise improves health. If it were a drug it would be by far the best drug for almost every condition. And it improves immune function. So that has tended to increase COVID deaths, as well as impair health and happiness overall and increase the death rate from all causes. If your goal is to reduce death, even to reduce COVID deaths, the last thing you should be doing is making it harder for people to exercise.

We even closed national and state parks for a time in the U.S. The Sierra Club has stopped doing group outings during the pandemic. In some states and nations, the stay-at-home orders have included orders not to go outside unless it is essential. In Italy in the spring 2020 people were not allowed to go outside unless necessary to walk their pets. The result was people exchanged their dogs so all the neighbors took turns taking the same dog for a walk so each neighbor could be outside!

Being outside and in nature rivals exercise and social interaction as the best strategy for improving your physical and mental health, including improving your immune system. So discouraging people from going outside and in nature was and is insane, and of course tends to drive us to being insane. It undoubtedly has tended to increase COVID deaths.

And discouraging people from being outside has no benefit in reducing COVID spread. Even indoors with confined air the evidence indicates small particle aerosol transmission of upper respiratory tract infections, in other words transmission across a distance greater than 3 feet or so, just does not happen (Gwaltney et al. and Chapter 14). The only way COVID or a cold or flu is transmitted outdoors is if you shake hands with an infected person outdoors or touch an object (not a tree) that an infected person has touched, and maybe to a small extent if an infected person sneezes on you from a short distance outdoors. To close national and state parks, where people are nowhere near anyone who is not their companion, was insane. There was no rational basis for that policy.

The headline for this section is not a misprint. The policy for fighting COVID was essentially to do everything possible to harm our immune systems. A sane policy would have been to do everything possible to *strengthen* our immune systems.

References:

1. Gwaltney Jr. JM, Moskalsik PB, Hendley JO. 1978. Hand-to-hand transmission of rhinovirus colds. *Annals of Internal Medicine* 88:363-367. https://doi.org/10.7326/0003-4819-88-4-463

Chapter 23

The Best Estimate of Number of COVID Deaths Prevented by the Lockdowns: Zero

In Chapter 3, I determined that the most COVID deaths our lockdown policies might have prevented is 400,000 in the U.S., because with 400,000 more deaths we would be at herd immunity. And I used an assumption of 200,000 COVID deaths prevented as the estimate to compare the benefit of the COVID lockdowns, COVID deaths prevented, to the harms of depression, suicides, unemployment, and money cost, etc. But did the lockdowns really prevent 200,000 COVID deaths? There is no evidence they did. There is no evidence that all the governmental mandates put together have had *any effect at all* on COVID transmission or COVID deaths. The best estimate for the number of COVID deaths the lockdowns have prevented is zero. Yes, zero.

First, there is no evidence that states and nations that instituted stronger restrictions or had better compliance with the lockdown strategy have had fewer COVID deaths or hospitalizations. For instance, Sweden, the one major nation that did not mandate social distancing or implement the lockdown strategy, has had fewer COVID deaths per capita than the U.S. and fewer than most of the major nations in Europe.

Florida and California are probably the most similar states to each other in terms of climate and population density, and they have been on opposite ends of the lockdown index: California has had perhaps the strictest lockdowns in the nation and Florida's governor has refused to implement almost any restrictions. And Florida has an older population than California, which should strongly tend to produce more COVID deaths per capita. Yet their COVID death rates are nearly identical.

Wisconsin is most similar to its three neighboring states of Minnesota, Illinois, and Michigan. Wisconsin's state-wide COVID restrictions were struck down by the state supreme court, so it has had fewer COVID restrictions than Minnesota, Illinois, and Michigan. Yet it has had fewer COVID deaths per capita than all three of those states.

Ohio has a Republican governor and has had fewer COVID restrictions than its neighbors of Michigan and Pennsylvania, which are both similar to Ohio in population, demography, and climate. Yet Ohio has the fewest COVID deaths per capita of the three.

None of those differences are large. And there are contrary examples. North Dakota has been rather restrictive and South Dakota extremely non-restrictive, and South Dakota has a somewhat higher COVID death rate. North Carolina has been more restrictive than South Carolina and has a lower COVID death rate. But overall, you cannot look at U.S. state comparisons and see any pattern that more or less restrictions have any effect on COVID deaths per capita.

More Restrictive State	COVID deaths / million population as of Feb. 25, 2021		Less Restrictive State
California	1303	1426	Florida
Michigan	1646	1099	Wisconsin
Minnesota	1158		
Illinois	1789		
Michigan	1646	1470	Ohio
Pennsylvania	1878		
North Carolina	1067	1646	South Carolina
North Dakota	1892	2124	South Dakota

So if you look at the COVID data comparing states and nations that took somewhat different strategies, there is no evidence that the entire lockdown strategy, including social distancing, has made any difference at all in COVID transmission.

Here is a chart of daily new cases in different counties in southern California with arrows showing the dates various restrictions were imposed or lifted in each county (Source: Hold2, LLC, Reference 3).

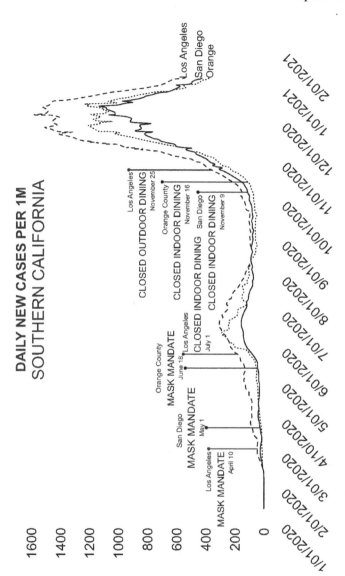

Does it look to you like any of the restrictions made any difference or correlate with one county doing better than another?

Here's a chart of COVID hospitalizations per million population in southern states, with arrows showing when mandates were imposed or lifted (Source: Hold2, LLC, Reference 3.)

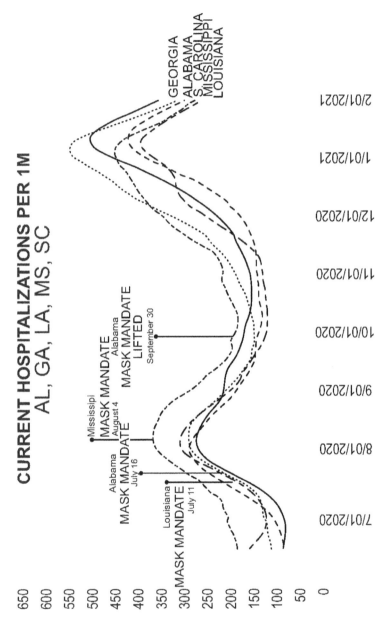

Does it look like imposing a mask mandate in Alabama or Louisiana made those states perform better than the other southern states? Does it look like lifting the mask mandate in Mississippi led to a spike in hospitalizations or led Mississippi to perform worse than the other southern states?

Here's a chart of COVID hospitalizations per million population in various midwestern states that took somewhat different approaches (Source: Hold2, LLC, Reference 3).

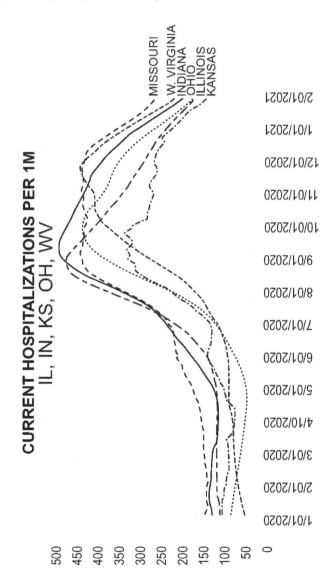

Is there anything to suggest that one state differs much from any other? Illinois generally had the tightest COVID restrictions of any of these states (Reference 2). Does it look like that led to fewer COVID hospitalizations in Illinois?

Republican governors have generally had slightly lower levels of COVID restrictions than Democratic governors—although there are many exceptions, especially of Republican governors with very tight restrictions, and every state has enacted pretty tight restrictions. Nonetheless, we can use Republican and Democratic governors as a surrogate of how tight the restrictions in different states have been. Here is a chart of rank of the 50 states plus the District of Columbia in COVID deaths per million population versus population rank (1 is low and 51 is high) for Republican and Democratic governors.

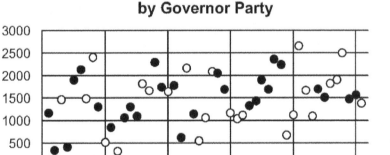

Does it look like the party of the governor has any correlation with COVID deaths per million?

Finally, here is a chart of the level of the rank of states in level of COVID restrictions versus rank in COVID deaths per million (Source: Reference 1, with data from Reference 2).

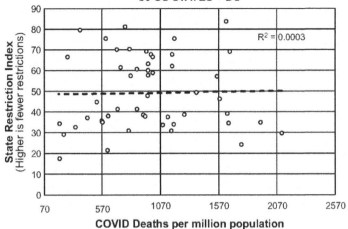

COVID DEATHS/MILLION POPULATION VS LEVEL OF COVID RESTRICION 50 US STATES + DC

There is no correlation at all of tightness of restrictions with number of COVID deaths per million. The slightly upsloping dotted line on the chart is the linear fit with the data. As you can see, there is no correlation. R^2 on the chart is a statistical measure of how tight the correlation of deaths to restrictions is, or in other words how good a fit that line is, and it is 0.0003. A statistically good fit would be 0.90 or higher. R^2 of 0.0003 means there is no correlation.

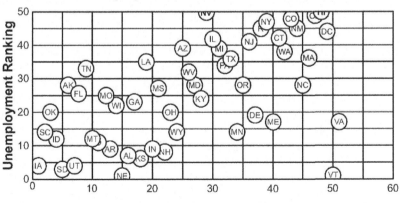

Unemployment versus COVID Restrictions

What *does* correlate with the tightness of COVID restrictions? Unemployment. Here's a chart of state rank in unemployment percentage versus rank in COVID restrictions index (Source: Reference 2).

Of the 26 states and DC with the most restrictions, 20 also rank in the top half of unemployment percentage. Of the 25 states with the fewest restrictions, 20 also rank in the bottom half of unemployment percentage. The P value for that comparison is less than 0.0001, or a less than 1 in 10,000 possibility the difference is due to chance.

Here's the evidence that the entire lockdown package—all of the government mandates put together—have had no effect at all on COVID deaths:

- Any chart of deaths, hospitalizations, or COVID cases plotted against time with marks indicating the times stay-at-home orders, the most extreme lockdown measure, are imposed and lifted—for any state or any nation you could choose—shows no evidence the stay-at-home orders have any effect on the trends. The trends do not go down when stay-at-home orders are imposed and do not go up when they are lifted. (Chapter 21.)
- Any chart of deaths, hospitalizations, or COVID cases plotted against time with marks indicating the times mask mandates, school closures, or any other restriction are imposed and lifted –for any state or any nation you could choose—shows no evidence the restrictions have any effect on the trends. The trends do not go down when restrictions are imposed and do not go up when they are lifted.
- Sweden, the only major western nation that did not impose lockdowns and imposed almost no restrictions at all, has fewer COVID deaths relative to population than the U.S., despite being a more northern and more urbanized country, both of which factors tend to result in more COVID deaths, and has fewer COVID deaths relative to population than most of the major countries in Europe, including the United Kingdom, France, Italy, and Spain. Other countries that imposed much less extreme COVID restrictions than the U.S., including Norway, Finland, Iceland, Korea, and Japan, had fewer COVID deaths relative to population even than Sweden and far fewer than the U.S. (Chapter 1)

- A chart of U.S. states by the severity of their lockdown measures versus COVID deaths per capita shows no correlation between the two whatsoever.
- For U.S. states, there is no correlation of COVID deaths per capita with the political party of the state governor, despite Republican governors generally imposing somewhat less stringent restrictions than Democratic governors.

So what is the evidence that the restrictions have reduced COVID deaths? I see none. I am happy to be corrected, but show me some data. Show me evidence. Don't just tell me, "Well, Anthony Fauci says these restrictions are making a huge difference!" OK, let Anthony Fauci show some evidence for that.

Why would all of our restrictions have made no difference?
The evidence discussed in previous chapters shows these points:

1. Wearing masks makes little or no difference to COVID transmission, and a mask mandate would make even less difference. (Chapter 15).
2. Closing schools makes absolutely no difference at all to COVID transmission. (Chapter 20).
3. Social distancing past three feet makes little if any difference, and we in the U.S. already kept three feet from each other because that is our standard social distance. (Chapter 17).
4. Only symptomatically ill people transmit COVID (or they are much, much more infectious than asymptomatic people), so only quarantining them would make any difference. Quarantining everyone for 2 months by stay-at-home orders makes it less likely that the symptomatic people would comply with instructions to quarantine themselves. Why should they, when they are ordered to quarantine whether they are sick or not? And why should they, when they are told that wearing a mask is just as effective as quarantining themselves? You might as well go out in public with the mask on—that's just as good, right? (Chapter 19).
5. The restrictions massively increased depression and unhappiness, as well as harming physical fitness and our diets, and that all hurt our immune function, which would tend to increase COVID deaths and COVID transmission (Chapter

22).

6. The one intervention that makes a large difference in transmission of COVID, as well as colds and flu, is hand washing, and that cannot be mandated or monitored. Furthermore, it was underemphasized by government authorities. (Chapter 16).

Based on all that, why would you expect the mandates to have decreased COVID deaths? Based on the fourth and fifth points, I would expect lockdowns to somewhat *increase* COVID deaths, if anything.

References

1. Rozmajzl, Anthony. Mises Institute, February 23, 2021. https://mises.org/wire/almost-year-later-theres-still-no-evidence-showing-governments-can-control-spread-covid-19

2. McCann, Adam. States with the Fewest Coronavirus Restrictions. Wallet Hub. March 2, 2021. https://wallethub.com/edu/states-coronavirus-restrictions/73818

3. Hold2, LLC. @Hold2LLC twitter account.

Chapter 24

Recommendations:
What We Should Have Done to Combat COVID

Our guidance to the public should have been guided by these facts known about upper respiratory tract infections and therefore suspected about COVID at the beginning of the outbreak:

1. Mask wearing makes little if any difference to transmission of upper respiratory tract infection. It does not even make a huge difference for professionals wearing an N95 mask perfectly and probably no difference for the public wearing a surgical mask imperfectly.

2. Certainly a majority, and maybe essentially all, upper respiratory tract infections are transmitted by direct contact, meaning getting the virus on your hands and then touching yourself on or near a mucous membrane of your face—eyes, nose, or mouth. The virus can get on your hands by shaking hands with an infected person, or more likely by touching a surface, such as a railing or your own body or clothing, that was touched or sneezed on or coughed on by an infected person.

3. Hand washing and use of hand sanitizers is the only intervention that has been shown to make a significant difference in transmission of upper respiratory tract infections, and it makes a very significant difference. Connected with point 2, if you are completely diligent about washing your hands and not touching your face with unwashed hands, you probably can almost completely eliminate your risk of infection. And therefore, if everyone were completely diligent about that, we could probably get the R for the epidemic below 1 and have case numbers decrease and the epidemic die out.

4. Asymptomatic people are much, much less infectious than symptomatic people and may be completely un-infectious.

5. Physically and mentally healthy people have stronger immune systems and are much less likely to get seriously ill, or ill at all, from an upper respiratory tract infection than less healthy people. And not only physical health but also happiness and mental health strengthen the immune system.

All of those points were known about upper respiratory tract infections generally prior to COVID and should have been expected of COVID and have now been confirmed for COVID.

Therefore, it is not 20/20 hindsight to say these should have been the recommendations:

- Wash your hands.
- Wash your hands (I'm repeating it because this is the most important recommendation).
- Don't touch your face unless you have just washed your hands (I know this one is hard).
- Quarantine yourself if you are feeling sick. Just assume it is COVID if the symptoms are consistent with it. Minimize contact with your housemates as much as possible while you are sick, and they should wash their hands more and keep at least three feet from you. You should wear a mask if you feel sick and if the mask does not make it harder for you to breathe, since it may catch your droplets and reduce transmission to the household. Alternatively, your housemates should wear a mask in your presence. It is probably not necessary for both you and your housemates to wear masks, and the masks should not be viewed as anywhere near 100% effective. It is more important for you and your housemates to wash your hands.
- And to promote your immune health:
  - o   Eat a healthy diet
  - o   Get some exercise—and the exercise does not have to be anything rigorous. Walking is probably the best exercise.
  - o   Make an effort to be happy and to make others happy:
    - ▪   Do things you enjoy.
    - ▪   Socialize with others more, not less, because it

will promote happiness for you and them and
improve the immune systems of both of you.

- Get out into nature.
- Go to your house of worship if that is something you enjoy.
- Go to a restaurant or bar with your friends, if that makes you happy.
- Go to your health club for sure, if that is something you do, because it will improve your health and your mood, which will improve your immune system.
- Smile more. It will make both you and others happier.

And I would actually recommend to the public that they not wear a mask, except when in the presence of someone with symptoms, which if symptomatic people stay home should only be if you are at home with them or if you are a healthcare worker in the presence of a COVID patient. Mask wearing will slightly decrease your oxygen and increase the carbon dioxide you are breathing, which will not be good for your immune system or your mood or your mental acuity. It is uncomfortable. And it decreases not only your own happiness but also that of everyone around you by signaling you are afraid of them and by not showing your face to them. The better thing you can do for others is to show your face, and preferably smile at them. That will make them happier, boosting their immune system, and making it less likely they will get sick from COVID or anything.

It was never wise to close schools, and completely inexcusable by the fall of 2020, by which time we knew that closing schools accomplished zero in reducing COVID deaths. That said, schools are known to be hotbeds of transmission of colds and flu to the community, so in the spring of 2020 before we knew closing schools makes no difference for COVID, it was defensible to close schools if your only goal was to reduce COVID deaths. It was still a bad idea because it was a big sacrifice for students for an uncertain benefit of maybe having a small effect of modestly reducing COVID deaths in the elderly. But if you ignored or did not care about the wellbeing of young people, as we apparently did not and do not, and only cared about COVID deaths, it was defensible in the spring of 2020 for the narrow goal of reducing COVID deaths. It was never defensible from an overall harm/benefit analysis, considering the wellbeing of children and young people as of equal value to the wellbeing of the elderly. By the fall of 2020 it was no longer even defensible in any sense at all because we knew it had no effect at all on COVID transmission or deaths.

Conclusion: What should our strategy have been?

Two prongs:

*First, and by far the most important, inform people that the evidence indicates that all upper respiratory tract infections, including COVID, are spread mostly, and maybe almost entirely, by virus getting on your hands and then you touching your face (mouth, nose, or eyes, near or on a mucous membrane). So you have the power. You control your fate. If you do not want to be infected, then wash your hands often, use hand sanitizer often, and try not to touch your face unless you just washed your hands.

Focusing on hand washing and the fact that most transmission is by the virus getting on your hands and then you touching your face has two huge benefits.

First, it is true and supported by the evidence, while the message that mask mandates or mask wearing in general reduces spread of the virus is false and not supported by the evidence. Dealing with the public honestly and with evidence seems like a good idea to me.

Second, it is empowering and does not divide us.

My message is:

> You control your own fate. Wash your hands and try to remember not to touch your face.

The CDC's message in contrast is:

> You are at the mercy of everyone else in society. Whether other people wear masks determines whether you get infected. If you get infected, it is the fault of kids going to school, or that kid playing basketball across the street without a mask, or that redneck wearing a "Don't tread on me" T-shirt at the grocery store who refuses to wear a mask. So you can and should fear and hate your neighbors. Everything is their fault! You should even fear your own children coming to visit you in your nursing home. It will be their fault if you get infected and die.

*The second prong of the strategy I would have used is to quarantine only symptomatic people, but not asymptomatic people even if we know they are infected or know they were in close contact with symptomatic COVID patients. And quarantine the symptomatic people only while they have symptoms or for 7 days, whichever is less. We do not need to test them for symptoms. If you have cold or flu symptoms we can assume you have COVID and ask you to quarantine yourself. If you want to be tested and the COVID test is negative, then you are free from quarantine. The quarantine can even be mandatory. We could have a $200 fine if you are caught in public sneezing and coughing. If you want to fight that fine you could get a COVID test to prove you were not infected at the time.

I am actually neutral or ambivalent on whether the quarantine prong is even worth it. It would divide us from each other, in that people may be on the lookout for sneezing persons and angrily demand that they quarantine themselves. And it would have a smaller effect than hand washing, which is in everyone's own control. But the evidence indicates it would help to reduce COVID cases and deaths and it is a relatively small thing to ask of people: just stay home for a week at most, and just when and if you are feeling ill.

That is a much smaller ask than:

- requiring every school and college student to stay home for over a year,
- closing every bar, restaurant, church, health club and other "nonessential" business and throwing 16% of the workforce out of work,
- mandating that every person cover their face in public for over a year so we cannot see each other smile, and
- issuing a stay-at-home order mandating that every person in society stay home for 7 weeks,

all of which, even put together, had apparently zero benefit in reducing COVID deaths.

Stop blaming other people. The neighbor kid playing basketball across the street without a mask is not going to infect you unless you go out there and shake his hand and then touch your mouth. The redneck with the "Don't tread on me" T-shirt who refuses to wear a mask in the grocery store is also not going to infect you. Your children visiting you in your nursing home are not going to kill you. Stop hating on other people! You control your own destiny; you do not depend on others.

Part 4
Miscellaneous Observations and Theories

Chapter 25

....

Lockdowns as a Pharmaceutical:
Comparison to the Drug Approval Process

It is enlightening to compare the COVID response of our state and federal governments to the New Drug Approval process. The societal response to COVID was in essence a response to treat and prevent a medical disease, COVID-19. That's what drugs do—they treat and prevent diseases. In fact, it is a perfect analogy to a vaccine. The lockdown response was intended to reduce incidence of and deaths from an infectious disease, exactly the purpose of a vaccine.

We have a very rigorous process, governed by statutes and regulations, and run by the Food and Drug Administration (FDA) in the U.S. and by a similar agency in every other country in the world, for the approval of new drugs, including vaccines. In that process, the FDA analyzes the benefits of and harms of a new drug, and the drug company sponsor has to show with good data that the benefit of the drug in treating the disease substantially exceeds the harms in side effects or adverse events.

The sponsor has to conduct, generally, a Phase 1 and Phase 2 clinical trial in small numbers of patients and then two Phase 3 clinical trials in generally 100 to 1,000 patients in each Phase 3 trial. Both of the Phase 3s have to show statistically significant efficacy, not only in treating the disease but if there is already a drug on the market you usually have to show that your new drug is significantly superior to the existing drug. And you, as the company sponsor, have to show the side effects or adverse events are acceptable. If the drug is to treat cancer and patients die without it, then a higher level of adverse events is acceptable than if the drug is to treat acid indigestion. But in any case, the benefit has to exceed the harm, and it probably has to exceed the harm by a large margin.

The example of the COVID vaccines is instructive. Each of these was only approved after it had been tested in 30,000 or more volunteers, about half of whom received placebo. Between the four approved COVID vaccines, there were probably over 50,000 patients who got the vaccines and 50,000 who got placebo. There was not a single death caused by the vaccines. If any one of those vaccines had caused three deaths, which would be less than 1 in 5,000, and maybe if it had caused one or two deaths, it would not have been approved, even though its benefit would then have still vastly exceeded its harm. COVID disease causes death in about 20 people per 5,000 infected. So a vaccine that killed 1 in 5,000 would still have a net benefit of preventing 19 deaths per 5,000 people dosed. No government would have approved that, though.

Yet, we as a society pursued and still pursue a lockdown policy that has this ratio of benefits to harms (from Chapters 2-12):

COVID Lockdowns Benefits and Harms			
Benefits	**Likelihood of benefit**	**Persons benefitted normalized to one**	**Person-years of life saved per one person benefitted**
Death from COVID averted	Up to 1 in 1,000 people, saving 4 years of life	1 (0 to 2)	4 (0 to 8)
Harms	**Likelihood of harm**	**Persons harmed per one person benefitted.**	**Person-years of life lost per one person benefitted.**
Depression caused	at least 1 in 5	at least 316	at least 120
Suicide and deaths of despair caused	1 in 5,000, losing 38 years of life	0.34	12.9
Decreases happiness	1 in 1	1,640	
Causes you to lose your job	1 in 6 workers	127	
Causes students to drop out of school or lose education	1 in 1 students.	350	
Cancer and heart disease deaths increased	1 in 10,000	0.1	0.5

Increased risk of domestic abuse or child abuse	Unknown, maybe 1 in 1,000		

It is insane. Can you imagine the TV ads for that drug?

COVID LOCKDOWN may, but probably does not, prevent death from COVID in as many as 1 in 1,000 people. Median age of persons whose death is prevented: 84.

Warning: COVID LOCKDOWN causes suicides or drug overdose deaths in at least 1 in 5,000 people, including children. Median age of suicides caused: 42. COVID LOCKDOWN has no benefit for children or anyone under age 50, but we require they take it anyway. COVID LOCKDOWN results in major clinical depression in 1 in 5 users. Your cost for COVID LOCKDOWN will be over $4,000. COVID LOCKDOWN causes a 16% chance you will lose your job. Students who take COVID LOCKDOWN will be unable to attend school for a year. You have a 100% chance of being less happy because of COVID LOCKDOWN. You are likely to lose contact with your friends because of COVID LOCKDOWN. You will be unable to worship God with others because of COVID LOCKDOWN. If single, you will be significantly less likely to find a partner because of COVID LOCKDOWN. You will be unable to visit your health club because of COVID LOCKDOWN and thus will get out of shape and fatter. COVID LOCKDOWN carries a significant risk of increased domestic abuse and child abuse. COVID LOCKDOWN significantly increases your chance of dying from cancer and heart disease. Consult Anthony Fauci if you have questions and before you stop taking COVID LOCKDOWN.

One weird thing about COVID LOCKDOWN is we have prescribed it for everybody, mandated it for everybody. It is like a drug that only benefits the elderly (if even them) and has terrible side effects for everyone who takes it, but we, the drug company, want to mandate that everyone take the drug anyway, including the 90% of the population who receive no benefit from the drug.

If you were on the FDA approval committee for this drug application, what would you do? At the least you would say, "How about you only prescribe this drug for the people who might benefit from it, instead of mandating everyone take it? And even for those for whom it

might be suitable, like people over age 65, how about we make it voluntary, like every other drug is?" Let the elderly at risk wear masks if
they want to. Let them isolate themselves if they want to. It makes no
sense to quarantine everyone.

The purpose of the lockdowns is the same as that of a drug: to prevent
a disease or lessen deaths or symptoms from the disease. The standard
for implementing the lockdown response should have been basically
the same as the standard for drug approval: The benefits must exceed
the harms, and if you are not sure, do not approve the drug or implement the lockdown response until you have reasonable certainty that
the benefits exceed the harms. For drugs actually, as the example of
COVID vaccines above shows, the benefits must be much greater than
the harms, not just a little greater.

The lockdown policy has harms that vastly exceed the benefits. It
is not even close. In addition to the economic and happiness harms, the
suicides and deaths of despair caused, alone, result in more lost person-years of life than are saved in prevented COVID deaths.

In addition, drugs do not get approved, ordinarily, until at least
three years of testing in humans. Even the COVID vaccines were not
approved until each had undergone about four months of testing in
humans. For drugs, we follow the precautionary principle: Do not implement an intervention until you are certain it is beneficial. Err on the
side of doing nothing.

With the lockdown response we did the opposite. We rushed in
with an enormous societal intervention, imposing what we knew would
be enormous economic costs and should have known would be an enormous cost to happiness and mental health, with at best no idea whether the benefits might exceed those certain enormous costs or harms. (In
reality, in addition to the huge economic cost that everyone knew was
coming, it was very predictable this would cause an explosion of clinical depression and a large increase in suicides, so you could be pretty
certain the harms would exceed the benefits.) It is like the opposite
of the precautionary principle: Implement the most drastic response
you can think of that you can be almost certain will be harmful, just
because you are panicked.

To continue with the vaccine analogy—and, again, the lockdowns
should be judged exactly like a vaccine since their aim is to prevent
disease and deaths, just like a vaccine—if you were offered a vaccine
for COVID, that had a 100% likelihood of making you less happy for a
year, a 16% likelihood it would result in your losing your job, a 1 in 5
likelihood of throwing you into moderate to severe clinical depression,

and a 1 in 5,000 risk it would cause you to commit suicide, would you take that vaccine?

If the current vaccines, which are 100% effective in preventing death, had that side effect profile, would you take them? The lockdowns are at best 40% effective in reducing deaths (if they prevented us from getting to herd immunity and thus prevented 400,000 deaths). Would you take a vaccine that was only 40% effective if it had that side effect profile?

Chapter 26

College and Pro Athletes and COVID

It is bizarre to me the restrictions professional and college sports have regarding COVID-19. Players are in a bubble, not allowed to interact with their families or the public. Players who are even in contact with someone who tested positive for COVID-19 are quarantined and cannot play, even if the player himself tests negative. Why? Why is it more unacceptable for an athlete to be infected with COVID than, say, a grocery store clerk?

I have never heard a clear reason given. Often it is said it is for the health of athletes. That is ridiculous! People in their 20s are at about the same risk, probably a slightly lower risk, of dying from COVID if they are infected than they are of dying from influenza or the flu if infected. (And to my knowledge, not a single professional or college athlete in North America has died of COVID.) So if we need to shut down competition because of the risk of death for athletes from COVID, then we should have never allowed professional or college athletics to begin with because of the (miniscule) risk of death from the flu. With COVID we do not allow athletes to play if they merely contacted an infected person, even if they are not themselves infected and are not sick. With the flu, it has never even been the case that a player who feels ill was encouraged to sit out competition or do anything to avoid infecting his teammates. In fact, up to now we usually glorified athletes who played while feeling sick with the flu.

So, at least logically, the restrictions on athletes and competition cannot be to protect the athletes. It can only be to protect the rest of society from being infected by the athletes. That makes no sense either. Maybe you can argue because of the hard breathing and close contact in most sports that athletes are more likely to infect one another than people in other occupations and activities. But I am not aware of any data that, in fact, athletes have been infected with COVID at a higher rate than others. In any case, even if athletes are infected at a slightly higher rate, they have no contact with the rest of the public during their competition, and outside of competition do not have a high rate of contact with the public in general and a low rate of contact with the elderly, who are the only people at high risk from COVID. If we are concerned about an occupation that has high contact with large numbers of people, we could start with sales clerks in grocery stores and retail stores. It would make more sense to test them every day and make them stay home from work if they are confirmed positive for COVID even if asymptomatic. I am not advocating that; that would be stupid too, but at least it would make more sense.

Chapter 27

The Effect of Lockdowns on Marriages and Intimate Partnerships

One underemphasized harm of the lockdown strategy is that it has made it more difficult to find a marriage partner and an intimate partner of any sort. If your goal had been to prevent people from getting married or prevent them from finding sexual partners or intimate partners, you could not have devised a much better strategy than the lockdown strategy against COVID.

I have not seen statistics, but it is certain that we have had fewer weddings since the start of our lockdown strategy. Large gatherings for weddings have been made illegal in most states and against church policy in most Christian denominations, and people have been subject to shunning and disapproval if they want to have or try to have a wedding with, really, anyone other than at most a few family members attending, and them wearing masks. So people have postponed their weddings. In a best case, that means one or two fewer years married, and in a worst case it means the couple decides not to get married and the marriage never happens.

Closing schools, churches, restaurants, bars, and health clubs, and encouraging or requiring people to work from home, and mask wearing in public, has made it much harder to meet people for either a new friendship or a new romantic partnership. Again, if your goal was to make it as difficult as possible for people to forge new relationships, this would have been exactly the policy you would have enacted. Then, if by some miracle, despite Anthony Fauci's best efforts, you do manage to meet someone new and want to go on a date, the only option available to you for the date often has been to take a walk outside (which can be challenging if you are in Minnesota in the winter or Seattle in the rainy season). You could not go to a restaurant or bar or coffee shop or movie or museum or baseball game.

We know married people tend to be happier than single people and tend to be healthier and live longer. We know more frequent sex (though perhaps not multiple sexual partners) correlates with happiness and health also. So the lockdown policy has caused an enormous harm in reducing marriages and intimate partnerships, as well as non-sexual new friendships.

Chapter 28

Surprises

I have been completely surprised by how we have reacted to COVID. When news that this new infection would reach the U.S., I did not expect anything like this response. I did not expect travel bans, stay-at-homer orders, closing schools—any of it. I thought our government would pretty much just shrug and continue with business as usual. We have never reacted like this to any prior epidemic. I suppose swimming pools were closed during the polio epidemic in some places. But that was about it for mandatory restrictions. The 1918 flu, which as I have calculated here was 15 to 30 times worse than COVID in person-years of life lost per capita (Chapter 13), resulted in almost no mandatory closures. The extent of the response was pretty much to keep windows open in school for better ventilation. So I have been shocked at this response and have felt again and again like a stranger in my own land. Here are some things that have surprised me.

* The courts upholding emergency powers by governors, months after the "emergency" started, after plenty of time for legislatures to meet and pass any needed legislation. In retrospect, though, this should not have surprised me. U.S. courts are very deferential to executive power.

* The courts upholding closures of churches and houses of worship, ignoring the most fundamental of our rights in the Bill of Rights. (The U.S. Supreme Court on 5-4 votes has now struck down some closures of churches, but on narrow grounds and after previously upholding the same bans before one more Trump-appointed Justice joined the Court. But over the course of the epidemic most executive orders closing churches have been upheld in most state and federal courts.) This also should not have surprised me. U.S. courts are very strong in upholding the rights of persons who are corporations but very weak in upholding

the rights of persons who are persons, especially if the persons in question are not rich.

* The closure of schools. Several things about this surprised me. One is that the teachers' unions were the loudest voice demanding schools be closed. Another is they were closed at all or that any politicians or officials would have proposed closing schools. Another is that parents have been rather compliant in this. Another is that the public has accepted it. And another is that students, both children and college and university students, have largely accepted it without objection, when they receive no benefit whatsoever from school closures.

* The public acceptance of mask mandates. I thought the American people did not like being told what to do and loved liberty.

* The public acceptance of stay-at-home orders. This is a huge—huge—infringement on liberty. By executive decree, with no statute passed by a legislature, the governors sentenced every person in their state, those persons having committed no crime and received no hearing or any due process, to a criminal sentence usually given for a 3rd drunk driving offense or gross misdemeanor assault, such as threatening someone with a rifle or beating your spouse when she has a restraining order against you. And by the way, this had no effect on COVID deaths or infections (see Chapter 21). There were almost no organized protests against this in Minnesota or in most states. Stunning to me. I thought Americans cared at least a little about personal liberty.

* That we seem to care nothing about children or young people and everything about the elderly. I thought it was the reverse.
    The only people at significant risk from COVID are the old and the sick, as I have elaborated here (Chapter 13). Closing schools and universities had no benefit whatsoever for children and young people, but a huge harm to them. It also, as it happens, had no benefit for the elderly (Chapter 20), but the school closures were sold and justified on the premise that they might have benefit for the elderly.
    Middle aged people and older complain about age discrimination in the workplace, which I think does exist. And the elderly and their advocates complain that we shunt away our old people into nursing homes and assisted living facilities and ignore them, which I heretofore thought was true. And people complain that we glorify youth and good

looks and belittle age and experience, which is certainly true among actors in TV and movies and I thought was true generally.

But the COVID lockdowns throw a wrench into the idea that we glorify the young and ignore and do not value the old. The majority of the sacrifices were made by children and young people, and all of the benefit, if there was any benefit, went to the old—mostly the very old in that the majority of COVID dead are over age 80.

So again, I thought we cared little about the very old and cared at least a little about children. It turns out we apparently care *only* about the old and care literally nothing about children in that we are willing to impose any sacrifice on them for no or minimal benefit for adults.

* That children, their parents, and young adults have accepted the enormous sacrifices imposed on children and young adults with little objection.

Children, of course, have to trust that their parents and adults will protect their interests. They are not responsible for standing up for themselves. So they are not to blame for not standing up for themselves against school closures. But I am a little surprised that even teenagers have not protested school closures much. And I am surprised and disappointed in parents, that parents have not stood up for the right of their children to attend school and get an education. And college students seem to have mostly accepted without protest the closures of colleges and universities.

Young adults also disproportionately work in the jobs that were hit most by the lockdowns, such as wait staff in restaurants. Despite all that sacrifice for no benefit, polling says young people are even more supportive of the lockdowns than older people in the U.S. This just shocks me. I guess young people have bought into the lies that they are at risk from COVID or that their sacrifice serves some purpose and substantially reduces COVID risk for the elderly. If so, they are wrong. Perhaps that is an indictment of our education system that they are not able to evaluate the evidence on that.

If young people expected to get some reciprocal sacrifice from the older generations, they obviously have been disappointed. Colleges are not offering any refunds. There have not even been any proposals, let alone serious discussion, of offering some financial benefit, like a government check, specifically to young people as compensation for their sacrifices. I have seen almost no letters to the editor from older people saying, "I do not want my grandchildren sacrificing a year of their lives and a year of education to try to eke out another year of life for me," which I think should be the overwhelming sentiment of the elderly.

Instead I see letters saying, "Those young monsters are playing basketball in the park across the street from me without masks! They are trying to kill me!"

* That I, Hugh McTavish, am the voice defending the interests of children and young people. I am not that comfortable around children and never considered myself particularly pro-kid. But now it feels like I am the *only* one who cares about kids.

* That I, Hugh McTavish, am the voice saying, "You know, interactions with other people is the major source of our joy. Isolating us all from each other and never socializing is a terrible idea." I am quite introverted. I generally dislike parties. It is bizarre to me that I am the one standing up for the importance of social gatherings and face-to-face interaction.

Chapter 29

The Dumbest Restriction

Perhaps the most irrational and misguided restriction any government has imposed is the requirement some governments have imposed, notably Minnesota's and Seattle's among probably others, that kids in youth sports wear masks when participating. Here are some facts relevant to that requirement:

- Persons under age 18 are at virtually no risk of death or serious illness from COVID and are at lower risk than they are from the flu (Chapter 13).
- Persons under age 18 essentially do not transmit COVID to others, so preventing their infection has no benefit to others (Chapter 20).
- Masks make little or no difference in preventing COVID infection or transmission, even when dry and worn properly (Chapter 15). Masks that are wet after breath condensation, rain, or sweat, as all masks become during exertion, are even more worthless, if it is possible to have less effect than none.
- Mask wearing makes it harder for the kids to breathe and more uncomfortable.
- Mask wearing either guarantees, or at least makes it more likely, that glasses and clear visors or eye protection (as all hockey players wear) will fog up, making it more likely the players will have an accident and hurt themselves, including possible serious accidents such as spine injuries from falling and crashing into the boards while playing hockey.

Chapter 30

The Big Lies

"We are all in this together."

Nonsense. We are all in this alone and apart. That was the entire point.

The stay-at-home orders, closing "non-essential" businesses, closing churches and restaurants and bars, encouraging or mandating working from home, and closing schools, of course physically separated us from one another. That was the point.

Mandating mask wearing has been the most emphasized intervention. Again, this separates you from others. You cannot see each other's faces and smiles or other facial expressions, which makes it much harder to bond emotionally with others for a moment, so we are more alone and apart.

It is just a lie that "we are all in this together." The entire point was exactly the opposite: to isolate us from one another.

"We are following the science."

Give me a break!

I am a *real* scientist. Science constitutes following the data. Science does not constitute standing in front of a microphone and saying "I have a Ph.D.," or "I have an M.D.," or "I am Anthony Fauci," "trust me, mask wearing reduces COVID. I'm not going to show you the data. Just trust me."

I am a real scientist, a Ph.D. biochemist and immunologist. I do not stand up at conferences or submit articles to journals and say or write, "These are my conclusions. I am not going to show you the data. Just trust me because I have a Ph.D." That would not go over well.

I imagine Anthony Fauci as Jack Nicholson in *A Few Good Men* screaming, "You can't handle the data!!" I would reply calmly, "No, I can handle the data."

I have shown more respect for you here: I have shown you the data.

The state and federal governments and the media generally have not.

In one round of closings in Minnesota, Governor Tim Walz ordered closing of bars and restaurants at 10 p.m. because, he said, the state had data that most of the COVID transmission in the state was occurring in restaurants and bars after 10 p.m. But the state declined to release that data. Obviously they did not have any such data. I cannot even imagine how you could possibly prove such a thing. In most cases you cannot know where or from whom someone was infected with the COVID virus, let alone what time of day. It is absurd.

After a week or two of only closing bars and restaurants after 10 p.m., when that, predictably, had no effect on COVID infection trends, the Governor ordered bars and restaurants closed completely and ordered health clubs closed completely. Again, no data or evidence was presented to support that decision. At that time, on November 19, 2020, when the step of closing health clubs was contemplated, Life Time Fitness sent an e-mail to their members saying their chain "has experienced 21.5 million member visits to its clubs across North America since May with 962 reported cases of COVID-19, equating to a rate of .00004. Additionally, we have conducted thorough contact tracing and have yet to identify a single case that originated in our clubs." "Following the science" would mean accepting that data or rebutting it with contrary data. The state did neither.

The data says hand washing and hand sanitizing is the only intervention that has been shown to reduce transmissions of upper respiratory tract infections. And it says certainly a majority and maybe nearly all transmission of colds and flu, and COVID, occurs by direct physical contact of the virus getting on your hands in some way, and then you touching your face. Therefore, by far the best recommendation to give to the public is "wash your hands."

The data said going into this that masks make either no difference or little difference in transmission of colds and flu, and the data we have gotten during COVID says that masks make either no difference or little difference in transmission of COVID.

The data says stay-at-home orders did not appear to slow the epidemic at all and accomplished nothing.

The data available by the summer of 2020 said that closing schools accomplished exactly nothing to slow the spread of COVID.

The data and science and common sense said closing schools, throwing 16% of employees out of work, isolating us from one another with stay-at-home orders and mask wearing, etc., would result in an explosion of clinical depression, suicides, and drug abuse and overdoses.

We have done anything *but* follow the science. We have ignored the science and ignored the data because it did not fit with the pre-conceived strategy and preconceived notions of the architects of the lockdowns.

As a scientist, I am also bothered that this entire response has given science a bad name. It has given it a bad name because our leaders and experts have not followed the science but have claimed to be doing so. Just as the Crusades gave Christianity a bad name by claiming that Christianity dictated going to war to kill and convert by force nonbelievers, when Jesus and the teachings of Christianity said no such thing, so Anthony Fauci and our leaders are giving science a bad name by claiming to be following science when they are in fact doing the opposite.

Maybe we should try actually following the science, instead of claiming to while ignoring it.

The bad things of 2020 and 2021 (unemployment, suicides, lost live music and sports, etc.) were "caused by the pandemic."

No. COVID deaths were caused by the pandemic. Everything else was caused by the lockdown response—the unemployment, the closing of businesses, the unhappiness, the suicides, the depression, the drug abuse, the lost weddings, the lost education, the end of live music, the end of attending spectator sports, etc., was all caused by the lockdowns. We, or more accurately our leaders, decided all of that was worth it to try to reduce COVID deaths.

You can judge for yourself whether those losses and sacrifices were worth it for the number of COVID deaths they prevented (if they prevented any). But it should never be forgotten that all of those bad things were caused by the lockdowns, not by the virus or the pandemic. The only bad thing caused by the pandemic was COVID deaths.

Chapter 31

Are the COVID Death Numbers Inflated?

In this book I have just used the official numbers for COVID deaths. But some have alleged or suspected that the number of deaths attributed to COVID are inflated. Are they? Probably at least a little.

The first issue is WHO guidance and U.S. CDC guidance for attributing cause of death to COVID which basically say, if you are not sure, attribute it to COVID. The CDC guidance (Reference 1) says,

> If COVID–19 played a role in the death, this condition should be specified on the death certificate. In many cases, it is likely that it will be the Underlying Cause of Death (UCOD), as it can lead to various life threatening conditions, such as pneumonia and acute respiratory distress syndrome (ARDS). In these cases, COVID–19 should be reported on the lowest line used in Part I with the other conditions to which it gave rise listed on the lines above it.

Part I of the Death Certificate lists the sequence of events that is judged to have caused the death. The lowest line is the ultimate or primary cause of death.

The Guidance in the appendix gives three examples of Death Certificates:

Example 1.
A 77-year-old male with a 10-year history of hypertension and chronic obstructive pulmonary disease (COPD), developed fever and cough four days before his death and tested positive for the virus that causes COVID.

Part I (direct causes of death):
>>> a. Acute respiratory acidosis, caused by
>>> b. COVID-19
Part II (other contributing conditions):
>>> Hypertension and chronic obstructive pulmonary
>>> disease.

Comment: That may be appropriate, but I think in a previous year where that person caught the flu shortly before death that would probably have been coded in Part I as acute respiratory acidosis caused by chronic obstructive pulmonary disease, or simply as a death caused by chronic obstructive pulmonary disease.

In the cause of death statistics for 2020, where each death can have just one cause, that person's death will be counted as caused by COVID. In a previous year where he caught the flu four days before his death, I think it would probably be listed as caused by COPD.

Example 2.

A 34-year old woman dies after having fever and cough for 10 days, the last four of which were spent in the hospital, and has inflamed lungs and a positive COVID test by PCR.

Part I (direct causes of death):
>>> a. Acute Respiratory Distress Syndrome, caused by
>>> b. Pneumonia, caused by
>>> c. COVID-19.
Part II (other contributing conditions):
>>> None.

Comment: This example is clearly correct. The death should be attributed to COVID. It is also extremely rare for a young person with no preexisting serious conditions to die of COVID, but it has happened.

Example 3.

An 86-year old woman had a debilitating stroke 5 years previously and was non-ambulatory since then. Five days before her death she developed a cough and fever and died at home five days later. There is no evidence other than the cough and fever that she had COVID.

Part I (direct causes of death):
>>> a. Acute respiratory illness, caused by
>>> b. Probable COVID-19

Part II (other contributing conditions):
Ischemic stroke.

Comment. That attribution may be appropriate but it is misleading. Most important, attributing this woman's death to COVID, even if she was infected with SARS-CoV-2, which we do not know, is misleading. She was 86-years old and had been in a wheelchair for 5 years since she had a stroke! It is hardly surprising that she died. Nor is it tragic that she died. Second, we do not know she had COVID. She may have had influenza or a common cold. This explains why no one is dying of influenza in 2020. There have been news articles saying, "No one is dying of influenza in 2020. That means the masks work!" No, it does not. It means everyone who is dying of influenza is having their death classified as caused by "probable COVID-19." The CDC is instructing physicians to classify deaths accompanied by fever and cough as caused by COVID unless the physician can basically prove it was caused by something else.

My father died two years ago. His death certificate is enlightening in this context and his death was under similar circumstances to Example 1 above. He was 91 and had had congestive heart failure for several years and passed away within a day after he swallowed fluid into his lungs, either a drink or saliva, and thus developed aspiration pneumonia. His death certificate lists
Part I (direct causes of death):
a. Aspiration pneumonia, caused by
b. Congestive heart failure.
Part II (other contributing conditions):
None.

That means his ultimate cause of death is considered to be congestive heart failure. In government statistics, that is the way it was counted. If his pneumonia had been caused by the flu, I think it would have been listed the same way, with pneumonia above the congestive heart failure and heart failure considered his cause of death. But if he had died this year from pneumonia that lasted one day after contracting COVID, under the CDC guidance above, his death would be listed as being caused by COVID, even if there was no laboratory evidence he had COVID. It would be listed as
Part I (direct causes of death):
a. Pneumonia, caused by
b. COVID-19

Part II (other contributing conditions):
Congestive heart failure.

The Federal government requires states to report every COVID-positive death even if the death was not caused by COVID (Reference 2). States are free to not report the death as being *caused* by COVID, but one could argue it creates an atmosphere of encouraging physicians signing the death certificate to attribute the death to COVID, since they have to note whether the person was known to be or suspected to be infected with the virus that causes COVID at the time of death, whereas they do not have to report whether a person was known or suspected to be infected with any other virus at the time of death or known or suspected to have any other medical condition at the time of death—just COVID.

Second point: Medicare pays hospitals 20% more for patients diagnosed with COVID-19 than for the same care for someone not diagnosed with COVID (Reference 3). Now, some have objected, "Yes, but there is no evidence this leads to inflated COVID numbers" (Reference 4). Sure. I am certain that, unlike every other person and business in society, physicians and hospitals are not motivated by money and do not have their decisions affected by being paid more for one answer than another.

References:

1. U.S. Centers for Disease Control and Prevention. https://www.cdc.gov/nchs/covid19/coding-and-reporting.htm

2. Pappas, Stephanie. "How COVID Deaths are Counted." *Scientific American*. May 19, 2020. https://www.scientificamerican.com/article/how-covid-19-deaths-are-counted1/

3. Ellison, Eyla. "Hospitals to get Medicare pay hike for COVID-19 patients." *Becker's Hospital CFO Report*. August 19, 2020. https://www.beckershospitalreview.com/finance/hospitals-to-get-medicare-pay-hike-for-care-of-covid-19-patients.html

4. Fichera, Angelo. "Hospital Payments and the COVID-19 Death Count." FactCheck.org. April 21, 2020. https://www.factcheck.org/2020/04/hospital-payments-and-the-covid-19-death-count/

Chapter 32

Censorship by the Tech Giants and Media

I started a blog about COVID, writing about the general ideas in this book that the lockdown approach was a mistake and was doing more harm than good, in March 2020, at the very beginning of this. I tried placing ads with *Google*, *Facebook*, and *Yahoo* (which had changed its name to Gemini or Verizon Media). None of them would accept any advertising to a website that said the lockdowns were a mistake. So I got no traffic.

In December 2020 I had the idea of starting a nonprofit (COVID Sanity, COVID-Sanity.org, please visit our website and sign the petition and donate :)) and getting other people involved, so it would be a nonprofit and a group of people saying these things, instead of one person. I thought then they would take our ads. But it did not seem to make any difference. What made a slight difference was hiring an online marketing agency to place our ads. Now the routine was that *Google*, *YouTube*, and *Facebook* would refuse the ads every time, my agency would appeal, the tech giants would refuse them again, my agency would appeal a second time, it would be rejected, they would appeal a third time, and usually by the third time, sometimes only by the fifth appeal, *Google* or *Facebook* would allow the ads. I do not believe we ever had an ad that was allowed on the first try and I do not recall ever having one allowed after just one appeal.

To allow the nonprofit I started to spread the facts about lockdowns, COVID Sanity, to appear in natural search on *Google* if you searched for "COVID Sanity" *Google* required us to submit our IRS letter with our tax ID number. We did that. Then they said that was not enough and wanted photographs of my house (the headquarters of the group) with professionally made signs saying "COVID Sanity" on my house. So I had to go have signs printed and pay for that, solely for that reason. We submitted photographs of the house with the signs. Then they let us appear for a few weeks. Then I got e-mails from them saying we had "violated terms of service," without saying what the violation was, and would be blocked henceforth. My marketing person said *Google* had never required either a copy of a letter from the IRS or a photo of the premises for any other client of hers.

We were not advocating violence, of course. And everything we said on our website was factually accurate and backed with peer-reviewed scientific data. Didn't matter. We were harassed every step of the way. Technically, we were allowed to speak. No one took down our website or our videos, yet. But the tech giants made it as difficult as possible.

Other experts actually were not so lucky. John Ionnadis is a respected epidemiologist at Stanford University. At the beginning of the lockdown he merely questioned whether it was necessary, and said publicly that COVID was not an existential threat and we risked doing more harm than good with the lockdowns. He made the analogy to our society being an elephant and COVID being a mouse, and the elephant being so frightened of the mouse that it ran off a cliff and killed itself. He had a video on *YouTube* that was viewed 1 million times. Then *YouTube* pulled the video.

This was the most pressing public policy issue, by far, of 2020. Many people, especially academics who have looked seriously at it, think on balance *Facebook* specifically and the new online world generally are bad things. They have decreased our attention spans and made us less happy due to comparing our lives to the *Instagram* posts of others. Obviously the new online world is not without its benefits. *Google* makes it much easier to find information. *Facebook* helps us connect with friends, although a better connection would be talking to them by phone or in person, and helps to find people with common interests to you. But most scholars and experts, including many of the executives in the tech world, think on balance technology has probably made the world a worse place and made people less happy.

Be that as it may, one of the best benefits, in principle, to the web and platforms like *Facebook* and advertising on *Google* and online generally, is to facilitate democracy and protest movements. In principle, these platforms make it easier for insurgents with unpopular opinions to organize, get their message out, resist despotic governments such as China's (and the U.S.'s?), and perhaps change public opinion with a message that TV networks and newspapers have ignored or refuse to disseminate. On COVID, the most important public policy issue of 2020 and the most important personal liberty issue since legally sanctioned segregation and racism, the online platforms and tech giants completely failed in that regard. They actively resisted dissenting opinions and refused even to take money from us. Their loyalty to lockdowns seemed to trump even their profit motive. (Actually it did not; their loyalty to lockdowns served their profit motive, as I will discuss in Chapter 37.)

Amazon refused, for a time, to publish a well researched anti-lockdown book by a respected author. Alex Berenson is a former *New York Times* reporter and best-selling mystery author. In the introduction to his book *Unreported Truths About COVID-19 and Lockdowns: Part 2*, he recounts that he completed the book and uploaded it to *Amazon* as a Kindle book and assumed it would be published and available in 24 or 48 hours, as Kindle books usually are. *Amazon* refused to publish it or allow it for sale. They sent him a message that said "Your book does not comply with our guidelines. As a result we are not offering your book for sale. . . . Please consider removing references to COVID-19 from this book. [Emphasis added.]" As Berenson notes, *Amazon* is a company that sells *Mein Kampf, The Anarchist's Cookbook*, and *Bestiality and Zoophilia: Sexual Relations with Animals*. So they don't generally censor anything. But they were going to censor an anti-lockdown book.

The story has a, sort of, happy ending. Elon Musk heard about *Amazon*'s decision and tweeted about it, so *Amazon* relented and published the book. Most of us don't have the benefit of being pals with Elon Musk.

If the tech giants will not even allow dissenting opinions on their platforms, or will practice favoring one political viewpoint over another, then they no longer have the one greatest benefit they theoretically can bring to the world.

They say they are trying to prevent incorrect information from being disseminated. Give me a break!! Some algorithm created by a fallible, biased human being, is supposed to determine what is true or false, or what political opinions may be expressed!! Twitter and *Facebook* both banned the President of the United States from their platforms!! I'm no fan of Trump, and while he was President he had plenty of means of getting his opinion out, but if the President of the United States can be censored, then anyone can be.

It seems to me that the way the tech giants have handled COVID and the debate (or in reality the non-debate because it was effectively censored) over whether lockdowns were wise policy, demonstrates that major steps need to be taken to reign them in. The tech giants should be broken up. They should be taken over by the government. They should be forbidden from censoring or removing any message, other than child pornography, perhaps other pornography, and explicit calls for violence. (And maybe not even those; maybe just report those people to the government for prosecution.)

If someone posts false and defamatory statements about a private or a public figure, let them be sued for defamation. If someone hints at a call for violence, without explicitly calling for it, and violence ensues, let them be sued for that. Let them be prosecuted for it if they have violated the law. But I do not want the CEOs of *Google*, *Facebook*, or *Amazon* deciding for me what messages I am allowed to see or allowed to send.

Mainstream Media

Television networks, newspapers, and major news outlets have not been any better than the tech giants in allowing dissenting opinion on lockdowns. I hired a public relations agent to place some pieces I wrote expressing the opinion that the lockdowns had done more harm than good, supported by some of the data in this book. I thought they were well written pieces. I am a Ph.D. biochemist and immunologist, so I am well qualified to write on this stuff. The anti-lockdown view is an opinion that is under-expressed in the media, obviously, so they should have an obligation or interest in publishing a contrary opinion and contrary data. And it is the most pressing public policy issue we have right now, so there would be enormous interest and controversy generated by publishing it, which would help to drive more eyeballs to their sites. So they should have a financial interest also in publishing anti-lockdown pieces. None of that mattered. My hired agent could not get anything accepted for publication in the Minneapolis *StarTribune*, St. Paul *Pioneer Press*, or even *MinnPost*, an independent on-line newspaper in Minnesota.

Then I tried to place an advertisement in the Minneapolis *StarTribune* showing some of the statistics in this book about suicides caused, depression caused, and COVID deaths prevented by the lockdowns. The *StarTribune* would not even accept our money. They refused to run the ad. I think that is censorship. Can they refuse to run an ad for a political candidate? I do not think so. So why should they be allowed to refuse to run ads expressing political opinions, let alone scientifically supported evidence, that the paper's management disagrees with?

Our nonprofit had the same experience with political websites on both the right and left. We attempted to place advertisements expressing the anti-lockdown views in this book directly on two liberal websites I sometimes visit—*Mother Jones* and *Talking Points Memo*. Both refused to accept the ads. We attempted to place advertisements online through an advertising broker that can place ads through a publisher on a consortium of both liberal and conservative political websites. The broker company could purchase ads at a discounted rate. We sent them a check, which they cashed, and they then said the publisher they worked through as an intermediary with the political websites would not accept the ads, and they refunded our money.

Here's an example of what I consider clear cut bias and—really—journalistic malpractice in the news media (not the story itself but the lack of coverage of it elsewhere). This story I found on *Fox News's* website and was originally reported by the *New York Post* (1), which, like *Fox News*, has a Republican or conservative political bias.

The story reports that Dr. David Nabarro, the World Health Organization's Special Envoy for COVID-19, said "We really do appeal to all world leaders: stop using lockdowns as your primary control method." "We in the Word Health Organization do not advocate lockdowns as the primary means of control of this virus." And, "The only time we believe a lockdown is justified is to buy you time to reorganize, regroup, rebalance your resources, protect your health workers who are exhausted, but by and large, we'd rather not do it." And "Lockdowns have just one consequence that you must never, ever belittle, and that is making poor people an awful lot poorer." And "Just look at what's happened to the tourism industry in the Caribbean, for example, or in the Pacific, because people aren't taking their holidays." And "It seems that we may well have a doubling of world poverty by next year. We may well have at least a doubling of child malnutrition."

If you get your news from any source other than the *New York Post* and *Fox News*, you never saw that story, because no one else published it. Do you think it is newsworthy when the person who is literally the very top public health official in the world on COVID-19, says "We really-ly do appeal to all world leaders: stop using lockdown as your primary control method," and "Lockdowns have just one consequence . . ., and that is making poor people an awful lot poorer"?

That story was buried by mainstream media. Even *Fox News* did not give it as much emphasis as I think was justified. I am a Democrat and do not generally have a favorable opinion of *Fox News*, but *Fox News* along with some other conservative news outlets like the *New York Post* were the only major news outlets that were even close to being "Fair and Balanced" in their coverage of the benefits and harms of lockdowns as a policy (or that covered the idea that lockdowns had harms really at all). Even the conservative outlets, as far as I am aware, have published nothing questioning whether masks and lockdowns have reduced COVID cases and deaths significantly, and as I have shown in this book the data is pretty clear that they have not. So I would say, not only is there legitimate question of whether mask mandates and stay-at-home orders and the lockdown approach generally have reduced COVID deaths, but the data is pretty clear they have not.

The major conservative media in the U.S. has done a decent job presenting some balance to the question of whether lockdowns were a wise policy. But the liberal or mainstream media of the *New York Times, CNN, MSNBC,* and most major newspapers like the Minneapolis *StarTribune* have failed completely. They have been nonstop cheerleaders for the lockdown policy and treat lockdowns as a fact of life like gravity that was inevitable, instead of a human policy choice that we could implement or not. They have also sent the message absolutely nonstop that COVID is the worst crisis ever and a complete disaster and that everyone should be terrified of getting it and dying from it and that any sane person will never visit their elderly parents again and if you do visit them you are trying to kill them and that children are likely to die from COVID and that it is inevitable and absolutely necessary that we had to give up gathering this year and give up live sports and live music and everything else we have given up and anyone who questions any of this is beyond the bounds of legitimate political discourse and probably a nut or a monster!

The headlines in Minnesota in the spring of 2020 were "People in Nursing Homes are Dying." I was not previously aware it was news, let alone front page news, that people in nursing homes often die. I wanted to shake those headline writers and say, "Would you rather it were people in schools??!!"

The media have acted like it is unprecedented for old, sick people to die and a tragedy when they do. There was a front page story in the Minneapolis *StarTribune* in the spring of 2020 that a 92-year-old physician had died of COVID, and as I recall his wife had died recently too. This was considered front page news. The story went on for many columns and onto another page with quotes from the couple's children about how great they were and what a tragedy this was that their 92-year-old father died. According to the story, this man was beloved by his patients, had many friends, beloved by his children, had been happily married to one woman for 70 years, and was financially successful. In other words, he had about as blessed a life as anyone could possibly have. But it was a tragedy that he only made it to age 92. And we must shut down society lest other 92-year-olds die.

References:

1. Salo, Jackie. WHO warns against COVID-19 lockdowns due to economic damage. *New York Post.* October 12, 2020. Available at https://www.foxnews.com/world/who-coronavirus-lockdowns-economic-damage

Chapter 33

Did Anthony Fauci and the Other Physicians in Positions of Power Advocating for the Lockdowns Commit Medical Malpractice and Violate Their Hippocratic Oath?

Short answer: Yes. But they get off on a technicality.

The Hippocratic Oath is an oath, allegedly written by Hippocrates in ancient Greece, that physicians take when they graduate medical school. Actually, these days some take no oath and others take variations on the Hippocratic Oath. But most take some variation on the Hippocratic Oath. The key, most widely quoted part of the Hippocratic Oath is, "First, do no harm." In other words, ensure that when you prescribe or perform some medical intervention, make sure the harm of the intervention is not greater than the benefit.

As I have discussed at length, the harms from the lockdown policy vastly—*vastly*—exceed the benefit. It is not close.

If a physician prescribed a drug that caused major clinical depression in 1 in 5 users, that drug better have one huge benefit.

If a physician prescribed a drug to a young person that caused 1 in 5,000 users to commit suicide, that drug better have a large benefit for that young person. The lockdowns have no benefit for young people and save probably zero lives of anyone, but certainly almost zero lives of young people.

In essence, Anthony Fauci and the other public health officials who are physicians prescribed to every person in the country a drug that causes major depression in 1 in 5 users in order to fight the risk of death from a moderately bad strain of influenza that is 1.7 times deadlier than the usual flu (and also a bit more contagious, and also we do not have a vaccine against it, unlike the flu). Would you take TAMI-FLU for the flu if there was a 1 in 5 chance it would throw you into major depression for five months and a 100% chance it would make you at least a little less happy for about a year? COVID is overall about 3-4 times deadlier than influenza by infection fatality rate, which I do not think is that large a difference, but it has a lower infection fatality rate than influenza for everyone under age 18 and about the same as influenza for ages 18-49 (Chapter 13).

So they, in essence, prescribed to everyone under age 50 in this country to fight the risk of influenza a drug that causes a 1 in 5 risk of major clinical depression and a 1 in 5,000 risk the young person will commit suicide. If that is not medical malpractice, it is hard to imagine what would be. If that is not a violation of the Hippocratic Oath, it is hard to imagine what would be.

For the elderly too, there is actually no evidence the lockdowns have prevented any deaths (Chapter 23). I have estimated, generously, here that they may have prevented 200,000 COVID deaths, but there is really no evidence for that. But if they have prevented 200,000 deaths, that is 1/3 as many as the number of COVID deaths that have occurred. In the over age 85 group, 1.32% had died of COVID by December 12, 2020, and by the end of COVID around 2% will have died from COVID. If we credit the lockdowns for preventing 200,000 deaths, then in the over 85 group the percentage who died would have been 2.7% instead of 2.0%, so the lockdowns prevented COVID death in 0.7% of the over 85 group. Is it worth it to cause 20% of them to go into major clinical depression to save the lives of 0.7% from COVID death? I don't think so. I at least think they should have had a choice. If an elderly couple living in a nursing home did not want to see their children this year because of fear of COVID, that would have been their right (although I think it would have been irrational because seeing their kids would have had no effect on their risk of COVID death). But if they did want to see their kids, I think they should have had the right to do that.

A better comparison than TAMIFLU would be the flu vaccine or better yet the COVID vaccines. Would you take the COVID vaccine if you were age 30, meaning at no risk of COVID death, and if it caused a 1 in 5,000 risk of causing you to commit suicide, a 1 in 5 risk of causing major clinical depression for you, and a 100% risk of making you less happy? Of course not. And the COVID vaccines are over 90%, and probably nearly 100%, effective in preventing COVID death, whereas the lockdowns have no or almost no efficacy. At age 85 would you even take the COVID vaccine if it had those side effects? I would not. Any physician who prescribed a vaccine for COVID with that side effect profile to a 30-year-old would be clearly committing malpractice. I think he or she would be committing malpractice even prescribing it to an 85-year old.

So certainly Dr. Fauci and the other physicians advocating for lockdowns committed medical malpractice and violated their Hippocratic Oath in regards to everyone under age 50 and really everyone under age 85. Even regarding the over-age-85 group I think they did, but I suppose you could make an argument lockdowns were worth it for that group if you value duration of life much more than quality of life and happiness.

It would be interesting if someone whose teenage child committed suicide over the lockdowns sued Fauci and the government for medical malpractice and wrongful death. I'm sure the case would be thrown out, but in a just world it would not be.

I believe that, since there is no doubt that the lockdowns caused more medical harm than benefit (even ignoring the economic harm and the mere mild unhappiness they caused for nearly everyone), there is also no doubt that Dr. Fauci committed medical malpractice and violated his Hippocratic Oath.

But I said he gets off on a technicality, and this is the technicality: He did not have an individual patient. The entire country was his patient, which means legally he had no patient. His legal defense would be that to commit malpractice he has to be providing medical care to an individual to whom he is acting as physician. In other words, he was acting as a government official, just like any non-physician, and not acting as a physician, so he cannot have committed malpractice or violated his Hippocratic Oath.

If he was physician to a particular 30-year-old and prescribed that he wear a mask at all times in public and stop going to health clubs and stop socializing and stop going to church if he was a regular church-goer and church was important to him, that would be malpractice toward that person. It would have no benefit for him and be likely to drive him into depression and possibly suicide. If he prescribed the same course of action to an individual 85-year-old, you could argue it is not malpractice. It might reduce that 85-year-old's risk of death from COVID somewhat and the risk of causing him depression might be worth it, at least arguably. It would still be poor medical advice. He should tell that 85-year-old to wash his hands and use hand sanitizer religiously, but not worry about masks. But maybe it's not malpractice.

So in summary, yes, Dr. Fauci is guilty of medical malpractice and violating his Hippocratic Oath in spirit, but he gets off on the technicality that he was not acting as a physician because he did not have a specific individual patient.

Chapter 34

Perhaps the Stupidest and Most Arrogant Statement Ever Made

D r. Anthony Fauci said in April 2020, "I don't think we should ever shake hands again." (1)

That's my nominee for the stupidest and most arrogant statement ever made. Maybe there have been dumber things said. Maybe there have been statements that were more arrogant. But for combining stupidity and arrogance, that ranks pretty high.

The handshake, or something like it, has been a custom in perhaps every society that exists on earth today and, to my knowledge, every society we know of in human history. But Anthony Fauci thinks he knows better than the consensus opinion of humans in every society that has ever existed. That's the arrogance part.

The stupidity part is partly the same. When every society that has ever existed has come to a different conclusion, maybe you are wrong. And is he vaguely familiar with the idea that touch is important to human beings? If he thinks we should eliminate handshakes, I assume he would have a conniption at the idea we should ever hug again. Has he ever heard of the studies on primates raised without touch? Has he heard about the outcomes of orphans in Romania who were raised in orphanages without touch? He attended medical school. Didn't they teach him any of this in medical school?

Louis Armstrong in his beautiful song "What a Wonderful World" sings:

"Friends shaking hands, saying 'how do you do.' They're really saying, 'I love you.'"

Louis Armstrong knew an awful lot more about human beings than Anthony Fauci.

References

1. https://time.com/5818134/anthony-fauci-never-shake-hands-corona-virus/

Chapter 35

Judicial Decisions and U.S. Civil Liberties

I have been stunned at the acceptance by the courts, as well as by the public, of government emergency powers and restrictions on civil liberties.

Governors across the country have claimed emergency powers. These have been challenged in court in probably every state and have mostly, but not entirely, been upheld by state and federal courts.

First, it does not seem to me to qualify as an emergency to have basically a new strain of the flu that is three-and-a-half times deadlier than the usual flu and about 1.7 times deadlier than ordinary flu if you have not received the flu vaccine (Chapter 13). Also, to put this in perspective, it is at least 15 times less deadly, in terms of person-years of life expectancy lost per capita (Chapter 13), than the 1918 flu, which did not produce a wave of restrictions on civil liberties or a wave of emergency-power edicts.

Second, the basis for emergency powers is or should be imminent danger, such that the legislature does not have time to meet and act, so the governor must act. That certainly was not the case here. Legislatures could have met and passed new legislation in a week or two, and if it was so obvious and unarguable that COVID was an existential threat and we must not allow churches to gather or people to be in public without a mask, you would not have had any trouble getting legislation passed that closed churches and mandated masks. Instead, as far as I am aware, not a single state in the union has passed its COVID restrictions by legislation. Everything has been by governors executing emergency powers. I think it is absurd to allow any emergency powers past a week or two, past the time when the legislature can meet.

Courts have not viewed it that way. Rights in the U.S. do not get much more fundamental than the right to practice your religion and the right to gather and peaceably assemble. Despite that, courts have upheld closing churches—and they have upheld the closures when the closures were by executive decree and were opposed by the majority of the state's legislators and could never have passed the legislature.

If I were a judge and I was faced with a lawsuit from someone suing for the right to leave his home or go to a church of his choice, in defiance of a stay-at-home order or an order closing churches, I would immediately rule in the plaintiff's favor and against the governor. I would rule I did not even have to consider the merits until faced with legislation passed by the legislature and signed by the governor, like any other statute. Even after such legislation was passed, I would rule the statute unconstitutional as an infringement on the First Amendment (freedom of religion and freedom of assembly), but I would laugh the government out of court until it at least has a statute passed by the legislature.

If courts are to uphold these extreme restrictions, I would say the government should have to show three things:

(1) A statute, not an executive order.

(2) An argument with evidence, not just the governor's say so, that COVID is an extreme threat that justifies waiving our rights. The evidence shows COVID is about three-and-a-half times deadlier than the ordinary flu and about 1.7 times as deadly as ordinary flu if you have not had a flu vaccine. I don't think that meets the standard for the level of threat needed to justify these restrictions on our liberties.

(3) Evidence that the restrictions accomplish or would be expected to accomplish a substantial reduction in risk of death from COVID. This also is lacking. As explained throughout this book, the evidence is that all of the restrictions taken together have had no effect at all on COVID deaths, let alone a substantial effect.

None of those three prongs were met. The government should have been required to show all three prongs were met to have these extreme restrictions upheld.

Chapter 36

The Vaccines

I will preface this advice by saying I am not a physician. For medical advice, ask your physician. But I will offer my free advice here anyway.

Do the COVID vaccines work? Yes, clearly. The data is not forged. Each of the four approved vaccines was tested on more than 10,000 volunteers with not a single death or serious adverse event attributed to any of the vaccines in clinical trials. They are each over 90% effective in preventing death or hospitalization from COVID. So unlike the lockdowns, the benefit-to-harm ratio of the vaccines leans vastly toward the benefits.

Certainly anyone over age 40 who has not been infected with the COVID virus should get the vaccine. Anyone over age 40 or 45 is at a 1 in 1,000 or greater risk of death if infected with the COVID virus. That is not super high, but high enough that I would want to get the vaccine. Over age 65 the infection fatality rate is above 1%, so fatality is a real risk if you are not vaccinated. So you ought to get vaccinated.

But that is your choice and you should have the right not to get vaccinated. You should have the right to travel by plane and do anything else whether you are vaccinated or not. In fact, no employer, business, or government should have the right to ask whether you have been vaccinated.

For adults age 18-40, they are at pretty trivial risk of dying from COVID and about the same risk as dying from the flu. So I suppose someone in that age group ought to get vaccinated, but it is not any more obvious that they should than it is that they should get the flu vaccine. Certainly they should have the right not to get vaccinated. The main argument for people in that age group to be vaccinated is for the benefit of others, not for their own benefit. Being vaccinated reduces, and probably almost eliminates, the risk they will be infected and carry the virus and then infect others. Being vaccinated in that age group helps get us to herd immunity, when this disease will be largely gone. However, the fact that being vaccinated helps get us to herd immunity and reduces the risk you will carry the virus and infect others does not make it a moral obligation any more than it is a moral obligation to get the flu vaccine. COVID, over all age groups, is about 3-1/2 times more lethal than the flu, by infection fatality rate. If you have not had either the flu or COVID vaccines, COVID is only 1.7 times deadlier than the flu. That is in the same neighborhood. So if you think it is a moral, and should be a legal, obligation to be vaccinated against COVID, regardless of your age or risk, you should think the same about being vaccinated against the flu.

For children under age 18, I do not think they should be vaccinated. They are at about a 1 in a million chance of dying from COVID if infected and at much lower risk of death from COVID than from flu. We have no evidence the vaccines have long term negative consequences, but we do not know they do not, especially the RNA vaccines and adenovirus vaccines. Those carry nucleic acids. It is not unreasonable to think the nucleic acids might integrate in the genome in some cells, and although unlikely, that could cause health problems later in life. We have the right and obligation to make decisions for children, since they are not fully able to make decisions for themselves, and therefore should err strongly on the side of not imposing a medical or other intervention that has a trivial benefit for them and some, though probably small, risk to them. This decision is much easier on closing schools, which has a huge harm to children and no benefit at all for them (or even for adults). With the vaccine it is a much closer call. The harm is small. The benefit for children is tiny, but there is probably a slight benefit in reducing the trivial risk of severe COVID disease. Also, children are essentially not carriers of COVID, as we saw in Chapter 20. They seem to very rarely become ill and rarely pass the infection to adults. So there is not even much benefit to adults from vaccinating children against COVID. But in my view the benefit to adults should not even enter the calculation. We should make the decision the same way we should have made the decision on closing schools and should make any decision about actions to take regarding children under our care: Does it benefit the children? Not, What's in it for me? Not, Does it benefit me to vaccinate my child?

Should people who have had COVID be vaccinated? No. That is an easy call. There is no benefit for them to be vaccinated and some risk for them and no benefit for the rest of us for them to be vaccinated. Fewer than ten people in the entire world have been infected with

SARS-CoV-2 twice. Once you have been infected, you are immune. That is abundantly clear. So there is no reason at all to vaccinate someone who has already been infected. Also, there is some risk for them to be vaccinated. Anecdotally, reports are coming out that people who already have had COVID are having strong reactions to the vaccine and becoming ill from the vaccine. That is as you would expect, since their immune system is already primed to react strongly to the vaccine. Apparently no one has died from the vaccine, but I see no benefit to them being vaccinated, so why should we ask them to take a risk of feeling lousy for a couple of days for no benefit to them or us?

For the purposes of choosing to get the vaccine or not, I would put into the category of "already had COVID" only those who (a) had or have a positive antibody test for prior COVID infection (whether they ever felt ill or not, since the antibody tests have very low false negatives) or (b) felt ill and had a contemporaneous positive PCR or antigen test for COVID infection. If you never felt ill and only have a positive PCR test at some time, there is a high likelihood the PCR test was a false positive. And if you felt ill with cold/flu symptoms but had no positive PCR or antibody test, it is about as likely that was cold or flu as COVID.

So my advice on who should get one of the COVID vaccines:

· Yes:

Over age 40 and not known to be previously infected with COVID.

Age 18-40 and not known to be previously infected. But the benefit of the vaccine for themselves is not huge for this group and is probably about the same as their benefit from getting a flu vaccine.

· No:

Children age 0 to 17.

Adults known (with certainty) to have been previously infected with COVID.

Should we mandate vaccines?

No, of course not. The vaccines work and have vastly more benefit than harm, and if you are at risk of death from COVID you certainly should get one. But that should be your decision.

And once you have been vaccinated, you have no interest in other people getting vaccinated. The vaccines give over 90% and probably 100% protection against COVID death. They are 80% effective against even being infected. You are now at no risk of COVID death (though still at 100% risk of death from something). It should not matter to you whether anyone else has been vaccinated.

Chapter 37

....
Who Is to Blame

I hesitate to criticize people for the lockdown response because I believe that in life everyone is doing the best they can with their current level of awareness. And we should be kind to each other and forgiving to each other. But at the same time, it is appropriate to do *post mortems* after disasters and figure out what mistakes were made, why they were made, and who made them. And for experts and leaders in particular, it is appropriate to hold them responsible and make them bear consequences for their mistakes and bad decisions.

So here are some of the organizations and people I am disappointed in over the lockdowns.

Anthony Fauci and U.S. CDC Leadership.

Mostly everyone was following their lead. These are the experts. We trusted their expertise, and they failed us abysmally. They are the first people to blame and should receive the greatest share of blame. It was their job to make good recommendations about how to respond to COVID and they made terrible recommendations of pursuing the lockdown strategy including recommending mask mandates, stay-at-home orders, closing schools (!!), forbidding large gatherings such as at church or at weddings, and closing non-essential businesses. They even recommended the insanity of closing state parks and national parks, where people are great distances from each other, when they knew or should have known that being outdoors is great for our mental health and great for our immune systems and would therefore reduce, not increase, COVID deaths.

They acted like COVID deaths are the only thing that matters in the world of health. They knew or should have known the lockdowns would increase suicides and drug abuse and vastly increase depression, but to this day they have not acknowledged that and apparently view those harms as either of no consequence or as simply not their concern. Their mission should be to promote health, not to prevent COVID infection or COVID death, and not even just to prevent death generally but to promote health more broadly.

There is no excuse for not acknowledging that the lockdowns would and have increased suicides, drug abuse and drug overdoses, alcohol abuse and alcohol deaths, and depression, and for not weighing that against any possible reduction in COVID deaths from the lockdowns.

Moreover, how much have the lockdowns reduced COVID deaths? How well has this strategy worked for that goal? Those seem like obvious and very reasonable questions to ask. The CDC has never made an estimate. They seem to have no interest at all in measuring or estimating how many COVID deaths were prevented, let alone in weighing that against the harms of the lockdowns.

What is my risk of COVID death? What is the overall infection fatality rate, the percentage of infected people who die of COVID, and how does that vary by age and health condition? The CDC has never made an official estimate of any of that. That is inexcusable. Why did I have to make those calculations for myself in this book?

What percentage of the population has already been infected by the SARS-CoV-2 virus as of now (asked at any date during the pandemic)? The CDC never attempted to answer that. That is a very, very basic and important question. It tells us how far we are from herd immunity. It gives us an idea of whether the lockdowns are preventing infections. And the answer is necessary to determine the infection fatality rate of COVID. The CDC never even attempted to get an answer to that question. Inexcusable.

Why did Dr. Fauci and the CDC leadership fail so terribly? Why did they not answer or even attempt to answer any of the questions above? Why did they have no apparent interest or concern in the harms of the lockdowns and weighing those against the benefits? I do not know. Someone in the media should ask them. It is not my job to defend them. They can defend themselves if they are able to.

The News Media

Basically the same criticisms that apply to Fauci and the CDC leadership applies to the news media. The only defense the news media have is they can claim their duty is just to make money and get eyeballs and views, not to inform the public. If the media want to claim they are just like any other business and are only seeking money and have no duty to inform the public, then they are excused on that cynical, bleak justification.

The same questions I raise above for Dr. Fauci and the CDC apply also to newspapers and other news media.

How much have the lockdowns reduced COVID deaths? How well has this strategy worked for that goal?

What is my risk of COVID death? What is the overall infection fatality rate, the percentage of infected people who die of COVID, and how does that vary by age and health condition?

What percentage of the population has already been infected by the SARS-CoV-2 virus as of now (asked at any date during the pandemic)?

What is my risk of COVID death? The media and Dr. Fauci have basically responded, "Oh, huge! You don't want to know! You could not handle it if we told you!" I would respond, "No, treat me like an adult. I want to know. Depending on how high that risk is, maybe I will conclude that it is not worth sacrificing a year of our lives to reduce that risk. In any case, I would like to make that decision for myself, based on the best estimates of the mortality risk, rather than have my governor and Dr. Fauci make that decision for me."

The media have no excuse for their failures. They employ science journalists. They should be able to evaluate the data. They should at least have the competence and courage to ask the questions listed above. When the government asserts that mask mandates and lockdowns have reduced the spread of COVID, you do not have to be Woodward and Bernstein to ask to see the data supporting that assertion. You just have to be a competent journalist. Apparently, we have none in the U.S.

The data on COVID cases and deaths are given daily. In Minnesota, for instance, here is a chart of COVID deaths and hospitalizations with arrows put on the chart of when stay-at-home orders were imposed and lifted.

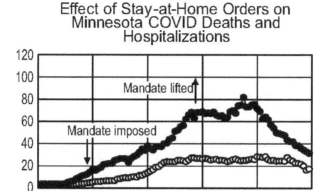

Effect of Stay-at-Home Orders on
Minnesota COVID Deaths and
Hospitalizations

—o— Deaths 7-day average   —•— Hospitalized 7-day average

It does not look to me like imposition of the stay-at-home orders slowed the spread of COVID, and it certainly did not stop it, and it does not look like lifting the orders caused any increase in the spread of COVID. If any journalist ever asked the Governor or our state Health Commissioner about this chart and to explain why they think the stay-at-home orders accomplished anything, I am not aware of it.

Governor Walz in Minnesota cited modeling predicting we would have 74,000 COVID deaths in Minnesota by the summer of 2020 if we did nothing and the lockdowns would reduce that by a third (we have 6,976 as of April 7, 2021). Those numbers were absurd at the time. A competent journalist would have pointed out they were absurd when they were made. By the summer of 2020 when we had had less than 5% of the deaths predicted, one might at least expect some journalist to ask the Governor at a press conference why he was so wrong. That did not happen to my knowledge.

The news media have given wall-to-wall scare mongering about this disease. Breathless predictions that we will have 74,000 deaths in Minnesota by the summer of 2020, that we will have a surge of cases after Thanksgiving or Christmas or any other holiday because of people traveling or meeting family, that Florida would experience an explosion of cases when its governor lifted restrictions, are repeated. When those catastrophes do not happen, no one follows up to report the error of the original predictions.

The newspapers have scare headlines in all caps PEOPLE IN NURSING HOMES ARE DYING, like that is a new development. I see that headline and want to shake the headline writer and scream at him, "Would you prefer it were people in schools?!!"

If you suggest that mask wearing has little if any effect on transmission of SARS-CoV-2 infection, you are labeled by the media as a COVID denier or an ignoramus, even though, as we have seen, that is what all the data says and that is what amounts to the official position of the medical community in *Cochrane Reviews*.

The media have fact checkers that have fact checked the assertion that COVID is less deadly than the flu. They correctly state that assertion is false. But they neglect to state or ask how much deadlier than the flu it is. Answer: three-and-a-half times deadlier and only 1.7 times deadlier when compared to the flu in unvaccinated people. They just leave it with the fact that COVID is deadlier than the flu and imply that if it is deadlier at all, then obviously we had to shut down society. That does not logically follow. If COVID were less than twice as deadly as the flu (and for people who have not received the flu vaccine and have not received any vaccine for COVID, COVID probably is less than twice as deadly as the flu), would it follow that we must shut down society and shut down the schools? If it would, then we should have been debating that every year for the flu. Three-and-a-half-fold is not that big a difference.

The WHO liaison for COVID said, "The only thing lockdowns are good for is making poor people an awful lot poorer," and "Lockdowns should only be used as a last resort." I think that was newsworthy. Maybe among the most newsworthy events of the past year. As far as I can tell, only *Fox News* and the *New York Post* covered that at all, and neither mentioned it for more than one day. (Chapter 32.)

The results of the definitive clinical trial on masks, a randomized study of 6,000 people in Denmark, came out and concluded that masks make "no significant difference" in likelihood of COVID infection. Maybe that was the most newsworthy event in 2020. It would rank high. It was not front page news in any major U.S. newspaper and was barely covered in the U.S. media.

The Minneapolis *StarTribune* almost every day on the front page for the duration of this epidemic has had a scare story about how terrible COVID is. They ran a front page story that a non-famous 92-year old died of COVID. Yet on the day that *Pfizer* and *BioNTech* applied to the FDA for emergency use authorization of the first COVID vaccine, the moment we had been waiting for about nine months, the *StarTribune* did not have that story on page 1. The editors of that newspaper literally thought that the death of a non-famous 92-year old from COVID was bigger news than the news that we would soon have a vaccine.

Governors and State Health Department Leadership

These parties have the partial excuse that they were trusting and deferring to the federal health leadership for recommendations and guidance. But the state health departments have expertise too. They should have been asking the same questions and making the same calculations of what the infection fatality rate of COVID is overall and by age, how effective the lockdowns were and how many COVID deaths were being prevented, and how much depression, suicide, and drug abuse and overdoses were caused by the lockdowns, and how those harms compare to the benefit of COVID deaths prevented. They did not.

The same criticisms apply to governors. They are not infectious disease experts, but they should have had the sense to ask the questions above and should have found experts who could answer them, within or outside their own health departments, since the CDC was not answering them.

The governors and other political leaders should also have tried to calm us and remind us that life will go on, that COVID strikes almost exclusively the old and sick and most people have little or nothing to fear from it. They should have been leaders. They should have acted like Franklin Roosevelt, when he said, "The only thing we have to fear is fear itself." Instead, they tried to inflame fears. They also tried to inflame divisions by focusing on mask wearing as the most pushed intervention, which we knew was almost entirely ineffective in reducing infections but very effective in dividing us from each other, causing us to fear one another and hate people who resist mask wearing, and providing scapegoats—governors could say, "All you people out there not wearing your masks or not wearing them properly, it is your fault!"

The governors and Dr. Fauci and the CDC leaders may have been motivated by a desire to be heroes and a desire to claim hero status. Toward that end, it helps to exaggerate how bad COVID would be, so when it is not so bad you can claim the entire difference is due to your heroic actions. For instance, Governor Tim Walz of Minnesota at the beginning of the outbreak cited a study he claimed said that if we did nothing, 74,000 Minnesotans would die of COVID and in the summer of 2020 two million Minnesotans would be infected all at once. Two million would be 40% of the population. Smallpox may have never infected 40% of a population all at once. Coronavirus is a common cold virus and there was never any evidence SARS-CoV-2's infectiousness is greater than the common cold (it turns out it is less infectious than the common cold and more infectious than influenza). The common cold never infects 40% of the population at once. 74,000 deaths would be 1.3% of the population of Minnesota. If we reached herd immunity at 70% of the population infected, to have 1.3% die you would have to have an infection fatality rate of 1.9%. Even the Imperial College of London researchers with their infamous erroneous projections of 2.2 million U.S. deaths from COVID estimated the infection fatality rate was 0.9% and wrote that that was basically a worst case scenario (Ferguson et al.). The idea that 1.3% of Minnesotans would die of COVID was absurd. The idea that 40% of any population would be infected all at once was absurd. But claiming that if we had done nothing, 74,000 Minnesotans would die of COVID allows Governor Walz to claim now that 6,976 have actually died as of April 7, 2021, that he is responsible for saving 67,000 lives! Hurrah, what a hero!

Teachers' Unions

As noted in Chapter 20, we knew by the summer of 2020 that closing schools had no effect whatsoever of reducing COVID infections or fatalities. We knew from before COVID reached the U.S. that children were at almost no risk of death from COVID and at lesser risk of death from COVID than from the flu. We decided to close the schools anyway, even in the fall 2020 to 2021 school year, knowing there was no benefit to doing so and enormous harm to children, unless you think schools serve no purpose, which I assume is not the official position of the teachers' unions. The party that pushed hardest and longest to close schools was the teachers' unions.

I am pro-union and am pro-teacher and was pro-teachers' unions, but as far as I am concerned teachers' unions can never live this down. They have ruined their reputation in my mind forever. They simply abandoned the children.

Why? Because they were afraid for themselves of dying from COVID. They should not have been. Anyone young enough and healthy enough to still be in the workforce is at very low risk of death from COVID and for everyone under age 40 the risk is about the same as that of dying from the flu. For that trivial risk, teachers' unions pushed to sacrifice a year or more of education for children, drive some children to suicide and drug abuse, and drive a huge percentage of children to clinical depression, probably more than the 19% driven to depression in the whole population. Inexcusable. If individual teachers were so irrationally afraid of this, they should have quit. But they should not have refused to do their jobs and demand to get paid anyway. (I am aware they were still teaching online and that might be even more difficult than teaching in person, but it is not what they were hired to do and it is less effective than teaching in person.)

Also, closing schools had no effect of decreasing risk to teachers. As reviewed in Chapter 20, studies show children *get infected* from adults, they mostly do not *infect* adults. And studies showed by the summer of 2020 that teachers in closed schools are at the same risk of COVID infection as teachers in open schools. So this cowardly and selfish move of closing schools did not even have any benefit for teachers.

The only excuse for teachers' unions is that they probably did not know these facts that children are at lower risk of death from COVID than from the flu and that closing schools has no benefit in reducing COVID infections or deaths of teachers or the community, since the CDC and the media did not publicize those facts. But maybe teachers and their unions should have inquired into those issues.

College and University Presidents and Administrators

The same criticisms directed at teachers' unions apply to college and university presidents and administrators who made the decisions to close colleges and universities, though to a slightly lesser extent. College students are not at lower risk of death from COVID than from the flu, as children are, but they are at the same risk. So they receive no benefit from closing colleges. It obviously is a significant harm to them, not just educationally but also socially. But the colleges and universities still demanded the same tuition payments.

College-age people are more likely to be symptomatically ill from COVID virus infection than children are, and symptomatic people are more likely to transmit the infection, so closing colleges probably did reduce infection of college professors and staff, whereas closing K-12 schools did not reduce infection of teachers and staff. And some professors and college staff are old or even elderly and at significant risk of COVID death. But the solution is not to close the college. The solution would be to allow professors over age 60 to take a leave of absence or maybe teach remotely. I would not view that as justified for any professors under age 60 and not in bad health.

Parents

Parents have the excuse that they were not told by the CDC or the media the facts that children are at less risk of COVID death than death from the flu and that closing schools has no effect on transmission of COVID to teachers or the community. But still, parents have a duty to stand up for their children. They knew their children were at very low risk of COVID death and knew that closing schools on balance greatly harmed their children. They knew this policy sacrificed the interests of their children to benefit their parents and grandparents. When a parent is asked to weigh the interests of their children against the interests of their retired and elderly parents, they should side with their children.

So, as a group, parents of schoolchildren should have stood up and opposed school closings more strongly than most parents did.

Leadership of Liberal Christian Denominations

I happen to be a churchgoing Episcopalian, and my faith and the Episcopal Church are important to me. It was a big chunk of my social life also pre-COVID. My parish has a slogan of "Free to Question," and when I was a teenager there was a poster with an image of Jesus and the words "He died to take away your sins, not your minds." Those sentiments appeal to me. The Episcopal Church has a proud tradition of supporting the civil rights movement and supporting environmental protection or care for God's creation. I have always been very, very proud of the Episcopal Church. (The Episcopal Church also has the most beautiful hymns and music of any denomination, in my opinion.)

I also happen to have been on the vestry of my parish, which is the lay governing body of the parish, when COVID hit. We soon closed the church and stopped meeting in person. We still had video worship but stopped meeting in person and did not allow more than immediate family to weddings and funerals. I opposed that, so I made a motion at our vestry meeting to reopen our church even when that was illegal as against the governor's mandate closing churches, which I thought and think was plainly unconstitutional. I was voted down 12-1. Then the governor lifted the order closing churches and the Roman Catholic Church and conservative Christian denominations began meeting. In fact, the governor probably lifted the order closing churches because the Roman Catholic Diocese of Minnesota announced they were going to defy the order and reopen. So now that it was legal to meet, I moved again to reopen our church and was voted down 12-1 again. Then the idea came to me to do a survey of our parish members asking them whether they wanted the church to reopen and asking, if church were reopened, whether they personally would attend church again. I figured even those afraid to attend church who personally would not attend would not begrudge the rest of us the privilege of meeting again. So I was confident if we did a survey we would have overwhelming support for reopening, although perhaps most would say they would not personally attend. I was voted down again 12-1 on even conducting a survey to gauge parish opinion on whether we should reopen. At that point I resigned from the vestry.

I should explain that the Episcopal Church is governed by diocesan bishops, in our case the Bishop for the Diocese of Minnesota. He had ordered all Episcopal churches in Minnesota to close and had not lifted that order. So we did not really have the power to reopen our church, or if we had, it would have been in defiance of the bishop and we might have been sanctioned. So in defense of my fellow vestry members, I think they did not want to defy the bishop, and secondly did not want to find out that the majority of our parish wanted the church reopened, since they were not going to reopen it anyway.

But I think it is to the credit of the Roman Catholic Church and of conservative protestant denominations that they reopened, and to the shame of the Episcopal Church and liberal protestant denominations generally that they have not. The churches that reopened sent a message that they take their religion seriously and that it is important to them; while the churches that have not reopened, even when they were legally permitted to do so, send the message—and I hate to say this—of our religion not being that important to us.

Churches exist largely to comfort and support people in difficult times—counsel and comfort them when they are depressed, grieve with them when a loved one dies, stand and pray with them through divorce and illness and other difficult times. In 2020, we had difficult times. And the Episcopal Church responded by saying, basically, "Whoa, these are hard times! You are on your own!"

Psychologists and Mental Health Therapists

Basically, the same comments I made for the liberal Christian denominations apply to mental health therapists. In the spring of 2020 I was depressed, in part because of the lockdowns and in part for personal reasons independent of COVID. But a large part of it was the lockdowns and the loneliness and isolation of not seeing people face to face. So I sought a psychologist to talk to. Very, very few of them were willing to see anyone in person. I finally found one who was, and she was great. But the vast majority would only see people by video.

Therapists are entitled to be afraid for their health and see people in person or not. But I am disappointed in those who would not see people in person, especially therapists under age 60 or so who would not see people in person. As I have elaborated here, most people were not at great risk from COVID and were at lower risk than they probably think they were at. Moreover, not seeing people in person, when you can keep three feet from them easily enough, has little if any effect on your risk of getting COVID. Maybe it is not a duty, but therapists should care about their clients and weigh the need of those clients for face-to-face interaction with a human against their own desire to protect their health.

Big Tech Companies

As elaborated in the Chapters 32 and 40, big tech companies profited mightily from the lockdowns and then censored and blocked the voices that opposed the lockdowns.

The Medical Profession Generally, But Mostly the Administrators

As mentioned in this book, as a result of the lockdowns we have had fewer cancer diagnoses and will have more cancer deaths as a result. The same applies for other serious diseases, and we have already had more heart disease deaths. The medical community says this is the result of people having an excessive fear of COVID infection (and whose fault is it that they have an excessive fear of COVID?) and therefore not going to the doctor for their checkups or when they have symptoms of cancer or some other serious illness. In other words, this is the patients' fault.

Not entirely. Hospitals and health systems have encouraged, or in some cases mandated, telemedicine instead of in person medicine. Doctors are less likely to make an accurate diagnosis in telemedicine because they cannot touch the patient's body or see the whole body, it is harder to read body language and facial expressions of patients, and patients just feel more rushed and are less likely to fully disclose. So the medical profession bears a significant portion of the blame for the excess cancer and heart disease deaths that we have had and will have as a result of the lockdowns.

The medical profession also bears the blame for suspending elective procedures, such as knee or hip replacement surgeries, over COVID. That seems to have accomplished nothing to reduce COVID deaths, since almost no hospital ran out of beds or equipment for COVID patients, and orthopedic surgeons were not going to be shifted to caring for COVID patients anyway. But it is a real cost. When you need one, getting a knee or hip replacement improves the quality of your life. That is worth something. Medicine is not just about preventing death, much less just about preventing COVID deaths.

The medical profession also bears a big chunk of the blame, along with CDC leadership and the media, for people's excessive fear of COVID and people therefore being afraid to go to the doctor, even when they have had a heart attack or have symptoms of cancer.

The decisions to promote or require telemedicine and to suspend elective procedures were mostly not made by individual doctors. They were made by administrators. So the blame falls on administrators and mostly not on doctors who were not administrators.

People and groups NOT to blame
Donald Trump

Yes, Donald Trump bragged about committing sexual assault. Yes, he is a pathological liar. Yes, he is a sociopath and a terrible, terrible human being. Yes, he incited a mob to storm the Capitol. Yes, he tried to overturn the 2020 election and would have stayed in power if he could have. Yes, he is a tax cheat and has probably committed felony tax fraud. But he is not responsible for COVID and he is not responsible for the misguided lockdown response to COVID. He could have done more to stop the lockdowns, but he probably could not have stopped them completely. The U.S. had about the same number of COVID deaths per capita as all the other big Western democracies. Trump is not responsible for those deaths. And we pursued the same lockdown strategy, which as I have elaborated here has caused vastly more harm than benefit, as other Western democracies.

Trump actually deserves some credit for mildly opposing the lockdowns. He seemed to sense they were a mistake. But he did not really follow through or do everything in his power to stop them and he never articulated why the lockdowns were a mistake. So I do not give him much credit. I would just say he behaved about the same as every other leader of a Western nation except for the leaders of Sweden.

CDC Staff and State Health Department Staff

CDC scientific staff have done their job competently. They have analyzed data and reported accurate, unbiased results. Their mission is to do that, not to recommend policy choices such as mandating mask wearing or not. Three CDC researchers authored a paper dated January 26, 2021 (Honein et al.) reviewing other studies on the effect of school closures and concluding that closing schools made no difference in reducing COVID infections among students or in the community. Despite that paper, Dr. Fauci and CDC leaders continued to recommend school closures and then recommended that if schools opened they should mandate mask wearing by students and social distancing. (No evidence supports either of those interventions in schools.) That is Dr. Fauci's fault; not the fault of CDC staff or those CDC authors recommending against school closures.

The CDC put out a press release that drug overdose deaths, after declining for several years, were up 16% for the 12 month period ending May 2020, including the first three months of the lockdowns (Reference 3). I would like to have seen the full numbers broken down by month or with other details, rather than just a press release. But the CDC and their staff deserve credit for releasing that information.

Likewise, the Colorado health department released a study concluding that depression had vastly increased in Colorado during the lockdowns (Reference 4). The authors of that study deserve credit for it.

The World Health Organization (WHO)

The WHO is an agency of the United Nations. It has no binding authority on any nation's government. It has released mostly accurate, unbiased work concerning COVID and fair recommendations, it seems to me. It recommends three feet or one meter of social distancing, not the six feet recommended by the U.S. CDC, and I have seen no data giving any reason to believe three feet is not enough. It has never recommended school closures. It's special envoy for COVID said, "The only thing lockdowns are good for is making poor people an awful lot poorer." And he said, "We recommend lockdowns only as a last resort." Its guidance emphasizes ventilation and being outdoors as ways to reduce risk of COVID and implies there is no significant risk of COVID infection when outdoors. It recommends mask wearing only when indoors. The WHO information says nothing about school closures.

The WHO has a video titled "How to protect yourself against COVID-19" (Reference 5) that says: COVID is spread mostly by droplets produced when an infected person speaks, sneezes, or coughs. The droplets are too heavy to travel far and fall to the ground within 1 meter, and "this is the reason person to person spread is happening mainly between close contacts." [The CDC does not acknowledge or emphasize that and claims a significant amount of spread may be happening by aerosols, meaning virus that floats in the air for hours, so you are infected by breathing air in a grocery store where an infected person breathed the same air 6 hours ago. That is contrary to the evidence. If that were a major source of spread, infection would be random and not clustered in households or among close contacts, as it is.] Therefore, the WHO video says, you should keep 1 meter from others, especially infected persons. It says that hands contact many surfaces and can pick up the virus, and you should therefore avoid touching your mouth, nose or eyes, since contaminated hands can transfer the virus from surfaces to yourself. It concludes, "The most effective way to prevent the spread of the new coronavirus is to clean your hands frequently with an alcohol-based hand rub or soap and water." So it specifically says hand washing is the single most effective intervention, unlike the U.S. CDC.

The WHO COVID website has these Facts:

"People should NOT wear masks while exercising."

People should NOT wear masks when exercising, as masks may reduce the ability to breathe comfortably.

Sweat can make the mask become wet more quickly which makes it difficult to breathe and promotes the growth of microorganisms. The important preventive measure during exercise is to maintain physical distance of at least one meter from others.

In contrast to that sensible guidance, Minnesota mandated that masks be worn in health clubs, playing tennis, and during high school sports, whether indoors or outdoors. Seattle required kids to wear masks during sports, even outdoors.

"Most people who get COVID-19 recover from it."

The CDC does not deny this fact, but they have not emphasized it.

"Water or swimming does not transmit the COVID-19 virus."

Many U.S. jurisdictions have closed swimming pools over COVID and I think the CDC recommended that or certainly did not recommend against it.

That is all very sensible and correct advice. My only quibbles would be that I think, although they state hand washing and sanitizing is "the most important" way to reduce COVID spread, they still overemphasize mask wearing, and that they do not recommend *against* school closures and stay-at-home orders, rather than merely being silent on those.

Who has been a hero
Pharmaceutical Companies and Scientists Who Developed Vaccines

Five companies, in less than a year, developed and brought to market four efficacious vaccines against COVID that essentially eliminate the risk of death from COVID. If government regulators had allowed it, the vaccines could have been released two months earlier than they were. And those companies are selling the vaccines at little or no profit. *Johnson & Johnson* and *AstraZeneca* have said they will make no profit from the vaccines, and *Pfizer* and *Moderna* are selling the vaccines at lower profit margins than normal. We should thank them.

References

1. Ferguson, Neil M. et al. March 16, 2020. Impact of non-pharmaceutical interventions (NPIs) to reduce COVID-19 mortality and healthcare demand. https://doi.org/10.25561/77482

2. Honein MA, Barrios LC, Brooks JT. Data and Policy to Guide Opening Schools Safely to Limit the Spread of SARS-CoV-2 Infection. *JAMA*. Published online January 26, 2021. https://doi.org/10.1001/jama.2021.0374

3. U.S. Centers for Disease Control and Prevention. https://www.cdc.gov/media/releases/2020/p1218-overdose-deaths-covid-19.html

4. https://www.cpr.org/2020/05/05/colorado-survey-finds-heightened-rates-of-depression-anxiety-and-stress-during-pandemic/

5. World Health Organization Video "How to protect yourself against COVID-19." Feb. 28, 2020. https://www.youtube.com/watch?v=1APwq1df6Mw

Chapter 38

Should We Be Wearing Masks After Most People Are Vaccinated?

Of course not!

It's hard to take this as a serious question, except it appears the mask mandates will continue, maybe forever if Anthony Fauci has his way.

Anthony Fauci and President Biden have both said that people will still be wearing masks at Christmas 2021.

Ross Douthat of the *New York Times* reported on February 23, 2021,

> Christmas of 2021: According to both President Biden and Dr. Anthony Fauci, together the two most prominent voices on public health in America right now, that's when we can hope for a return to normalcy, the beginning of life after the emergency.
>
> Even that not-exactly-optimistic prediction comes with hedges and caveats. Next Christmas won't necessarily be the end of pandemic restrictions, according to Biden—just a time when "significantly fewer people having to be socially distanced, having to wear a mask." Likewise, Fauci has described his hope as "a degree of normality" by the end of 2021, with the possibility of widespread masking persisting into the following year.

First, masks make little or no difference, so it never made sense to mandate mask wearing. But let's pretend masks work.

By June 1, 2021, really even by May 1, 2021, everyone who wants to be vaccinated will have been vaccinated, certainly everyone at any significant risk of death from COVID who wants to will have been vaccinated.

The vaccines are over 90% and maybe 100% effective in preventing death, which should be the only thing we are really concerned about with COVID, not suffering with flu symptoms for 2 weeks.

They are also over 90% effective in preventing virus transmission, i.e., being infected and becoming symptomatic enough that you can infect others.

To start with, COVID is 1.7 times deadlier than the flu, if you have not been vaccinated against either. Then the vaccine cuts that risk by over 90% (really by 100%). Once you have received the vaccine, what are you worried about?

Even if masks worked, once you have been vaccinated, there is no rational reason to wear a mask either to protect yourself or to protect others. You cannot die of COVID and you pretty much cannot infect others.

As for whether unvaccinated people should wear a mask to protect other unvaccinated people (vaccinated people need no protection), if you have chosen not to be vaccinated, that is your right, and by June 1, 2021, or really May 1 anyone who wanted to be vaccinated could have been and thus could have protected themselves, so why are you obligated to protect them by wearing a mask when they could give themselves 100% protection and chose not to do so?

There is no rational reason for continuing mask mandates past June 1, or really May 1, 2021, and no rational reason for anyone to wear a mask even now if they have been vaccinated or been previously infected.

So when Biden and Fauci say they want us to wear masks and continue with some variant of the lockdowns into 2022, you have to believe the motivation is not to reduce COVID deaths. We will have almost no COVID deaths after June or so, and the few deaths we have will be people who either were on death's door anyway and were not really killed by COVID, or people who chose not to get vaccinated, as is their right. There must be some other motivation besides to reduce COVID deaths.

Chapter 39

Did the FDA Delay COVID Vaccine Approval to Hurt Trump?

I am a Democrat and I am glad Trump lost the election. But did the FDA deliberately delay approval of any COVID vaccines until after the election to prevent Trump from getting political benefit from good vaccine news? It is not an unreasonable question.

I think the FDA made two decisions that were not justified and that both had the effect of preventing vaccine approvals until after the election.

First, the FDA decided not to allow "challenge" clinical trials that involve deliberate infection or challenge of volunteers with the SARS-CoV-2 virus after they have been vaccinated to test the efficacy of the vaccines. The FDA apparently decided challenge clinical trials would have been unethical.

The FDA argument would be that COVID is too dangerous to deliberately infect volunteers and volunteers cannot give informed consent for that. In a challenge trial the volunteers would all be healthy young people, in their 20s and maybe 30s. People age 25-34 have a 0.022% infection fatality rate from COVID, which is the chance of dying if infected (Chapter 13). That is 2.2 deaths per 10,000 infections, and nearly all of those deaths would be from people who are very obese or have other serious pre-existing conditions. If you deliberately infected 200 healthy people in that age group, with half being in the placebo group, the chance of 1 person dying would be 2% if there was no effort to screen out sick volunteers and much less than that if you took only healthy volunteers. Against that unlikely one death, you could probably have significant results two months earlier and have the vaccine approved at least one month earlier than in a traditional clinical trial, where you have to dose thousands and then wait for them to be infected by chance and for a few in the placebo arm to get ill. A one-month earlier approval would have prevented as many as 90,000 COVID deaths in the U.S., since we have about 3,000 deaths per day in this winter peak. So you have an unlikely 1 volunteer death versus preventing as many as 90,000 deaths in the general population. I don't see how it is unethical to risk (if you think less than 2% is a major risk) that one volunteer could die when that is balanced against saving 90,000 lives.

The better argument for the FDA's decision is that maybe a challenge trial would not have given useful information. Young people get sick so rarely that you may not have had much difference in sickness between the placebo and vaccine groups. You would have relied on virus counts in the body, and virus counts in the body may not correlate with risk of sickness or death. Still, I think it would have been better to do challenge clinical trials and get earlier approval.

Second, the FDA decreed that manufacturers must have a median follow up of two months in the Phase 3 pivotal clinical trials. That means manufacturers had to wait until two months after they had 50% enrollment in their clinical trials (if they had planned 30,000 people in the trial, they could not apply to the FDA until two months after the 15,000th person was enrolled) (Reference 1). That 2-month requirement was announced with less than two months to go until the election and had the result that no manufacturer could apply for emergency use authorization of their vaccine until just days after the election.

The timing seemed a little suspicious to me in that it had the effect of guaranteeing no one would apply for approval until just days after the election. And there was nothing magical about two months. The FDA could as easily have required just one month of follow up. A large number of people would still have had two months of follow up, and most adverse events connected to the vaccine should happen immediately after the vaccine doses, not between one and two months after the vaccine dosing. And again, a one-month earlier approval might have saved 90,000 lives.

Now, against that evidence, Trump appointed the FDA Commissioner, and both Trump and the Commissioner could have overridden those suspicious decisions.

So, I'm glad Trump lost, but Republicans can be legitimately suspicious about both of the FDA decisions discussed above.

Chapter 40

Conspiracy Theories

We have seen here that the best estimate is that the lockdowns (meaning the whole package of mandates, including mask wearing, closing schools, closing businesses, and stay-at-home orders) have had zero effect on COVID cases and deaths—not even a small effect, but zero effect (Chapter 23). And even if they had prevented us from getting to herd immunity, that would have prevented 400,000 deaths in the U.S. (Chapter 3), which would have been a huge number of course, but is only about 1 in 1,000 Americans, and the majority of those dying from COVID, and therefore the majority of those whose lives we even potentially are saving with the lockdowns, are very old and very sick. Against those potential COVID deaths maybe averted with the lockdowns, the lockdowns threw 16% of workers out of work, 1 in 5 Americans into moderate to severe depression, and caused suicides and drug overdose deaths that unquestionably will result in greater lost person-years of life than even the maximum number of person-years of life you could have believed at the outset of this that the lockdowns could potentially save in averted COVID deaths. And the unemployment, depression, and suicides were not a surprise. Those were entirely predictable outcomes of the lockdowns. Perhaps more relevantly, the lockdowns have made billionaires richer and worsened economic inequality in the U.S., which was also predictable. So it is not unreasonable to believe those outcomes were intended.

This leads to conspiracy theories. Does that mean the Rockefellers and other members of the secret societies met in Davos, perhaps with the head of the CIA, and decided to release the SARS-CoV-2 virus and had a secret vote on whether to direct all heads of state in the world to implement lockdowns? That seems unlikely to me. But I have observed that the Rockefellers and Bill Gates and other billionaires, and the CIA, and the biggest corporations, tend to get what they want out of government a lot more often than I do.

So it is very relevant to ask why we implemented this lockdown strategy when it was entirely foreseeable ahead of time, and if you had any doubt the evidence was clear two months into this, that the lockdowns were causing vastly more harm than benefit? It leads me to ask who benefited. Who gained power and who made money? Answer: Billionaires and tech giants principally, to a lesser extent big corporations generally, and the rich but less than super rich individuals, and governors and presidents and prime ministers around the world. Who lost power? State legislatures and Congress in the U.S., and legislatures and ordinary members of parliaments around the world. Who lost power and money? Ordinary citizens around the world lost freedom. The bottom 80% or so of the economic pyramid in each country lost money, especially the bottom 20%. The less developed nations in the world, especially those dependent on tourism, lost economically. The wealthiest nations did OK economically. Those persons prone to depression and suicide and drug and alcohol abuse lost their lives. A few people fortunate enough to still be living in their 80s may have had their lives extended by one to four years on average by the lockdowns (or the expectation could reasonably have been that they would, although as I have explained here, the data indicates the lockdowns had no effect on COVID deaths), although they were also thrown into depression by them.

I think you have to assume these outcomes were intended. The billionaires in the U.S. increased their net worth from $3 trillion to $4.3 trillion during the lockdowns (Reference (1)). If that was not intended, then they sure seem to get lucky a lot.

Also, now that the COVID vaccines are available, there is no longer any excuse for the lockdowns, or will not be by June 1, 2021, by which time everyone at risk of COVID death who wants a vaccine will have been vaccinated. But President Biden and Anthony Fauci have both still claimed mask mandates will be needed until next Christmas! It's insane. If you want mask mandates after June 1, 2021, (or really any mandates or restrictions at all) then your reason is not to prevent COVID deaths. It is something else. (Really, if you want mask mandates now your reason is not to prevent COVID deaths since the data shows mask mandates have no effect at all on COVID cases or deaths. But after June 1, I do not see how you can even pretend with a straight face that is the reason.)

So let's look at some of the conspiracy theories.

This was to prevent Donald Trump's reelection.

I am a Democrat, so if that was the reason, I am glad it succeeded. But for me it would not be worth the horrendous harms the lockdowns have caused. I would not be willing to cause the deaths of about 100,000 Americans by suicide or drug overdose, throw 16% of the workforce out of their jobs, and throw 1 in 5 people into depression, in order to prevent Donald Trump's reelection.

As discussed in Chapter 37, two decisions by the FDA—to require 2 months of follow up after 50% enrollment in each vaccine trial, and to not allow challenge vaccine trials where volunteers would be deliberately infected or challenged with the virus after taking a vaccine—both had the effect of preventing any FDA approval applications for a vaccine until after the election, and preventing that probably made Trump's reelection less likely. And I do not think either of those decisions is justifiable on a cost-benefit or benefit-harm analysis. So it is not unreasonable to think those decisions were motivated partly by a desire to prevent Trump's reelection. On the other hand, Trump appointed the FDA Commissioner, and he and Trump both theoretically had the power to override those decisions.

The lockdowns certainly harmed the economy, and that was very foreseeable, and a bad economy hurts the incumbent, so some have argued that the purpose, or at least a purpose, of the lockdowns was to damage the economy in order to hurt Trump's reelection chances. I hope not, but it is consistent with the facts—except that most Republican governors embraced lockdowns with almost as much enthusiasm as Democratic governors. I also think voters generally understood that the lockdowns were what damaged the economy and therefore did not blame Trump for the bad economy as much as they otherwise would have.

China engineered and released this virus as a bioweapon.

If so, it was the world's worst bioweapon. It is barely more lethal than the flu and focuses like a laser on killing only the oldest and weakest people.

China, or someone, released this virus as a test to see if whole populations of western nations would be compliant enough to accept wearing masks for a year or stay at home for 2 months over a trivial risk, or to see if nations would basically commit national suicide over a trivial risk.

Bingo! If that was the plan, this was a huge success. The only major country it did not work on was Sweden.

Seriously, though, this actually makes more sense than that this was developed as a bioweapon. It has shocked me how compliant people have been with these restrictions over something that really is a trivial risk and for people age 50 and under is about the same risk as the flu. If you wanted to carry out a test run to see if you could get mass compliance with extreme restrictions on behavior and liberty and extreme changes in a culture overnight, this would have been a great test run. And it was plainly a huge success. I would not have predicted you could get this level of compliance or that virtually every country in the world would overreact to a disease not much deadlier than the flu.

This was done or supported by big tech companies to accumulate even more power and money.

I would have thought *Facebook* and *Google* and *Amazon* would have been happy with the market share they have. But perhaps not. The lockdowns have been great for them. For the calendar year 2020, the stocks of *Google* (up 29%), *Facebook* (31%), *Amazon* (74%), *Apple* (78%), and *Microsoft* (40%) all did much better than the broad S&P 500 index (16%). Since all of those are part of the S&P 500, the index as a whole would be even worse in comparison if you excluded the five tech giants I listed. And we saw in the chapter on censorship (Chapter 32) that *Google*, *Facebook*, and *Amazon* have all actively tried to suppress anti-lockdown messages. If I had not witnessed it myself, I would have thought it was a baseless conspiracy theory that these enormous companies would actually bother to try to suppress voices like John Ionnadis, Alex Berenson, and myself. What threat could we possibly be to them? But they did.

The tech companies have benefited from the lockdowns because the lockdowns have driven our lives even more to the online world than they already were and tended to crush small local brick-and-mortar stores and businesses. The big tech companies have actively tried to suppress anti-lockdown messages and labeled those messages with biased "fact checks" that are not put on any other political message, whether conservative or liberal.

I would not have thought that big tech would be so greedy and power hungry that it would not have been satisfied with the money and power it already had. But the facts are consistent with conspiracy theories that big tech was somehow behind the COVID lockdowns. Big tech companies have supported the lockdowns and acted to suppress anti-lockdown messages, and their power and money has grown because of the lockdowns.

The massive increase in depression is not a bug; it is a feature.

The increase in clinical depression caused by the lockdowns is absolutely stunning. In my view, this is by far the worst consequence of the lockdowns. Western industrialized societies already had the highest levels of depression of any societies in human history. The lockdowns tripled those levels. They threw 19.3% of the U.S. population or 63 million Americans into moderate to severe depression. The amount of psychic pain and human suffering that represents just staggers the mind. And the idea that anyone could intend to cause that, especially anyone in power, is very disturbing.

But, as I wrote in Chapter 5, if you had set about to design a policy to maximize depression, the lockdown policy in response to COVID is almost exactly the policy you would design. Do everything possible to prevent face-to-face human interaction and touch. Close bars and restaurants and churches. Mandate or encourage working from home. Close the schools. Ban large weddings and discourage all weddings. Bar or discourage people from going to health clubs and getting exercise. Bar or discourage people from going to national and state parks and even getting outside. Ban or discourage handshakes and hugs. Sentence the entire population to home confinement, which for many is solitary confinement (which many consider torture) for two months by stay-at-home orders. To the extent you cannot prevent face-to-face interaction, mandate that people wear masks so they cannot see each other's faces and smiles and constantly have a visual reminder of how awful this year is. If your goal were to maximize clinical depression, almost the only other thing you could do would be to ban having pets.

Since this policy was so perfectly designed to maximize depression, we have to consider the likelihood that that was the intent behind it. Either that was the intent, or the architects of the policy are completely incompetent and have no understanding of human beings and what makes them happy.

Why would the powers that be want to maximize depression? It does not make a lot of sense to me. One conspiracy theory I heard is they (sorry to slip into "they," but consider it shorthand for "the powerful elements in society") want to break our will to resist in order to institute an international government. As it happens, I personally favor an international government. (Please buy my prior book, *Ending War in Our Lifetime: A concrete, realistic plan*). International anarchy has not worked too well the past 10,000 years and now we plainly need more international cooperation to address environmental problems that are global and do not stop at national borders.

But anyway, if the goal was to psychologically break us so we would accept even more restrictions on our behavior and accept more authoritarian government, it is fair to say that the lockdowns may have helped to achieve that goal. Depressed people do not tend to fight back or stand up for themselves.

Summary

None of these conspiracy theories is very convincing to me. I do not think there was a secret meeting of some club consisting of the most powerful people in the world and they decided to do this. And it is a lot of trouble to go to as a test run to see if massive societal changes could be implemented overnight and would be tolerated. And the big tech companies and the billionaires were already doing pretty well, so would they really be so greedy and evil to do all this to add a relatively small amount of power and wealth? And is anyone really so evil that they intended to throw 1 in 5 people into clinical depression?

But the data is consistent with each of those hypotheses. And it really is less consistent with the hypothesis that this was all intended solely to reduce COVID deaths and all the harms were just viewed as acceptable collateral damage.

First, the harms vastly exceed the benefit of the rather small number of COVID deaths we might have prevented, so any fair-minded assessment would have concluded in the spring of 2020, if not before the lockdowns were implemented, that the harms would vastly exceed the benefits and not be acceptable collateral damage. Second, the data indicates the lockdowns have had zero effect of decreasing COVID deaths. There is as much chance they increased them as decreased them. Yet the governments keep telling us they are reducing COVID deaths, in plain contradiction to all the evidence.

Moreover, the governments keep pursuing the lockdown policy even after the evidence is in that shows it has no effect on COVID deaths but an enormous effect on increasing unemployment, depression, and suicides. And most shocking, governments seem to want to continue the lockdown policy even after everyone who wants a vaccine will have been vaccinated, when there will no longer be any plausible justification for the lockdowns—*if the intent of the lockdowns is to reduce COVID deaths.* But if the intent was really to cause depression, increase the power and wealth of big tech, or some other consequence of the lockdown policy, then it makes sense government would want to continue it after the COVID threat is over.

Notice that the government has never released (1) an estimate of how many COVID deaths the restrictions are preventing, (2) any charts or data or actual arguments for the proposition that the restrictions have prevented COVID deaths, or even (3) a systematic study and survey to determine what percentage of the population has been infected with the virus, and (4), tied to (3), what the infection fatality rate of COVID is for the population as a whole or for the various age groups. I find that suspicious and telling. I believe the reason for (1) is that the data shows the answer is zero COVID deaths prevented. The answer to (2) is that there is no data that shows the restrictions have dramatically reduced COVID deaths or reduced COVID deaths at all. Number (3) has not been done because the answer would be embarrassing in showing that a large percentage of the population has already been infected despite the lockdowns, so the lockdowns could not have made much difference, and embarrassing in allowing anyone to calculate the infection fatality rate and determine that COVID killed only 0.4% of infected people overall, and that is only about three-and-a-half times more than the flu. And the answer to (4) is that it is embarrassingly low. If people knew the infection fatality rate was less than 0.1% for everyone under age 45 and was only about three times the rate of the flu, they might not think this was all necessary.

References:

1. *Inequality.org,* citing statistics from *Forbes.* https://inequality.org/great-divide/updates-billionaire-pandemic/

Chapter 41

The Emperor Has No Clothes

As I wrote in the introduction, I have been surprised about so many things in this response and have often felt like the little boy in the "Emperor Has No Clothes" story: The media is saying, and everyone around me seems to believe, that this lockdown response was necessary and beneficial and the Emperor is wearing a beautiful suit as he parades through town. I have been standing there saying, "Huh?, he's buck naked!"

The news media and *Facebook* and *Google* have basically engaged in censorship, doing all they could to belittle and silence voices that opposed the lockdowns. We had never done anything remotely like the lockdowns before, but when it started it was treated as if it were a fact of life, like gravity. It was treated as if it was so obvious that this was necessary that there was no need to justify it or explain why it was necessary. When that happens, you should be suspicious. When a salesman gets angry or defensive when you ask about less expensive options or competitors or when you ask him why you should buy his product, run. When you are considering hiring a contractor and ask for references and he refuses to supply any, saying, "I do not want to bother any of my prior clients; they are busy," run. Hire a different contractor. The reason they won't answer your questions is that what they are selling does not stand up to scrutiny.

The lockdowns do not stand up to scrutiny. The imposing and lifting of mask mandates and restaurant closures and stay-at-home orders made no apparent difference in the trends of COVID cases and deaths, as we have seen. But no one in the media ever points that out or asks about it, and the governors and government health leaders never address that. The CDC said masks made no difference and recommended against the public wearing them, and then they switched and said everyone should wear a mask at all times and implied masks were the main weapon against this and the most effective intervention. But that does not stand up to scrutiny. The medical consensus, as represented by *Cochrane Reviews*, was that masks have no effect on transmission of respiratory viruses. And the governors and CDC never showed any evidence or data to explain their 180 degree turn in position. And when we look at the data, it shows masks make little or no difference, which explains why the CDC and governors do not want to talk about the data.

The CDC and governors have never made any estimate of how many COVID deaths are being prevented by lockdowns, which can be explained by the fact that the evidence suggests the lockdowns did not prevent any deaths. They have no data to suggest otherwise and would not have been able to support any estimate that the lockdowns have prevented, really, any deaths.

When it comes to the harms of economic losses, destroying certain businesses like restaurants, and—on the rare occasions it is mentioned—human harms of massively increased depression, increased suicides and drug overdoses, and increased domestic abuse, it is always phrased that these are "caused by the pandemic." That's nonsense. They are caused by the lockdowns. The only thing bad caused by COVID is COVID deaths and illness. Everything else, including closing schools and the lost education, was caused by the lockdown policies. Our leaders never explicitly said this, because it would not sound good, but they <u>decided</u>, and <u>decided</u> should be emphasized, that all these harms were worth it for some other good, which could only be reduced COVID deaths. But they never said that because it would not stand up to scrutiny. If you acknowledge you decided that increasing depression and suicides and destroying education for a year was worth it to reduce COVID deaths, it naturally leads to several follow up questions: How many COVID deaths are we preventing? How much was depression increased? How many suicides and drug overdoses are we causing? How much economic loss, how much money, is it worth to prevent one COVID death? Why is it worth it to sacrifice the interests of every child in America for the interests of a portion of the elderly? Those questions cannot be acknowledged because the answers would not look good.

The only hope for the defenders of lockdowns is that those questions are never asked. It is therefore very important to silence and discredit anyone who dares to ask those questions, anyone who dares to ask to see data and evidence that this strategy has produced more benefit than harm. That's the "Emperor Has No Clothes" story. Everyone can see the emperor is naked. If your job is to maintain the reputation of the emperor, your only hope is to convince everyone to doubt their own eyes or convince them it will be ruinous for them to state the obvious, so they are either gaslighted or cowed into going along with the official story. It's a tenuous situation. If a few people tell the truth and are not ruined, the dam will break. Soon everyone will acknowledge the obvious. I still have some hope that will happen with the lockdowns.

Actually, though, the path the emperor's defenders have taken is not so much to gaslight us into believing the lockdowns have reduced COVID deaths, or even to threaten us with some sort of reputational ruin if we ask the questions above, it is more to convince us we have no choice or power, and therefore, resistance would be futile. Along those lines, they act like the lockdowns were a natural consequence of a law of nature. They were going to happen and there was nothing anyone could do to prevent them. The same strategy is used to defend free trade and free immigration and the power of big tech and big corporations and rapid technological and cultural change: It is treated as if these are all facts of nature and government could do nothing about them, so it is pointless to ask whether these things are beneficial or harmful. Almost never are any of those things defended on the merits. So with the lockdowns. The lockdowns cannot be defended on the merits. So the best strategy to defend them is to pretend we had no choice and that we the people have no power and that the government itself has no power. That strategy has worked to allow free trade and free immigration and to allow ever expanding power of big tech and big corporations and rapid technological and cultural change. And it has worked for lockdowns. It works because most of us feel we do *not* have any power. So the government and media telling us, "You have no power and no choice, so don't bother asking questions," is pretty believable.

Maybe we should stop letting the powers that be tell us we have no choice and no power.

Part 5
Comparison to Other Epidemics and Disasters

Chapter 42

....

Comparison to Other Epidemics and Disasters

It is interesting to compare the toll, in person-years of life lost relative to the population of the society, of COVID to other epidemics in history, such as AIDS, smallpox, the Black Death, tuberculosis, and yellow fever, and to current leading causes of death, such as cancer, heart disease, suicides, and drug overdoses. This helps to put COVID in perspective.

COVID

There were 362,634 COVID deaths in the U.S. in 2020 and we will have about 600,000 by July 1, 2021, and I would expect almost none after that. Any deaths after that will be either people who were on death's door anyway and were not really killed by COVID, or people who chose not to get the COVID vaccines and accept their risk. I have estimated 4 years lost life per COVID death on average in the U.S. (Chapter 2). Deaths of 0.362 million persons times 4 year/death divided by 328 million population equals 1.6 days life span lost per person to COVID in 2020. 0.600 million deaths times 4 years/death divided by 328 million population equals 2.7 days of life span lost to COVID per person in the U.S. for the whole epidemic.

For the comparisons below I will use in all cases an assumption that the life expectancy is 80 years and the age distribution of the society is even across the age spectrum. That is not true of course, but this allows us to compare different times and nations without in effect discounting past lives because they had a shorter life expectancy or discounting current lives in less developed countries because they have a shorter life expectancy. Also, while past societies and current less developed countries had and have shorter life expectancies, that is largely because of higher infant mortality. If you made it to adulthood in those societies, your life expectancy did not differ so much from ours today.

Influenza or Flu

There are about 60,000 influenza/pneumonia deaths per year in the U.S. It kills children at a higher rate than COVID does, so average life lost per death is probably about 5 years instead of COVID's 4 years. That is 300,000 person-years each year and works out to 0.3 days per year and about 24 days over the course of an 80-year life.

1918-1919 Flu

The 1918 flu (extending into 1919) killed 675,000 people in the U.S., according to the CDC, out of a population at the time of 103 million (Reference 1). According to the CDC, the 1918 flu had high mortality in persons under age 5 and age 20-40, as well as age 65 and up (Reference 1). Stories on it often say the young died at a higher rate than the old. So I would estimate the average death cost at least 16 years and maybe as much as 32 years from an 80 year life. 675,000 deaths times 16 years lost per death divided by 103 million people equals 0.104 years or 38 days. If the average life time lost per death was 32 years instead of 16, it would be double that. About 75% of the deaths seem to have been in 1918 and 25% in 1919. So the peak year of 1918 would be 28 days to 56 days of life time lost.

AIDS

At the peak of AIDS deaths in the U.S. there were 181,000 deaths from 1988-1992, or 36,000 per year in that period (Reference 2). As many as 95% of persons diagnosed died of the disease. The median age was very young, about 35, with 45 years of life expectancy remaining at that age. U.S. population at that time was 250 million. That works out to 2.4 days of lost life span per person per year at that time. Deaths held at approximately that rate for almost a decade, so over the course of that decade it represents a total of about 20 days of lost life time.

For the world as a whole, in the peak year for AIDS deaths of 2004, there were 1.7 million AIDS deaths in a population of 6.4 billion (Reference 3). That is 2.6 days of lost life span per person for the entire world. I have not been able to find accurate data for the hardest hit countries of Haiti or sub-Saharan Africa, but I would guess you could multiply that by at least five in those countries and in their worst years they were losing at least 13 days life span per person per year to AIDS.

Cholera

The worst recent cholera outbreak recently was in Peru in 1991, here 2,909 people died from a population of 22.5 million. That is 0.013% of the population. A reference says 49% of cholera deaths are under age 15 and 33% are over age 60. From that I would roughly estimate each death represents 50 years of lost life. That works out to 2.4 days of lost life expectancy per person in the population of Peru.

Typhoid fever

The U.S. CDC says there were 226 typhoid deaths per million population in 1906 and 210 in 1907 over the entire U.S. That is a death rate of 0.022%. The age profile of typhoid deaths, from my tiny amount of internet research, is mostly under age 1 and over age 30. So I will say average of 20 years life expectancy lost per person. That would work out to 1.6 days per person in each of 1906 and 1907 or 3.2 days over the 2-year period.

Ebola

The worst outbreak of Ebola was 2014 in Liberia. There were about 10,000 deaths in a population of 4.25 million in that country, which is 0.235% of the population dying. The case fatality rate is quoted as 70% in children 0-4 and 15% in adults 18 and up (WHO, Reference 4). Infection is somewhat more common among children but seemingly fairly even across the age spectrum. So I will say an average of 20 years life expectancy lost per person. That would work out to 17 days of lost life time per person in Liberia from Ebola in 2014.

Black Death or Plague, Middle Ages

I will quote Wikipedia on this:

> According to medieval historian Philip Daileader, it is likely that over four years, 45–50% of the European population died of plague. Norwegian historian Ole Benedictow suggests it could have been as much as 60% of the European population. In 1348, the disease spread so rapidly that before any physicians or government authorities had time to reflect upon its origins, about a third of the European population had already perished. In crowded cities, it was not uncommon for as much as 50% of the population to die. Half of Paris' population of 100,000 people died. In Italy, the population of Florence was reduced from between 110,000 and 120,000 inhabitants in 1338 down

to 50,000 in 1351. At least 60% of the population of Hamburg and Bremen perished, and a similar percentage of Londoners may have died from the disease as well, with a death toll of approximately 62,000 between 1346 and 1353. Florence's tax records suggest that 80% of the city's population died within four months in 1348. Before 1350, there were about 170,000 settlements in Germany, and this was reduced by nearly 40,000 by 1450. The disease bypassed some areas, with the most isolated areas being less vulnerable to contagion. Plague did not appear in Douai in Flanders until the turn of the 15th century, and the impact was less severe on the populations of Hainaut, Finland, northern Germany, and areas of Poland. Monks, nuns, and priests were especially hard-hit since they cared for victims of the Black Death.

The physician to the Avignon Papacy, Raimundo Chalmel de Vinario (Latin: Magister Raimundus, lit. 'Master Raymond'), observed the decreasing mortality rate of successive outbreaks of plague in 1347–48, 1362, 1371, and 1382 in his 1382 treatise *On Epidemics (De epidemica)*. In the first outbreak, two thirds of the population contracted the illness and most patients died; in the next, half the population became ill but only some died; by the third, a tenth were affected and many survived; while by the fourth occurrence, only one in twenty people were sickened and most of them survived. By the 1380s in Europe, it predominantly affected children.

The Great Plague of London of 1664-65 is said to have killed 100,000 people, which was a quarter of the city's population, again according to Wikipedia. The age profile of the dead is said to be indiscriminate, by the skeletons in a cemetery that was used only for the dead of 1664-1665, but other data cited in the paper suggests the dead leaned toward older adults (Reference 5). That would suggest lost life time of about 20 years per fatality, had the life expectancy been 80 years.

With a quarter of the population dying and a lost life time of 20 years per death, that would be 5 years lost life time in the population per person from Black Death deaths in a single year. Given that there is abundant data that the population of Europe declined due to the Black Death, the average time of life lost per year per person in those periods of population decline would have to be more than 1 year per person each year for a several years and probably for decades. (If it were not more than 1 year per person per year for a sustained number of years it could not cause a population decline, it seems to me, unless women were having fewer than 2 children per woman.)

I would guess in some places or nations in Europe in the Middle Ages, over an 80-year span Black Death cost 20 years of life time per person or averaged a quarter year lost per person per year.

Smallpox

The most devastating epidemics in history seem to have been smallpox, particularly among Native Americans. When the Pilgrims arrived in Massachusetts, the native populations in the area apparently essentially vanished in a few years. The Pilgrims commented on this in their journals, and wrote that it was evidence of the "providence of God" for them. Some sources say that was due to an unknown disease that was not smallpox. But certainly smallpox devastated Native Americans across the continent.

In Boston in 1721, 8% of the population (of mostly white citizens) supposedly died from smallpox.

Wikipedia makes a number of claims about smallpox. Most of this is not in refereed scientific literature or academic publications, so I take it with a grain of salt. But among the claims are that it killed 25% of the Aztec population in Mexico in 2 years around 1520, that it killed an estimated 400,000 Europeans each year in the 18th century, that in 1862 an outbreak killed 50-90% of the Natives in the region of British Columbia. It asserts that 400,000 Europeans died from smallpox per year in the 1800s. It says most people in Europe became infected during their lifetimes, and about 30% of people infected with smallpox died from the disease in the 1800s.

Smallpox death rates were highest among young children and otherwise pretty even across the age spectrum (Reference 6). That would mean about 50 years of life lost per death.

In periodic peak years in Sweden in the 1700s, before a vaccine, 7 people per thousand died of smallpox (Reference 7). With an average life time lost of 50 years per death, that would be 128 days of lost life span per person in those peak years.

If there were Native American populations that suffered 25% loss of population in one year or a few years, which seems certain to be true, then that would be 12 years of life span per person lost over that time span. If smallpox cut a population by a third or more, which seems certain, than the toll would be worse than the Black Death and might have been 25 or 30 years of life span lost per person in a society over an 80 year span.

Tuberculosis

Tuberculosis (TB) or "consumption" as it was known, was the most feared disease in the U.S. for most or all of the 1800s. It is an infectious bacterial respiratory disease. These days there is a vaccine available, but it is not a great vaccine, and the disease is treatable with a recipe of three antibiotics given together for at least 6 months. It still kills 1.5 million people worldwide each year.

According to Wikipedia, in the 1800s TB killed as many as about 900 per 100,000 people in cities in Europe and North America. According to Wikipedia the death rate was higher for young people generally than old. So let's say in places it killed 0.9% of the population every year, and perhaps 0.5% of the population of entire countries like the U.S. each year, with 20 years average life span lost per death. That would be an average of 36 days of life span lost every year per person and in peak years or cities perhaps 66 days of life lost per person. Let's say the 36-day peak toll continued for 30 years, then it would be 4.9 years of life lost over an 80-year span of a life.

Cancer

The American Cancer Society estimates 608,500 cancer deaths in the U.S. in 2021 (Reference 8). From the data in Reference 9 from the U.K. government, I calculate the median age at death from cancer as 77 and the average age about 74. The life expectancy at age 74 is 12.5 years. 12 years x 608,500 deaths divided by 328 million people in the U.S. is 8.1 days lost life span per person. That is every year.

Heart disease

Heart disease kills almost exactly the same number of people per year as cancer in the U.S. currently. Average age of first heart attack is 65 in men and 72 in women. I had a hard time finding the average age at death from cardiovascular disease, but 74 seems like a reasonable number, same as cancer. If life expectancy remaining is the same as with cancer, then heart disease also causes 8 days of lost life span per person each year. I think that may not be a fair figure. It is easy to imagine a person who dies of COVID not contacting and never being infected by the virus and ask how much longer that person would have lived. It is almost as easy with cancer, where one can imagine the particular tumor that killed the person never developing. With heart disease it seems harder to consider that way. If a particular heart attack had not happened and had not killed a person, how much longer would that person have lived? Well, are we to assume he still had the same blood vessels and some clots in his vessels, one of which caused this heart attack? Then one would imagine another heart attack would have probably come along pretty soon. Or are we to imagine a counterfactual world where he had great blood vessels and no clots anywhere in his body and no cardiovascular disease? That seems like too far from reality to be relevant. But I will stick with the 8.1 days average life span cost per person each year. By the logic above you might want to cut that somewhat.

Suicide and drug overdoses

In 2018 there were 48,344 suicides in the U.S. (Reference 10). There were also 67,386 drug overdose deaths, and over 95,000 alcohol caused deaths that elsewhere in this book I have included with suicides as "deaths of despair" or *de facto* suicides. But here let's just include the actual suicides. The median age at death of suicides is 42, with 38 years of life expectancy remaining (Reference 11). 48,344 suicides times 38 years lost life per death divided by 328 million people in the U.S. works out to 2.0 days of lost life span per person in the U.S. If the drug overdose deaths are also at a median age of 42, then they add 2.8 days of lost life.

Note this means that *every year* suicides and drug overdoses, each, cost more person-years of life than COVID did in 2020.

Vietnam and 9/11
Vietnam War

In the next chapter I will go into these numbers more, but in the Vietnam War there were 58,220 U.S. military killed (Reference 12), and perhaps over 2 million Vietnamese (Reference 13). I will only consider the U.S. troop deaths here. Assuming an average age at death of 22, they had about 58 years of life expectancy remaining. It works out to 6.2 days of life span lost per person in the U.S. population over the entire war.

The deadliest year for U.S. troops was 1968 with 16,952 U.S. military deaths that year. That is 1.8 days of life lost per person in the U.S. population in that year.

9/11 attacks on New York

2.,977 people were killed in the 9/11 attacks (excluding the hijackers). Most were working in the World Trade Center, so I would assume an average age of 42, the midrange of working age. That would be 38 years life expectancy remaining. U.S. population at the time was 285 million. It works out to 0.14 days of life span lost per person in the U.S. The population of the New York City metropolitan area is 20 million, so assuming nearly all the 9/11 dead came from that group it is about 2.1 days of lost life time per person in the New York City metropolitan area.

| Disease | Time of life lost per person | |
	1-year peak	80 year lifetime or entire epidemic
COVID in U.S.	1.6 days (2020)	2.7 days
Influenza in U.S.	0.3 days	24 days
Cholera, Peru 1991	2.4 days	
Ebola, Liberia 2014	17 days	
Typhoid fever, U.S. 1906-1907	1.6 days	3.2 days
1918-1919 flu, U.S.	28 to 56 days	38 to 76 days
Black Death		
London 1604	5 years	
Many places in Europe, maybe entire countries or the entire continent, Middle Ages	1 year	20 years
Smallpox		
Native Americans (some tribes or communities, not the entire Native American population of the Americas)	12 years	25 years
Smallpox, Sweden 1700s	128 days	5 years
Tuberculosis, U.S. 1800s	36 days	5 years
AIDS		
U.S. 1985-1994	2.4 days (1990)	20 days

Haiti or Southern Africa at peak	13 days	75 days
Entire World 2004	2.6 days	
Cancer, U.S.	8.1 days	1.8 years
Heart disease, U.S.	8.1 days	1.8 years
Suicides, U.S.	2.0 days	160 days
Drug overdoses, U.S.	2.8 days	224 days
Vietnam and 9/11		
Vietnam War, U.S. deaths only.	1.8 days (1968)	6.2 days (1961-1973).
9/11 attacks, for U.S. population	0.14 days	
9/11 attacks, for New York metro population.	2.1 days	

References:

1. U.S. Centers for Disease Control and Prevention. https://www.cdc.gov/flu/pandemic-resources/1918-pandemic-h1n1.html

2. CDC. https://www.cdc.gov/mmwr/preview/mmwrhtml/mm5021a2.htm

3. U.N. AIDS World AIDS Day 2020 Fact Sheet. https://www.unaids.org/sites/default/files/media_asset/UNAIDS_FactSheet_en.pdf

4. https://www.who.int/csr/don/19-december-2019-ebola-drc/en/#:~:text=Of%20persons%20who%20have%20died,older%20were%20in%20the%20community.

5. DeWitte, SN. Age Patterns of Mortality During the Black Death in London, A.D. 1349–1350
J Archaeol Sci. J Archaeol Sci. 2010 Dec 1; 37(12): 3394–3400.
htts://doi: 10.1016/j.jas.2010.08.006
PMCID: PMC3094018

6. https://www.statista.com/statistics/1107867/smallpox-share-small-

pox-total-deaths-by-age-great-pandemic-historical/

7. Edwardes (1902) A concise history of small-pox and vaccination in Europe. H.K. Lewis, cited in https://ourworldindata.org/smallpox

8. American Cancer Society. Cancer Facts and Figures 2021. https://www.cancer.org/research/cancer-facts-statistics/all-cancer-facts-figures/cancer-facts-figures-2021.html

9. Cancer Research UK. https://www.cancerresearchuk.org/health-professional/cancer-statistics/mortality/age#heading-Zero

10. American Foundation for Suicide Prevention. https://afsp.org/suicide-statistics/

11. Wikipedia. https://en.wikipedia.org/wiki/Suicide_in_the_United_States

12. National Archives. https://www.archives.gov/research/military/vietnam-war/casualty-statistics

13. Wikipedia. https://en.wikipedia.org/wiki/Vietnam_War_casualties. citing Rummel, R. J. "Statistics of Vietnamese Democide", Lines 777–785, http://www.hawaii.edu/powerkills/SOD.TAB6.1B.GIF, accessed 24 Nov 2014

Chapter 43

Is the Lockdown Strategy the Worst Public Policy Mistake Ever?
Comparison to the Harm of the Vietnam War

Is the lockdown strategy the worst public policy ever?
It depends how you define "public policy." If you consider Hitler's concentration camps and genocide to be a "public policy," no, that was a lot worse, as was the Armenian genocide, Pol Pot's genocide in Cambodia, and every other genocide. And as was the cultural genocide and land stealing in the U.S. of Native Americans, and in Canada, Australia, and New Zealand and other places of the aborigines or natives.

And let's stipulate that slavery was a lot worse, if you consider slavery to be a "public policy."

I would argue also that the policies that collectively have led humans to occupy and use for their own purposes nearly every square inch of usable land on earth, leading to a sixth mass extinction event in human history are, collectively, worse.

I would argue also that the policies that have led us to alter the climate and to increase CO_2 concentration in the atmosphere from 280 parts per million (ppm) in the 1700s prior to industrialization to 411 ppm now are collectively worse.

It is hard, however, to compare those environmental damages to the deaths and lost time of life caused by the lockdowns. It is comparing apples to oranges. It is comparing what is primarily damage to other species versus damage to human lives. And for human damage, it is comparing damage mostly to future generations to damage in a single year or two year period of our current human lives.

For the U.S., the clearest example of what most people would agree was a disastrous public policy choice was the Vietnam War. The war killed 58,220 U.S. service members and about 2.15 million Vietnamese. The purpose of the war was to prevent Vietnam from falling into communism, but Vietnam wound up going communist anyway, with no perceptible harm to the U.S. from them doing so and arguably no harm to the Vietnamese from them doing so. It seems to me that most Vietnamese wanted their country to be communist, and that probably should have been their choice.

Unlike the genocides or slavery, the Vietnam war was a legitimate public policy choice. I would accept that the U.S. politicians who pursued it genuinely wanted the best outcome for the U.S. people on the whole. They may not have cared much or at all about the Vietnamese people, but I do not believe they were purely evil men like Hitler or Pol Pot. They were ordinary elected leaders and government officials making a legitimate public policy choice.

So it is interesting to compare the harms in human terms of time of life, lost both to early deaths and time spent depressed, caused by the Vietnam War and caused by the COVID lockdowns. Have the lockdowns done more harm to the American people than the Vietnam War did?

Vietnam War

In the Vietnam War there were 58,220 U.S. military killed (Reference 1). Additionally, a midrange estimate of 2.15 million Vietnamese were killed in 1954-1975 in the conflict, including both soldiers and civilians killed by the U.S. military and by Vietnamese fighting on both sides (Reference 2).

Just looking at the U.S. military deaths in the war, 58,200 was 0.029% of the U.S. population of 200 million as of 1968. Assuming an average age at death of 22, they had about 58 years of life expectancy remaining. That works out to 6.2 days of life span lost per person in the U.S. population over the entire war. (For the 2.6 million U.S. service members who served in Vietnam, the lost time of life for those 58,200 deaths works out to 1.3 years per service member, but for the U.S. population as a whole it is only 6.2 days per person.)

Men who served in Vietnam, as in all wars, were at higher risk of post-traumatic stress disorder and were purported to be at higher risk of suicide, drug overdose, and, I would assume, depression. Some evidence apparently indicates it is not true that Vietnam veterans were at higher risk of suicide than the general population (Reference 3). But assuming they were at higher risk of deaths of despair and clinical depression after returning from the war, how many days of lost life might that have represented?

There were 2.69 million U.S. service members who served in Vietnam and about half of those or 1.3 million were either in combat, close support of combat, or exposed to enemy attack at some time. Let's assume the other troops essentially had the experience of service members in peacetime and thus were at no greater risk of suicide, drug abuse, or depression. For the 1.3 million who were ever in or near combat, if we estimate 10% more of those than of the general population later had depression or killed themselves one way or another, and those 10% on average lost 10 years of life either to depression or suicide or *de facto* suicide of drug and alcohol abuse deaths, that would be 130,000 persons x 10 years lost life = 1.3 million years of life lost. Divided by an average U.S. population in their later lives of about 250 million is 1.9 days of life lost per person in the entire U.S. population (not per Vietnam veteran). Obviously there is a lot of uncertainty in that estimate, but probably the lost time of life due to suicide, drug and alcohol death, and time spent in depression among Vietnam veterans who survived the war is less, cumulatively, than the lost time of life of the U.S. service members who died in the war.

COVID Lockdowns
Deaths of despair

How many additional deaths of despair above our normal baseline level will the lockdowns cause? We had more than a 200% increase in moderate-to-severe depression in the spring of 2020 caused by the lockdowns (Chapter 5). The CDC put out a press release saying that for the 12-months ending at the end of May 2020 there were 81,000 drug overdose deaths and that this was a 18.2% increase over the prior 12 month period, which had been a 4% decline from the year before that (Reference 4). Since drug overdoses had been declining, my guess would be the 18% annual increase for the 12 months ending in May 2020 occurred entirely in the three months of March-May 2020, during COVID after the unemployment and social isolation hit. If so, then it was a 72% increase during those 3 months.

With a 200% increase in depression and probably a 72% increase in drug overdose deaths in the first 3 months of the lockdown, I think it is very reasonable to estimate we will have a 40% increase in all deaths of despair in the first year of the lockdowns, a 20% increase in the next year (even without lockdowns continuing), and a 10% increase in the third year. It takes some time after people become depressed, unemployed, and/or addicted to drugs and alcohol, for their lives to unravel and for them to finally kill themselves. So you would not expect all of the deaths of despair caused by the lockdowns to occur during the lockdowns. They will come in over a few years.

For 2018, there were 67,386 drug overdose deaths, 48,344 suicides, and over 95,000 alcohol caused deaths, of which over 40,000 were classified as "100% alcohol attributable" (references 5-7). That is a total of 210,000 deaths of despair per year, or 155,000 if you exclude indirect alcohol-related deaths such as liver cancer and cirrhosis of the liver. Let's use the lower 155,000 figure as the basis for our estimate. Assuming a 40% increase in the first year, 20% in the second year, and 10% in the third year, it would be 109,000 excess deaths of despair. The median age of suicide is 42, with 38 years of life expectancy remaining. So 109,000 deaths times 38 years is 4.14 million lost years of life. Divided by 328 million U.S. population is 0.0126 years or 4.6 days of lost life due to the suicides and excess deaths of despair caused.

Depression

The lockdowns caused an increase in the percentage of the U.S. population suffering from moderate to severe clinical depression from 8.5% of the population pre-lockdowns (which is terrible enough) to 27.8% in the spring of 2020 during lockdowns (Chapter 5). That means the lockdowns threw 63.3 million Americans into major clinical depression just in the first 3 months of the lockdowns. The average time spent in depression is 20 weeks or 0.38 years, so, if we consider time spent depressed as lost time of life, the lockdowns caused a lost time of life to depression of 63.3 million people times 0.38 years = 24 million person-years. Divided by 328 million people in the U.S., that is 0.73 years or 26.7 days per person in the U.S. That is just the depression caused in the spring of 2020. If we assume the lockdowns over the remainder of the more than one year we have endured this caused just half again as much depression, then they have caused a total of 40 days of life time lost per person in the U.S. in time spent depressed.

COVID deaths averted

But against the deaths of despair the lockdowns caused and the depression they caused, we should balance the COVID deaths they prevented. Unfortunately, the best estimate of how many COVID deaths they have prevented is zero (Chapter 23). If the lockdowns reduced COVID cases and deaths, show me the evidence. Show me the data. There is no evidence for it in the data.

Comparing the Numbers

The benefit side of the ledger of the Vietnam War for the U.S., most of us would agree, is zero. Vietnam became communist anyway, and that did not harm us.

The harm ledger, ignoring harms to the Vietnamese (since the U.S.

officials pursuing this were not concerned with harms to the Vietnamese, so I am viewing this from the U.S. perspective), has deaths of U.S.
service members in combat and later deaths from suicide and drug and
alcohol abuse (deaths of despair) and later (or during the war) depression in U.S. Vietnam veterans, in excess of the deaths of despair and
depression in the general population.

As calculated above, I come up with these figures

Table. Days of life lost per person in the U.S. population

	Vietnam War	COVID Lockdowns
Combat deaths	6.2 days/person	
Deaths of despair caused by lockdowns		4.6 days/person
Depression caused by lock-downs		40 days/person
Deaths of despair and depression together caused by serving in Vietnam	1.9 days/person (rough estimate, perhaps as many as 6 days)	
Total time of life lost	8.1 days/person (perhaps 8 to 12 days/person)	44.6 days/person

The combat deaths in Vietnam represent more time of life lost per person in the entire U.S. population than the deaths of despair caused
by COVID lockdowns, but not by too much. When you add in the depression for the lockdowns and the depression and subsequent deaths
of despair caused by service in Vietnam, the lockdowns have and will
have caused several times more (around five times more and probably
at least three times more) lost time of life per person in the general population. So I think it is pretty unarguable that the lockdowns
caused and will have caused, in slightly more than a year, quite a bit
more damage to lives of U.S. citizens than the Vietnam War did in 12
years of U.S. military action there (although if you add in the damage
to lives in Vietnam, the Vietnam war would be worse).

Maybe recognizing the lockdown mistake can help unite us
I am a liberal. But we liberals tend to be a little self-righteous and
convinced we are always right. We have been generally right in his-

tory. Liberals were right to fight for an end to slavery, right to fight legalized racism in the civil rights movement, right about the need for environmental protection, and right to oppose the Vietnam War. Conservatives were on the wrong side of history and morality in all of those. But with lockdowns, it has been conservatives who have opposed them, and perhaps without exception at least among elected officials, liberals have supported the lockdowns and claimed anyone who opposed them was ignorant and anti-science and unethical. On this one, conservatives were right and liberals were wrong.

As this book has shown, the lockdowns have caused vastly more harm than benefit. It is not remotely close or debatable. The lockdowns have even caused more harm, maybe 5 times as much net harm, to U.S. citizens in one year as the Vietnam War caused in 12 years. So this was a pretty big disaster, bigger even than Vietnam. Maybe that will generate a little humility among liberals and help to unite us.

References

1. National Archives. https://www.archives.gov/research/military/vietnam-war/casualty-statistics

2. Wikipedia. https://en.wikipedia.org/wiki/Vietnam_War_casualties. citing Rummel, R. J. "Statistics of Vietnamese Democide", Lines 777–785, http://www.hawaii.edu/powerkills/SOD.TAB6.1B.GIF, accessed 24 Nov 2014

3. Pollock DA, Rhodes P, Boyle CA, Decoufle P, McGee DL. Estimating the number of suicides among Vietnam veterans. *Am J Psychiatry.* 1990 Jun;147(6):772-6. https://doi: 10.1176/ajp.147.6.772 PMID: 2343923

4. U.S. Centers for Disease Control and Prevention. https://www.cdc.gov/media/releases/2020/p1218-overdose-deaths-covid-19.html

5. U.S. Centers for Disease Control and Prevention. https://www.cdc.gov/drugoverdose/data/statedeaths.html#:~:text=In%20 2018%2C%2067%2C367%20drug%20overdose,2018%20(20.7%20 per%20100%2C000).

6. American Foundation for Suicide Prevention. https://afsp.org/suicide-statistics/

7. U.S. Centers for Disease Control and Prevention. https://nccd. cdc.gov/DPH_ARDI/Default/Report.aspx?T=AAM&P=1A04A664-0244-42C1-91DE-316F3AF6B447&R=B885BD06-13DF-45CD-8DD8-AA6B178C4ECE&M=32B5FFE7-81D2-43C5-A892-9B9B3C-4246C7&F=&D=

Part 6
Philosophical Musings

Chapter 44

Why Have We Fallen for the Lie That Face-To-Face Contact Is Not Important?

I blame philosophers and our bizarre obsession as a species with proving that we are categorically different from, and superior to, all other animal species.

During this year of lockdown, we seem to have bought into a number of related lies: Face-to-face contact is not important. Remote video meetings are just as good as in-person meetings. We do not need to see others faces, so it is no harm if they are wearing masks. We do not need to touch other humans, so it makes no difference if we give up handshakes and hugs. Remote learning works just as well as in-person instruction, so closing schools makes no difference to our children and college students.

All of those statements are absurd and we all know they are absurd. Before this began, there had been plenty of studies showing that remote learning is much less effective than in-person instruction, and some studies suggested remote learning is almost worthless. If remote learning were not less effective, everyone would have been sending their kids to on-line schools and college students would have chosen on-line colleges like the University of Phoenix instead of in-person schools like your local major state university, since the on-line schools are cheaper. For that matter, no one would have been worried about teacher-to-student ratios in in colleges or K-12 schools.

Romanian orphans became very disturbed and often sociopaths because they did not receive human touch and human interaction growing up.

Famous studies in monkeys showed that monkeys raised with a wire mannequin acting as a mother dispensing milk to them became completely psychologically disturbed.

We all know how good a massage feels, and how great it feels for a loved one to stroke our skin or for us to stroke their skin.

But somehow, too many otherwise intelligent people have bought into the lie that touch, in-person contact and meetings, and seeing one another's faces are not important. Why would so many believe such an absurd thing that conflicts with their own personal experience? I think part of it is our fetish as a species with trying to prove we are not animals and we are categorically different from other animal species and categorically superior to them. For some reason, the fact we are an animal species, very similar to others, is a threat to our psyches. We are like a pathetically insecure narcissist that is obsessed with proving he is different from and superior to other people.

An outgrowth of the belief we are not animals is the belief that we have to understand and control everything: We must sterilize our environments because then we cannot get sick. We can understand the idea that sterilization or masks prevent disease: Disease is caused by viruses and bacteria, right?, so if we just kill all the viruses and bacteria in the world, then we cannot get sick. If we block the viruses and bacteria from us with masks, then we cannot get sick. And we cannot see through a mask, so how could anything possibly be so small that it could easily pass through a mask, right? That's easy to understand; it makes logical sense.

In contrast, we cannot fully understand our immune system, so we do not really trust that it will fight disease for us and that we do not have to do much other than support it a little.

If we are basically robots or computers, then we just have to be kept clean. We do not need to socialize or touch other robots or computers. But if we are animals, like squirrels, my God!, how do you keep a squirrel clean! They are filthy little creatures. I'm not like them! And then we would have to socialize with and touch other squirrels!

But the reality is we are animals. We do need our mother's touch and smile growing up, and we continue to need touch and smiles when we are adults.

Another aspect of being animals is we do not fully understand how we work. We understand how computers and robots work. We do not understand how our bodies work. We cannot even explain how we walk. We just do. Somehow we know how to do it and learn without an instruction manual or going to school to be taught how to walk. We do not know how our immune systems work, and that makes us uncomfortable. We would rather rely on our own power than just trust in nature and the way were created. We would rather rely on our own power (our own brilliant enormous brains!! See how big my brain is!!) than trust in the universe or a higher power.

Philosophy professor Crispin Sartwell had a piece in the *New York Times* recently (Reference 1) titled "Humans Are Animals. Let's Get Over It" and subtitled "It's astonishing how relentlessly Western philosophy has strained to prove we are not squirrels." I recommend you find it. Here's one quote I liked: "The Great Philosopher will, before addressing himself to the deep ethical and metaphysical questions, pause for the conventional, ground-clearing declaration: 'I am definitely not a squirrel.' This is evidently something that needs continual emphasizing."

Whenever I see a sentence that begins, "The unique thing about humans is . . .," I know it is wrong. Unless it is some trivial thing like we are the only species that does crossword puzzles.

Common ways that sentence goes are, "We are the only species that uses tools." Not true. Chimpanzees use tools. Crows use tools. Some species even modify objects such as sticks to make them more suited as tools.

"We are the only species that uses language or can learn language." Not true. Chimpanzees and gorillas have learned American Sign Language. Dolphins can be taught to communicate to humans and they certainly are communicating to each other with their clicks. Prairie dogs communicate information about predators to other prairie dogs by their whistles and vocalizations, including apparently details such as what species of predator it is and how close it is and what direction.

"We are the only species with souls." How do you know other species do not have souls? I think they do.

"We are the only species with a sense of humor." Not true. I've seen my dogs playing jokes on each other. Other primates have been seen playing jokes. Koko, the first gorilla who learned sign language, would tell jokes.

"We are the only species that grieves." Nonsense. Our younger dog, Matilda, obviously became depressed and grieved when our older dog, Sally, died. Mother elephants and mother whales have been observed to stop eating and obviously become depressed when their offspring die.

"We are the only species with a sense of morality." I do not think so. Dogs seem to have a sense of ownership of "their" bones or toys and object when they are "stolen" by another dog. So they seem to have a sense of ownership and a sense that it is wrong to steal. And they get angry at each other when playing with another dog and the other dog plays too rough and hurts them. My dogs have been angry at me when they think I have wronged them.

But I think the most frequently cited "unique" trait of humans is that we are supposedly the only species whose members know they will die. I don't think that is true. I think my dogs knew they would die. At least one of them probably knew it and accepted it more than I did.

But more to the point, do humans really know they will die? You certainly would not know it by observing our societal reaction to COVID. This is a disease that focuses like a laser on killing almost exclusively the oldest and sickest people in society. But we shut down society to fight it. We acted like it was unprecedented for old and sick people to die. There were headlines in my local newspaper screaming "Most COVID Deaths are in Nursing Homes!" We have acted like it is unprecedented and tragic for the elderly to die, instead of something that has happened to every elderly person who ever lived and that will happen to all of us.

A certain very wise person said 2,000 years ago "Leave the dead to bury the dead." He was crucified for saying that and similar things. If he were alive today and submitted an op-ed to the *New York Times* about COVID with the title "Leave the Dead to Bury the Dead," first, it would never be accepted for publication, but if somehow it were published, he would be figuratively crucified for saying it. (We probably would not actually string him up to a cross now because we are beyond that. But cancel culture would get him. His tweets would be searched for any other outrageous things he had said.)

We have gone astray before with this belief that we are not really animals and the hubris that we are better off relying on our reason than our instincts or our animal nature. One way we went astray is to feed babies with formula instead of breast feeding them. We figured, "Breasts are so dirty. Better to use a sterile formula that we understand and know exactly what goes into rather than messy milk coming out of a gross body organ, especially when we do not fully understand what is in the milk." That was a popular practice in the 1950s and 60s in the U.S. It continued to be pushed on less developed countries for years by the manufacturers of formula because they could make money on it, whereas mother's milk is free.

We do too many cesarian section births still, and they used to be more popular. Again, I think that this stems from a belief that we know better than evolution or God does. If we do not understand all the benefits of natural childbirth, then those benefits must not exist.

Most importantly, the belief that we are not really animals and are superior to all other species and all creation leads us to mistreat the earth and all other species. We do not sufficiently value other species (not just animals but all forms of life) and their contributions to our lives, such as sacrificing their lives so we can eat them, and cleaning our pollutants in the case of plants and worms and bacteria.

References

1. Sartwell, Crispin. Humans are animals. Let's get over it. *New York Times*. Feb. 23, 2021. https://www.nytimes.com/2021/02/23/opinion/humans-animals-philosophy.html

Chapter 45

....

Philosophical Musing

C OVID and the lockdowns have revealed, I believe, flawed aspects of our societal outlook on life.

<u>The beliefs that we are machines and have unlimited time (i.e., we do not have to die and whatever we did not do or enjoy in 2020 or 2021 can be done later because we have unlimited time in life).</u>
The lockdown response to COVID reveals, I think, that we don't really accept that we are mortal and have a limited time on earth that we should enjoy while we can. I think that may stem from believing we are not really animals but more like machines or gods.

The belief we are not a species of animal but are categorically different from and superior to all other animals is at the root of our estrangement from nature and terrible treatment of the environment. Just as racism and the belief that whites were categorically different from and superior to blacks, allowed, or perhaps caused, whites to enslave, torture, and kill blacks with impunity and with little moral compunction, so speciesism and the belief that we are categorically different from and superior to all other species of life has caused us to degrade the planet and cause a 6th wave of mass extinctions.

Instead of realizing we are a species of animal, much like any other, and part of a community with every other species, no more superior to those species than we are superior to the other humans in our human communities, we believe we are more like robots, or computers, or gods than animals.*

That belief I think is the fundamental error and has led us astray

---

* Note, I happen to think we are gods, or more accurately God. You are God. I am God. And there is only one God because there is really only one of us here. But I also think a wolf is God, and my dog is God, and a butterfly is God, and probably a rock is God. So the belief you and I are God does not mean we are superior to other species.

in our treatment of the earth. But it seems it may have led us astray in COVID and the lockdown response. Robots and computers can be fixed indefinitely and are not mortal. It seems we believe, "OK, so we are sacrificing everything we enjoy in life for a year. It's not that big a deal. We'll get married next year. I'll start my business next year. I will take singing lessons or join that choir next year." That only makes sense if you think you are going to live forever. If we are going to live forever, then deliberately deciding not to enjoy your life and live it to the fullest for a year makes sense. If we only have 80 years or so, not so much.

This is revealed most starkly in what we have mandated for group homes for the elderly and in what the elderly have voluntarily chosen to do in many cases. We have forbidden visitors from outside the homes. Residents were forced to eat meals alone in their rooms rather than in the common area with their friends, the other residents. Some of that was mandated; some of it was voluntary for the elderly even when they had a choice. I hope I would not make that decision when I am in my 80s. To me it makes no sense when you should know and accept you have a limited time left to live, that you would choose to be miserable for a year and not see your children or loved ones for a year in hopes of eking out another year of life. Moreover, the isolation probably did not reduce their COVID risk at all. The only thing that significantly reduced their COVID risk was washing their hands and their caretakers and other contacts washing their hands. Moreover, SARS-CoV-2 infection is hardly a death sentence even for the very old. The infection fatality rate is 9% for persons over age 85. I think this isolation was a terrible decision when made voluntarily and a terrible thing we have done to the elderly when we forced that isolation on them. It can only be explained by a vastly excessive fear of death and by a seeming belief that death is optional and can be prevented forever.

So I think COVID has revealed that we do not really accept we are mortal and therefore do not believe that time passes and we should enjoy life while we can. I suspect the belief we are not mortal stems from this belief we are not really animals but more like robots or computers. Robots and computers and other machines can be fixed forever (theoretically). They do not have a fixed lifespan. (In reality machines cannot be fixed forever and are not really immortal either, but that probably does not enter our thinking.)

Or maybe it does not have to do with believing we are machines but is just a characteristic of humans that we do not really accept we have a limited time on earth and that when time passes it is gone and we cannot get it back. In any case, I think COVID and the lockdown response we chose demonstrates we do not really accept either (1) our mortality or (2) that time passes and cannot be regained and the only time we have is now.

Non-acceptance of reality.

The lockdown response to COVID shows we have a problem accepting reality and accepting bad things.

Byron Katie wrote a book titled *Loving What Is*. She says she is described in her community in a very windy place in Wyoming as "the woman who loves the wind." Most of the residents think it is too windy there, so they spend some of their time complaining and wishing it were less windy. Do you think that has much effect on the wind? Katie realized it is better to love the wind, be glad it is windy. You get the same amount of wind either way, but you enjoy your life more with the latter approach.

That is an approach taught in Buddhism and by many modern self-help and spiritual authors and by Jesus and the authors of *Ecclesiastes* and the *Book of Job* and by all great spiritual traditions. Accept reality, and more than just accept it, love it and embrace it.

COVID was reality for us in 2020 and 2021. Maybe instead of fighting it in a way that apparently did not reduce COVID deaths but caused all kinds of other harms, we would have been better off accepting it.

A similar sentiment is expressed in the famous Serenity Prayer of Reinhold Niebuhr. It's most succinct form is:

God grant me the serenity to accept the things I cannot change,
Courage to change the things I can,
and Wisdom to know the difference.

COVID deaths turned out to be something we could not change, and we did not have the wisdom to realize that.

We acted like it was an entirely novel thing for a large number of people to die of an epidemic infectious disease, and totally unacceptable. Of course it is not novel; far worse epidemics have happened in history, including the 1918 flu about a century ago. But maybe we thought with all our advances in science and medicine it shouldn't happen to us.

It also was not that big a catastrophe. At the risk of being called heartless, it killed almost exclusively the sick and old. It is about three-and-a-half times more lethal than the flu (and only 1.7 times more lethal than the flu if you have not received a flu vaccine), which I do not view as that categorically different.

We behaved like a guy dumped by his girlfriend who falls into total depression and is unable to move on. He would be better off realizing, "Oh well, that is unfortunate, but it was not a perfect relationship anyway; I can be happy without her; I can find another girlfriend; and even if I don't I can be happy."

Just accept reality. Even try to love it. And have the wisdom to know what you can change and what you cannot. We had a lot of COVID deaths in 2020 and 2021. We were going to have those whether we did the lockdowns or not, and, as we have seen here, the lockdowns made little if any difference in the COVID death numbers. We would have been better off accepting reality, accepting that sometimes bad things happen, and having the wisdom to understand the limits of our power and what we can change and what we cannot.

We could and did develop a vaccine to COVID, and that made a difference. So we were right to pursue that. That was something we could change.

Mandating mask wearing, ordering everyone to stay at home for two months, closing churches and restaurants and health clubs, giving up attending sports and live music for a year, etc., did not make any difference, except to make us miserable and cause suicides. Much like the jilted boyfriend who pines over his ex, which does not do him any good, just makes him miserable longer, and just wastes and ruins time of his life, we pursued an approach that wasted and ruined time of our lives for no positive purpose.

It has also felt like we went into a society-wide ritual mourning over COVID, like we were a wife whose husband died and societal mores dictated that we wear black and a covering over our face for a year. Everyone was mandated to be miserable for a year and give up everything they enjoy to show that we all understood a terrible thing has happened to us. But the widow wearing black for a year does not bring her husband back, and high school students giving up their schooling, sports, and extracurricular activities for a year does not bring any of the COVID dead back. (It also did not prevent any COVID deaths).

Jesus had better advice: "Leave the dead to bury the dead." Enjoy your life while you are here and do what you can while you are here.

Part 7

The Good News:

The Rapid And Enormous Changes and Sacrifices We Made in the Lockdowns Show What Great Things We Could Do If We Pursued Better Goals

Chapter 46

....

If We Can Remake Society on a Dime and Undertake These Sacrifices Over COVID, We Can Do Anything!

Setting aside the wisdom or lack thereof of the lockdown response to COVID, I have been completely surprised that the U.S. society was willing to make these enormous sacrifices and change on a dime in response to a crisis, in this case COVID-19. As I have elaborated here, I don't think it was really a crisis and I think the data clearly shows the lockdown response caused far, far more harm than good. But one positive we can take from this is societies the world over showed they would make almost any sacrifice and turn on a dime to massively remake their societies in response to a crisis.

All my life, when I and like-minded people have called for change in response to the causes I have cared about—principally environmental crises for me, but also racism, militarism, and income inequality—our calls have been met by the establishment and the powers that be by responses like these:

On global warming:
"Well, to address global warming would cost too much money. People aren't willing to make even small economic sacrifices for the earth. It would also require a total change in our way of life. Our way of life is to burn oil. That's never going to change. You cannot expect the economic system to change quickly."

On overpopulation and habitat loss:
"Who cares?" "What do I care about butterflies or salamanders?"
"People have the right to have as many children as they want. You cannot infringe that absolute right."
"The economy trumps everything else. No one will sacrifice their job or be willing to make any economic sacrifice to allow other species

to live and have the needed habitat to exist. Any politician who called for it would lose the next election."

On racism:
"Be patient. Racism is ingrained. And whites will never make any sacrifice for blacks or be willing to pay really any cost at all as reparations for slavery and a century of ingrained racism. Nobody alive today ever owned slaves, so whites alive today will respond that it is not their fault and they should not have to pay."

On militarism and excessive wars:
"The military contractors have too much power. And they own Congress. So it is not going to change."

All of these responses are defeatist and based on a claim that radical or rapid change is not possible and that most people will not make even modest sacrifices for a greater good. Our enormous, drastic, overnight response to COVID shows that is a lie.

Other things we could do

After showing we were willing to give up live music, spectator sports, meeting others at restaurants and bars, attending worship in person, the right to appear in public without covering your face, the right to have a wedding that all your friends attend, the right to have a funeral that all your friends and all the friends of the deceased attend, our jobs for 16% of the workforce, our lives for about 100,000 people driven to suicide and drug overdose deaths, our happiness for really everyone but especially the 19% of us driven to moderate to severe depression, and about $4,000 of economic cost per person, I do not ever want to hear again in response to demands for change needed to address any serious problem in society: "That's not realistic. No one would ever make the needed sacrifice. You cannot change society at all, and certainly not quickly. It would cost too much money. It would cost too many jobs."

So in that spirit, the following chapters offer some proposed solutions to a few of the most serious problems in society that would involve (1) far less loss of personal liberty than the lockdowns imposed, (2) far less economic cost than the lockdowns imposed, (3) far greater benefits to happiness than the lockdowns caused, and (4) far more net extension of life than the lockdowns caused.

This is shooting fish in a barrel. Anything that caused a tiny net extension of life would cause far more net extension of life than the lockdowns, since the lockdowns caused a massive net *loss* of life due to life time lost to suicides and drug overdoses caused significantly exceeding any life time saved due to prevented COVID deaths. Anything at all would cause less loss of happiness than the lockdowns caused, since I cannot imagine any better intervention to destroy happiness than the lockdowns and cannot imagine any other intervention that could even possibly drive 19% of the population into major depression. It would be hard for any intervention to cause more economic loss than causing 16% of workers to lose their jobs and causing $4,000 economic cost per person. And it is hard to imagine any policy proposal that would involve a greater loss of personal liberty than losing the right to leave your house, as the lockdowns imposed. So here goes.

Chapter 47

Values

I think it is very useful before I lay out some policy proposals to lay out my values and argue for them. When you live your life and make any major decision such as what career to pursue, which employer to work for, what colleagues and friends to associate with, who to marry and whether to marry, whether to have a child or children and how many to have, as well as more minor decisions, you should know your values and your priorities. Likewise, in guiding our society and making decisions of what direction our society should go and formulating policy proposals and choosing between them, we need to first know what our values are and which values are more important than others.

Here are mine, in order:

1. Caring for the planet and other species

I believe this should be our first and primary value and responsibility, above even happiness for ourselves and other humans. The Bible says humanity has dominion over the earth, and we do. Maybe we did not completely at the time the Bible was written, but we certainly do now. All other species are at our mercy. We are condemning many to extinction. That is our choice. That is not something that just happened; it is something we are deciding to do.

When we decided to plow up 99.9% of the native prairie of North America, we decided to condemn native prairie grasses and birds and mammals that live exclusively in that ecosystem to extinction or to drastically decrease their numbers. When we put DDT into the environment, we made bird egg shells thinner and caused mutations and reproductive problems that drove many bird species to near extinction. Thankfully, when we realized that was going on, we banned DDT. But we continue to use other pesticides that have negative consequences for wildlife, and thereby we are deciding to impose those harms on wildlife. When we cut down rainforest, we are deciding to harm every species that lives in the rainforest and to drive many to extinction.

Those species and the individuals of those species are under our care, just as our minor children are. Since we find ourselves in the position of having dominion over every other species, we have a moral obligation to be enlightened and benevolent rulers, not tyrants. When you decide to have a child, you have the moral obligation to care for that child and put his or her interests above your own for 18 years. You do not need to totally sacrifice your life and your interests, but the happiness and welfare of your child should take priority over your own. Likewise, since we are in the position of having control over the destiny and lives of every other species on earth, and because we chose to be in that position by developing our technology and power and expanding our numbers and cutting down forests to covert them to fields, and generally remaking the environment to suit our interests—we have a moral obligation to care for the environment and every other species, and that moral obligation supersedes our own interests.

2. Happiness, and specifically per capita happiness, not gross total happiness

It seems self-evident to me that happiness is more important than duration of life or money. Would you rather be rich but miserable or middle class and happy? Would you rather live to 85 and spend 10 years with major depression or die 1 year earlier at 84 but be basically happy with maybe one year or 12 months scattered over the course of your life spent in depression? I think we all would choose the second option in both of those cases.

So happiness is more important than money or a long life.

And it is per capita happiness, not gross happiness, that is important. That is, the number of humans is of no importance to me, within reason. I place no greater good on a world with 7 billion humans, all happy, than one with 1 billion or 100 million humans, all of them happy. At some point fewer numbers would be worse, all other things equal. Maybe a world with 100 million humans, all happy, would be better than one with 1 million humans, all happy.

But one with 6 billion humans, three quarters or 4.5 billion happy and one quarter or 1.5 billion unhappy, is definitely worse than one with 3 billion humans, all happy. Let's say in the first case we judge that the 1.5 billion unhappy people negate 1.5 billion of the happy people, so you are left with total net happiness of 3 billion happy people. The second scenario also has total net happiness of 3 billion happy people, but with no unhappy people. I have no difficulty saying the second scenario is preferable.

And I think 100 million or 1 billion humans on earth is plenty. I place no higher value on a world with 1 billion humans than one with 100 million, even if both have the same average level of happiness and both have few or ideally no unhappy people. I do place a higher value on a world with 200,000 wolves in the lower 48 states and 2 million wild bison and several million meadowlarks, etc., than one with only a tiny number of each of those species, barely above extinction in the lower 48 states, or in the world entirely in the case of meadowlarks.

Happiness for humans, of course, includes and requires adequate food and shelter for everyone, as well as a certain amount of money.

3. Human wealth, but per capita wealth, not gross wealth, and income equality above per capita wealth

The Kingdom of Bhutan has made news by changing the official goal of the society to "gross domestic happiness" instead of "gross domestic product." They are on the right track, but as noted above I would choose per capita national happiness as the goal, rather than gross national happiness.

Gross domestic product or gross national product I view as not very informative or important. A society that spends a lot of money on divorce lawyers and has a high divorce rate has a higher GDP than an otherwise identical one that has fewer divorces and spends less on divorce lawyers, because money spent on divorce lawyers contributes to GDP even though it probably has a negative effect on happiness. As they say, the best things in life are free and money cannot buy happiness. Many things we spend money on have a negative effect on our quality of life or happiness, such as entertainment that glorifies or promotes racism, sexism, violence, and anger, and advertising that makes us envious and unhappy with our current lot in life. So GDP is a poor guide to the health of a society and a poor goal in government.

But money and consumption do have a positive effect on happiness and are important. Studies on happiness of persons within one society show the following correlations with money: As income rises from abject poverty to having enough money for adequate food and shelter, happiness rises dramatically. As it rises further to about the average level of most of your peers (which is higher if your peers are doctors and lawyers, than if few of your peers went to college) happiness rises, but less dramatically than it did in getting to have enough for food and shelter. As income rises above the average level of most of your peers, happiness rises slightly if at all.

Between societies there is probably even less correlation of rising average income with happiness. Societies where nearly everyone has enough to live on are happier than ones with widespread poverty. But after a society has enough wealth and income for everyone to have a materially decent life, further wealth slightly increases happiness but not very dramatically. More important to happiness is income and wealth equality. A society with a fairly even distribution of wealth and income is happier than one with greater inequalities. This is suggested by what I said in the previous paragraph that as an individual your happiness rises as your income rises from poor but adequate to average for your peers, but then rises less rapidly with income above that. What we care about is comparisons to others, not our absolute level of income. We would like to have about as much money as most of our fiends and family and our peers, but we do not care so much about being richer than them.

So, as a guide for public policy, more money and more GDP is good, but not that important. More important is a relatively equal distribution of wealth, income, and opportunity.

But I will say that money and consumption do contribute to happiness and are important. The most important issue and problem for me is overpopulation. Many of my fellow environmentalists say population is not important if we would all just consume less and stop eating meat. Well, I like to eat meat. Humans are carnivores. I think there is nothing wrong with eating meat, as long as the livestock we raise are raised humanely and have decent lives before we kill them and eat them. I think my right to eat meat trumps your right to have three or more children. As long as none of us have three or more children, we can all keep eating meat and be as rich as we want. But if we keep having three or more children forever, at some point none of us can eat meat, all of us are poorer, other species cannot even exist, and ultimately none of us can have three or more children anyway.

Most of my fellow environmentalists say environmental destruction or impact (I) equals P x A x T, or I=PAT, where I is environmental impact, P is number of people or population, A is average level of affluence, and T is impact of technology. I think that equation is meaningless. If affluence were such an important factor, then Africa and poorer areas of the world should be less environmentally degraded than the U.S. I don't really think they are. They have contributed less to CO_2 emissions and global warming, and that is pretty proportional to affluence x population, regardless of technology. But they have as high or higher levels of extinction and habitat loss, which appears to me to be pretty much just a function of population, regardless of affluence or technology. In fact, as they become more affluent, through tourism dollars for instance, they become less likely to hunt gorillas or poach other wildlife or practice slash and burn agriculture that cuts down the rainforest, and their environmental impact decreases. In any case, I think preaching that we should all be voluntarily poorer and give up meat and air travel and large houses and other things we enjoy is not likely to be accepted. I would instead say, "Be as rich as you want. Eat meat. Enjoy your life. Just don't have three or more children."

4. Duration of life

It is important we be healthy. I would promote health, and that means principally exercise and a healthy diet. But duration of life is not so important. I would put it below wealth or affluence in my values. We would all like to live longer. But we are all going to die. We are mortals. It is terrible when a teenager or 30-year-old dies. It is bad but less terrible when someone dies at age 50 or 60. But whether someone dies at age 85, 90, or 100 does not seem very important to me. In the COVID lockdowns we have acted like duration of life is far and away the most important thing, far more important than happiness or having a job or economic wellbeing; and we have acted like it is an equal tragedy when an 84-year-old in a nursing home dies of natural causes as when a 40-year-old dies of suicide or a drug overdose. I disagree. I think as a society we should have a goal that everyone live to age 70 and most people past age 80, and health while we are alive is an important goal, but in general, duration of life is a far less important goal than happiness and quality of life and a somewhat less important goal than money and affluence.

That hierarchy of values and priorities guides the policy proposals that follow.

Chapter 48

....

Extinction, Habitat Loss, and Overpopulation

This, not global warming, is the biggest environmental problem facing us today. And environmental problems are easily the biggest problems of our time, so habitat loss and species extinction is the biggest problem or crisis in the world today.

We are undergoing the 6th wave of mass extinctions in Earth's history (Kolbert). The previous five were caused by meteorites striking the earth, supervolcanoes erupting, or other natural causes. The current wave of mass extinctions is caused by one species—our species. It is caused by humans filling the planet and overusing land and ocean resources so there is not enough land and habitat left for the other species on earth. It is principally caused by habitat loss and overharvesting resources, which I view as a type of habitat loss, such as overfishing, overhunting, overharvesting timber, and too intensely farming and ranching (overgrazing and not practicing restraint in farming—not using crop rotation, depleting the soil and impoverishing biodiversity in the soil, overapplying fertilizer, resulting in water pollution and dead zones in the Gulf of Mexico and elsewhere, and overusing herbicides and insecticides).

To a lesser extent it is caused by pollution, particularly insecticides and pesticides. The pollution of releasing chemicals such as bisphenol-A (BPA) that disrupt hormones may be responsible for amphibian extinctions, particularly, and increased numbers of malformed amphibians and fish and amphibians and fish with deformed or malfunctioning reproductive systems. Humans also are suffering from malfunctioning reproductive systems. Women begin menstruating at earlier ages than previously, and men have much lower sperm counts than previous generations. That may be, and I suspect is, primarily because of synthetic chemical pollution of our environment and particularly hormone-disrupting chemicals. But I am more concerned about the harm we are doing to other species than to ourselves. They did nothing to bring this on themselves.

Insecticides, particularly neonicotinoids, seem to be responsible for a huge decline in insect numbers and extinctions of insect species (Wagner). If you were around in the 1960s, 70s, and even 80s, and you are like me, you remember driving though the countryside in the summer at that time and your windshield would be covered with dead insects. Today, you can drive all day in the summer and hardly have an insect on your windshield. I had not noticed that until it was pointed out to me a few years ago, but it is absolutely true.

One type of pollution that is responsible for some species extinction and that will be responsible for more in the future is CO_2 pollution (and methane pollution) causing global warming. But the sixth wave of mass extinctions was well underway by 2000, at which time temperatures had barely started to rise. Global warming is responsible for almost none of the extinctions that have already happened, and we would have this sixth mass extinction event to almost the same extent whether global warming ever happened or not. This mass extinction is caused primarily by habitat loss and overuse of natural resources such as soil, fish, grasslands, and water. To a lesser extent it is caused by pollution, particularly insecticides and herbicides and hormone-disrupting chemicals. To a still lesser extent it has been caused by CO_2 pollution and global warming, although that may surpass other types of pollution in the future. It will not surpass habitat loss ever as the primary driver of extinctions.

Habitat loss, in turn, is caused simply by overpopulation. I know people say, "Well, if we would stop eating meat, if we would be voluntarily poorer, travel less and consume less resources, maybe we could slow the extinctions some and slow the environmental degradation some and still have 7 billion people on earth. So that means overpopulation is not a problem."

It is also said that not that many people suffer from hunger and the number of people suffering from hunger and starvation is a lower percentage of the world population (although perhaps a larger absolute number of persons) than in previous times. So that means the world can support 7 billion people and overpopulation is not a problem. And it is said that people on average are richer now than they were at any previous time in history, so that means overpopulation is not a problem and Malthus was wrong. And the price of oil has gone down recently, contrary to the predictions of those of us who worry about overpopulation.

Everything in the last paragraph is just focused on humans. So even if true that overpopulation has not worsened the lot of most humans (and I think that is not true) it has certainly worsened the lot of every other species on earth that is not cultivated by humans (livestock and crops), with a few exceptions such as rats and cockroaches that benefit from humans. Other species have rights too. Other species have interests too. We recognize that with our dogs: that it is morally wrong to abuse a dog because it makes the dog unhappy and the dog has legitimate interests and we want our dogs to be happy. Well, I think wolves have legitimate interests too, and I want them to be happy. I think pigs have legitimate interests too, and I want them to be happy (that is, they should be able to turn around in their crates, preferably be able to go outside and roll in the mud, while they are alive, although I think killing them for meat is perfectly legitimate, just as it is legitimate for wolves or bears to kill a wild boar for meat). I think salamanders and frogs and fish and butterflies and mosquitoes and trees and plants of all types have legitimate interests. I want them to thrive. For any species, a world with a million or more individuals of that species is better than a world with fewer than 100, even if the species does not ever go completely extinct. I want to see every species thriving across its entire native range, not just saved as a museum piece with 1,000 individuals left but not in immediate danger of extinction.

We treat wolves in the U.S. as if we only want them to exist as museum pieces, barely above endangered status. Wolves exist only in a few states. In the Midwest, they exist only in northern portions of Minnesota, Wisconsin, and Michigan. They used to exist across all of North America, throughout the entire area of every state in the U.S. (before they were states). We have about 2,700 wolves in Minnesota and fewer in Wisconsin and Michigan. They are the apex predator of North America, equivalent in our ecosystem to lions and tigers in Africa and Asia. They have been classified as endangered in the lower 48 states, but courts have said they are no longer endangered, that 2,700 in Minnesota is enough, 500 in Wisconsin is enough, and we can resume hunting them. In fact, a federal court *ordered* Wisconsin to resume hunting them without delay when the Wisconsin Department of Natural Resources (DNR) wanted time to study where to set the quota and how many wolves could be killed. So our goal apparently is to keep wolves just on the edge of extinction but not extinct. As soon as their numbers recover enough to not actually be in imminent danger of extinction, we resume hunting them to "cull their numbers."

That would not be my goal. My goal would be for wolves and every other species to recover across their entire historic range, meaning for wolves to have a population of at least 10,000 wolves in, not only Minnesota, but also Colorado, Iowa, Georgia, Missouri, Ohio, and every other similarly sized state. I would like to see wild bison (not bison on farms) across at least every state of the prairies, from Montana to Minnesota, Colorado to Illinois, and Arizona to Texas, if not most other states.

Humans directly use for our own purposes the large majority of suitable land on earth. Forty percent of earth's land area was used for agriculture (including farming and grazing) as of 2005 (Foley et al.). It would be more now. That is 40% of total land area, including all the unusable land such as mountaintops, deserts, Antarctica, Greenland, arctic tundra. Another 3% is urban areas. Most of the remaining arable land is forest that is frequently harvested for timber and therefore is also properly classified as primarily used by humans. Another portion is used for mining. Probably not more than 10% of the world's land area is potentially suitable for human use and remains unused. That should be at least 50%.

My modest proposal is that we humans share the earth with the other species. It is a value we should have learned in kindergarten. It is selfish to take the large majority of land on earth for our own use. Half should be enough for us. We should leave half the earth, at least, for use exclusively by the other billions of species on our planet instead of our one species. *Homo sapiens* is like a psychopathic billionaire who alone owns 90% of the wealth on earth and complains it is unfair if anyone suggests he should be taxed or give anything to charity.

Philosophers and humans generally constantly seem obsessed with what makes humans unique, as noted in Chapters 43 and 44.

Humans are just not unique. We are primates, mammals, and animals. The belief that we are unique and the bizarre obsession with proving we are categorically different from every other form of life and not really animals, but more like robots or computers or gods, is at the root of how terribly we treat the earth and every other species on earth. Just as racism and the belief that blacks were not really like whites and not really human allowed whites to enslave, torture, and kill blacks, so speciesism and the belief that we are categorically different from every other species of animal and not dependent on other species of life allows us to mistreat other species and the earth.

That said, after saying humans are not unique and that the belief we are is the root of nearly all evil, I will now contradict myself. If we demonstrate an ability to leave half or more of earth for the exclusive use of other species, we might legitimately say that we are the only species that had the power to control the entire planet and voluntarily

chose to give half to other species. It would really be something to brag
about. Maybe then we can legitimately say we are unique.

Proposal 1: Give up 50% or more of each habitat of the earth to the exclusive use of other species.

The catch with my call for 50% of the earth to exclusive use of other
species is it has to be at least 50% of every *habitat*. It does not count to
say, "Well, Antarctica is probably 10% of the earth, and we don't use
that. Add in Canadian tundra, and Russian tundra, and the Sahara
desert, and mountains, and maybe we get to almost 50%!" No. Leaving
Antarctica alone and calling it a wilderness does not do gorillas or lions
or salamanders any good. We have to leave at least 50% of every habitat unused, and I would define habitat narrowly as a local habitat. In
Minnesota, for instance, these habitats exist:

- Northern conifer forest. Pines, spruces, and fir. Historically
  was dominated by white pine but now mostly spruce and fir.
  Mostly northeastern portion of the state.
- Northern deciduous forest. Birch and aspen. Northeastern
  portion of the state.
- Big woods. Maple- and ash-dominated forests. Southeastern
  portion of state.
- Oak savannah. Scattered oaks over grasslands. Central east-
  ern portion of the state.
- Marshland. Over whole state, especially common in north-
  west portion.
- Prairie. Northwest and southwest portions of state.
- Deep lakes. Water tends to be clearer. More common among
  lakes in the northern portion of the state.
- Shallow lakes. More plant matter, less oxygenated lakes.
  Scattered over the state.
- Rivers (should be divided further into trout streams and oth-
  er types of rivers).
- River bluffs. The southwest portion of the state has bluffs
  over the Mississippi River that have some rattlesnakes.

Half or more of the historical area (not just the current area) of each
of these habitats should be reserved for other species. The tallgrass
prairie has nearly disappeared under the plow, so there is barely any
left. I am not talking about protecting what is left but rather giving up
cultivation on half or so of the farmland so it can revert to prairie. Minnesota has 10,000 lakes. Half of those should have completely pristine

shorelines with no homes or buildings or farmland on the shore and little or no fishing. That is what it would mean to share half the habitat with other species.

Those habitats are scattered across the state, so half of each region of the state would be protected. We should also connect every protected area with a corridor probably at least 100 yards wide, which should not be difficult if 50% of the area is protected. Many species need those corridors to be able to move from one area to another. So for native wildlife to spread to and repopulate every area where it should be, you have to have those corridors.

A similar plan protecting half the land area should be in place in every other state and every nation. And the protected areas across different states and nations should have contiguous wildlife corridors, allowing wildlife to migrate not only between adjacent counties but from one end of a continent to the other.*

We do not need to intervene to reestablish these habitats. We could hire people to plant native grasses, but it is not essential. Nature will take care of it in time, and in most cases probably very quickly. This is documented in *Wilding* by Isabella Tree. Isabella Tree and her husband stopped farming their large English estate, and the book describes the remarkably fast return of nature to the estate, with little intervention by humans, including various species that had disappeared or nearly disappeared from that part of Britain returning to the estate. This happened with no planning and almost no intervention by humans. But the return of large herbivores such as certain deer, cattle, and boar, was key. Their dung and their actions of hooves tearing up the soil created habitats to allow certain plants and insects to return. Their eating plants had huge effects on the ecosystem. They were not able to bring in any apex predators (and the apex predator in Britain is apparently the badger, which seems kind of pathetic compared to lions and tigers and bears and wolves), but bringing native predators back to a landscape may be even more important than large herbivores.

---

* I will just brag a little about my home state here. Minnesota has somewhat unusually varied habitats. We are at the juncture of the three biggest habitat zones in North America. We have the prairies running from western Minnesota south to Texas and west to the Rocky Mountains. We have the northern boreal forest running from northeastern Minnesota north to Hudson Bay and east and west to the Atlantic and Pacific. And we have the Eastern deciduous forests running from Central and southeastern Minnesota east through the northeastern U.S. to the Atlantic. We also have 10,000 lakes and are on the largest freshwater lake (by surface area) in the world, Lake Superior. I understand that most other states are somewhat pitiful in comparison, but I'm sure your state is nice too. On the other hand, our football team has never won the Super Bowl.

When wolves were brought back to Yellowstone, they culled the elk so the elk were not overbrowsing on willows and other shore plants, then the streams stopped eroding and streamside vegetation came back in Yellowstone, which in turn cleaned up the water in the streams and made better habitat for trout. I'm sure similar spectacular recoveries and changes would happen if you brought back bison and wolves to southern Minnesota.

This habitat recovery plan is not just for the land. We should protect at least 50% of each local ocean habitat—each area of tropical reefs, each cod fishery area, each breeding area for Orcas, etc. Half of each of these areas should be off limits to fishing and off limits to oil drilling or other resource extraction. That would allow the fish populations and other species populations to recover. The fish would move from the protected areas to non-protected areas, so the fish harvests in the non-protected areas would be higher than now and sustainable.

I should also emphasize that I mean <u>exclusive</u> use of other species. I would allow hiking and tent camping in these areas, but no mining, resource extraction, logging, farming, or garden cultivating at all. I would also allow no hunting or fishing at all. In principle maybe you could have very limited fishing or hunting, but it would have to be only recreational, of course, and very limited in scale in order to not significantly affect the ecosystem. I don't trust us. Better to just say none at all.

How could this be implemented? If you want half the lakes in Minnesota to have no homes or buildings on their shoreline, you will have to remove a lot of cabins and presumably buy out their owners. If you want to revert half the farmland of Minnesota to prairies and forests, you will have to buy out that land from the current owners. For the buildings, you do not actually have to spend any money or effort tearing down the buildings. You could just leave buildings in place to eventually rot. But what about the current owners and current farmers? To minimize the number of people forced to move or sell, I would try generally to protect less populated rural areas versus suburban and urban areas. And I would try to focus the protection more on areas with large farms than smaller farms, again to minimize the number of people displaced. You would not need to displace people immediately or really at all in their lifetime. You could probably in all cases allow the people who currently own the land to own it and use it as they are currently using it until their death, at which time I would purchase it at fair value with the proceeds going to their estates. I would pick the areas we want to protect, designate those as protected, and then inform the owners of the land in those areas that the government will buy them out at fair value, and they can take that offer now or at any time until their death. They are free to continue to live and farm where they are as long as they like. But if they want to sell, they cannot sell to a third party; they have to sell to the government and the government will then allow it to revert to nature.

Is that feasible? Can we produce enough food to feed our population if we give up farming half our current farmland? Yes, we can, but we do ultimately have to reduce the population.

First, under my plan people could continue to farm their land for the rest of their lives. So area under cultivation would not immediately drop off a cliff. Also, we would preferentially buy out larger tracts of land to minimize the number of people displaced; and on a per acre basis, small farms produce more food than large farms. So reverting half the farmland to nature would decrease production by less than half. Moreover, more labor intensive farming can more than double the productivity of land. Devoting more labor, more people, to cultivating the remaining land, by sustainable practices such as terracing, no-till farming, composting, etc., can increase the yield per acre with the added benefit of revitalizing rural economies and rural societies by putting more people to work in farming, without any increase, and possibly a decrease, in pesticide and fertilizer use. It's a win-win-win: better environment, better rural economy, same or better food production. And rural people, moreso than city people, would have the added privilege of seeing wolves and bison, as well as all kinds of birds and flowers and wildlife, on a regular basis.

Proposal 2: Reduce the human population

But to give back half the land we currently live on to the use of other species will ultimately require us to decrease our population, you say. So what? We also have to decrease our population if we continue to use all of the earth. Let's say the sustainable population of the earth using all of the earth is about 1 billion people, which I think is about right. That is a greater than 80% decrease from our current 7.7 billion. Using only half the earth instead of all of it would actually not have much effect on the sustainable human population. We need the ecological services supplied by nature to clean up and reprocess our pollution. Leaving half the earth to other species is basically necessary to have those ecological services available to us at all and certainly increases the efficiency of those ecological services so the remaining half can support a larger density of humans than it otherwise could. So giving up half the earth to other species does not actually cut the sustainable human population in half. It may not cut it at all. It may increase it because maybe the sustainable human population is almost zero if we insist on using every inch of arable land and degrading the planet as much as possible. But let's say it does cut the sustainable human population in half. So then the sustainable human population is 500 million instead of 1 billion. Who cares? Why is that worse?

Many say overpopulation of humans is not a problem and we do not need to limit population, so let's confront their arguments.

My basic argument that overpopulation is a problem and human population must be limited is simply that we live on a finite planet. Nothing can grow forever on a finite planet.

Those who argue population growth is not a problem and population does not need to be limited now or in the foreseeable future argue a few points.

The price of oil and other resources has not risen as much as feared. True, and I cannot explain that.* But it does not negate the fact that we live on a finite planet and population must be limited at some point. And some resources, such as copper, have soared in price as population has grown. So has the price of farmland and land generally, which is the most basic and most important resource.

Hunger has fallen. The percentage of the world population starving or hungry has fallen, but the number of hungry people has not fallen and the percentage hungry has risen since 2014 (Reference 5). Over 690 million people globally are undernourished (Reference 5). I think that is still too many. It is said that enough food is produced to feed everyone if we just distributed it perfectly and none of it went to waste or if everyone would give up meat. None of that is going to happen. Distribution of every good is imperfect. We live in a world of money, and if people do not have enough money to buy food, they are likely to go hungry. There is always waste. And people like meat, they are not going to give it up, and I don't think they should have to. If we had fewer people in the world, it would be easier to raise enough food for everyone, everyone could eat meat if they wanted to, and we would not have to farm every square inch on earth to feed everyone, allowing other species to have their habitats back and simply live. Moreover, I do not think the point of life is to cram as many people onto the earth as possible as long as they are not literally starving.

We will just move to another planet. It is hard to take this one seriously, except that some otherwise intelligent people, most notably Ste-

---

* The probable explanation is that prices do not respond smoothly as a resource declines. They do not rise until the resource is in extremely short supply, so price is a poor signal of declines in a resource.

phen Hawking, while he was alive the world's most famous physicist, have said this. I don't think Hawking was actually advocating this but just saying it was feasible and an option. It does not seem like much of an option to me. Mars has little if any water and no oxygen. It seems to me a colony would have to be supported from earth and could never have significant numbers. Any planet outside our solar system would be light years away and we have no way to get there with current technology or any technology we could reasonably envision. Also we do not know whether there even is any planet outside our solar system as good as earth for our needs. No matter how much we destroy the earth with runaway global warming or widespread nuclear war, earth will still have oxygen, water, soil, and many areas with temperatures humans tolerate. It would still look like a paradise if we discovered it outside our solar system and be far more hospitable to humans than anything we know of.

"Malthus has been proven wrong." This is a very popular claim. Thomas Malthus wrote a book titled *An Essay on the Principle of Population* in 1798 that inspired Darwin and provided cornerstone principles for Darwin's theory of evolution. Malthus observed that an increase in a nation's food production tended to be followed by an increase in population, which left the people as hungry and malnourished as before. He observed that population of humans, and all animals, can increase geometrically but theorized that food increases only arithmetically, so humans reproduce up to the level the current food supply can support. He also predicted widespread famine, and his critics claim the world has never had widespread famine since Malthus and this proves Malthus was wrong. That claim seems doubtful to me. But more to the point, Malthus's theory is basically that humans and any species have essentially unlimited capability of reproducing, and if they exercise that capability they will bump up against the food supply and there will be a struggle for existence. This is the cornerstone of the theory of evolution. If Malthus was wrong, then Darwin and modern biology are also wrong.

No one ever points that out in defending Malthus. I suspect if the Malthus critics were confronted with that, they would respond, "OK, maybe Malthus's theory was right when applied to every other species of life, but humans are categorically different from every other species; we are not really animals, so it does not apply to humans." Again, I think this is the fundamental error in human thought—believing we are not like other species of life and categorically different. From that error, flows all our environmental destruction and most of our other problems.

Most importantly, even if human overpopulation has not caused any problems for humans yet—is not responsible for the high price of land and housing, is not responsible for any share of the hunger that exists on earth today, and is not responsible for, or contribute to, poverty or inequality of wealth—it is unarguably a problem for the earth itself and almost every other species of life on earth.

So I take it as true that overpopulation is a problem and human population must be limited at some point. I further take it as a true that there is an optimum population size, at which human welfare is optimized, even ignoring the issue of whether welfare of any other species or the earth matters other than insomuch as welfare of other species and the earth's ecosystems benefits humans. At a given level of technology, such as the level we are at now, there is a level of population for any nation and for the world as a whole at which these goals are met, as much as possible:

- Hunger and starvation do not exist or are minimized
- Highest possible level of average material wealth
- Relative equality of income and wealth, and equality of opportunity
- Highest personal freedom (at lower population levels it matters less or not at all whether you burn leaves or hunt bison, for instance, because fewer people are doing those things and the impact is less, so they may not need to be regulated or banned)

The optimum human population may rise with technology development, but it does not rise forever on a finite planet. And at any given level of technology, it is possible for a nation to be overpopulated.

Furthermore, when a species, such as deer or hares or foxes, is above its optimum population in a local environment, its population must come down—through starvation and lowered reproduction because of inadequate nutrition or through intraspecies fighting and killing—and the higher above the sustainable optimum population level it goes, the farther below that optimum it must fall. When deer are overpopulated, they eat back the brush until there is not enough food for the deer and the numbers fall or crash until the environment can recover. The further above the optimum the numbers get, the further below the optimum they must fall before the food source can recover. This is the phenomenon of overshoot and collapse.

The same applies for humans: Perhaps the optimum sustainable human population was 2 billion, and if we had approached 2 billion slowly and plateaued at that level we could have stayed at that population level for centuries, but since we have overshot it, the population will have to fall below 2 billion in order to be sustainable. It will have to fall to perhaps 1 billion.

Others have estimated the optimum sustainable human population as 1.5 to 2 billion (Daily et el.), but that was in 1994, and since we have overshot that by 4-fold, the optimum sustainable human population is probably less than that now.

It is not controversial that deer or wolves or any other wild species have an optimum population level in a local environment, for their own quality of life as well as the ecological health of their environment. For some reason it is controversial that the same applies for humans. Again, the error that we think we are unique and the laws of nature do not apply to us.

It is not terribly important what is the exact optimum human population, but the important thing to recognize is it that some optimum level does exist and it is less than our population now. If we had a lower population with the current human technology, we would have less hunger, be wealthier on average, have more equal distribution of wealth, and have fewer restrictions on our personal liberty. We should also recognize that because we have degraded the environment, the sustainable optimum population is less now than it would have been if we had stopped population growth at some lower level such as 2 billion people.

If we protect 50% of every native habitat and reserve at least 50% of land in every habitat to the exclusive use of other species, humans will have about half as much land to use as we use now. That will require some decrease in population. But the bigger decrease will be needed just to optimize our wealth and wellbeing and because we have overshot the optimum population. I would estimate an indefinitely sustainable population for the world would be not more than 2 billion, and that the optimum population of the world would be less than that, probably 100 million to 1 billion.

The United States is overpopulated too, to about the same extent as the entire world. (Sometimes people argue overpopulation is only a problem in the developing world.) Even setting aside the health of our environment and the welfare of wild species, if the U.S. population were lower, we would have higher wages for unskilled workers (the law of supply and demand: fewer workers would mean more competition for them and higher wages) and therefore more equality of income, wealth, and opportunity (see Chapter 51); we would have higher average wealth and income; and we would have less hunger and poverty.

Population growth in the U.S. and the Western world generally is due entirely or almost entirely to immigration. Our natural population growth from births is near zero. So to reduce population in the U.S. the first task is reducing legal and illegal immigration to as low as possible. We should take our fair share of refugees, especially refugees from environmental crises we created and war zones we created. But we should not take any, or almost any, immigrants just seeking better economic opportunities. We should not allow any illegal immigration.

And then we need to have fewer children.

Immanuel Kant is considered the greatest western philosopher of modern times. His categorical imperative is: *Act only according to that maxim by which you can at the same time will that it should become a universal law.* That is essentially, the Golden Rule: *Do unto others as you would have them do unto you.* I also consider morality to be to act so as to create the greatest good: that is, our actions are judged by their consequences. A moral action is one that promotes happiness and welfare for humans as a whole (and other species, I would argue) and in immoral action is one that has negative consequences for people and other species as a whole. This means what is moral and immoral varies by circumstances.

Kant gives the rule that one should always tell the truth, and gives the example that is scarily prescient of the holocaust that you are sheltering in your house a person who is hiding from one who wants to kill him. The would-be killer knocks on your door and asks if the person whom you know he wants to kill is in your house. According to Kant, since one should always tell the truth you should answer, yes. I and most people think that is absurd. It is generally ethical to tell the truth, but it depends on circumstances.

Today, it is unethical to have three or more children, and since we need probably a 90% drop in human population to get to our optimum, I would argue it is always unethical for anyone on earth to produce more than one child for the next century or so. Once we are at the optimum population, it will be ethical to have up to three children (since some will have zero or one), but probably still unethical to have four or more. At certain times, it could be ethically required to have a large number of babies. I have heard that genetic evidence suggests at one time humanity was almost wiped out by some cataclysmic event and we may have been down to 200 or fewer breeding female humans in the world. At that time, no doubt it was a good thing to have a large number of children. We are not living in that time now.

Many say, "Live simply that others may simply live." Or, Do not eat meat because it takes more land and grain to produce meat than to produce the grain or other vegetables and eat those directly. The problem is, even if we all chose voluntary simplicity or even poverty and chose to give up meat, we would still eventually, if not now, have to limit our reproduction and population. We might as well limit our reproduction now so we can all eat meat and be as wealthy as we want.

How can government or society reduce procreation?

Studies show the most effective things are access to contraceptives and improvements in the rights and standing of women. When women have economic opportunities and have the power to decide for themselves how many children to have, they have fewer children.

But that may not be sufficient on its own. Beyond improving women's rights and economic opportunities and access to contraceptives, I think the most effective measure is simply peer pressure and acceptance of the ethic I am advocating for here that we should all have no more than one child, and certainly no more than two children, for at least the next century, and that if you have more than that, you are selfish and infringing on the rights of others to have rich, healthy lives and to have a child of their own and for their child to have a decent life, and you are infringing on the rights of other species and of all of us to live within a healthy environment. The world would change if when people have a third or fourth child, instead of receiving congratulations and warm wishes, people received frowns and the silent treatment or a response of, "Well, aren't you selfish." (I have never had the guts to say that, but I do not congratulate people for having a third or fourth child.)

I do not recognize a right to have as many children as you want. It is a right to have a decent environment. It is a right to have enough to eat. It is a right for other species merely to exist and not go extinct. Those rights trump your right to have as many children as you want.

I am fine with China's one-child policy. Indeed, it is certainly the best policy China has enacted in a century and has done great good for the people of China and the world. In fact, *it is probably the single most successful and beneficial public policy in history.* Policies should be judged by the goal of producing the greatest good for the greatest number, right? What better measure is that? *By that measure, China's one-child policy has to be the single best policy intervention in history.* The one-child policy existed from 1979 to 2015, when it became a two-child policy. In that time, China's per capita GDP went from $156 to $8,067, a 52-fold increase. Of course, the one-child policy was not solely responsible for that, but it would not have been possible without it. For comparison, over 1979 to 2015 India's GDP per capita went from $224 to $1,606, a 7-fold increase. So China did more than 7 times better than India in per capita GDP growth, and it is not unreasonable to say that entire difference may be due to the one-child policy.

To reduce population in the U.S. and the world:

- Reduce or eliminate immigration, other than humanitarian refugees.
- Improve women's rights and economic opportunities in the less developed world (in the U.S. I think this has pretty much been accomplished)
- Insure access to contraceptives
- Promote an ethic that it is selfish and morally wrong to have three or more children, and really even two children, for probably the next century. (Obviously I am talking about procreation here; adoption is another matter, and it is noble to adopt as many children as you can effectively care for.)
- And the proposal below.

Population Proposal for U.S.: A Maximum Three-Child Policy

Mandatory surgical sterilization (tubal ligation for women and vasectomies for men) after a man has biologically fathered three children or a woman has given birth to three children.

Overpopulation is by far the largest problem in the world, and the greatest thing anyone can do for the world is to have fewer children — zero is better than one, one is better than two, and two is better than three. So this would have enormous benefit.

It would have enormous benefit for the environment and other species. That is my primary concern.

But it would also have enormous benefit for us humans. It would have a large benefit for the children in ensuring each child has adequate parental care and that care is not diluted across too many children. It would help ensure each child has adequate financial and material support. A father who has fathered four or more children, sometimes with four different women, is not in a great position to pay adequate child support. Studies have shown that all outcomes are better for children in small families than large families. Children raised in small families are less likely to go to prison, make more money on average as adults, and are more likely to graduate from high school and college. And those patterns persist across the board: only children are more successful than those in 2-child households, who are more successful than those raised in 3-child households, etc.

This measure would directly reduce births in theory by 13% in that 13% of U.S. births are currently the fourth or greater child born to the mother. But probably a bigger benefit in my mind is that it would signal our societal disapproval of having a large number of children, and that would tend to lead people to follow that social pressure either from fear of social pressure or changing their own thinking of the desired family size, to make them more likely to stop at one or two children.

This, of course, is a coercive step. If you want to think of it as a punishment, that is fine with me. In my mind it is a punishment for having three children; and I believe it is wrong to have three or more children, so it is appropriate to punish people for having a third child. Many are likely to stop at two children to avoid this involuntary medical intervention.

The benefits of this are vast. We need to reduce the human population, and if we do not, nature will do it for us by increasing the death rate. It is preferable to reduce the birth rate.

The harm is simply an infringement on liberty, an infringement on your "right" to have as many children as you want. But I do not think that is a right. Or if it is a right, it is trumped by the rights of others on whom it impinges: the right of your first three children not to have to share resources and parental attention with even more children, the right of other species to not go extinct, the right of other people to a healthy environment and to experience wilderness, the right of future generations to a healthy environment, the right of others to have a healthy world and environment for their children and descendants and not have that infringed by your irresponsible behavior, and the right of others not to have to pay more taxes for schooling and care (and likely welfare and future imprisonment) for children that it was irresponsible of you to bring into the world.

As an infringement of personal liberty, I think that is a smaller infringement on liberty than being ordered to not leave your home for 51 days or being forbidden from gathering with others to worship God. Also, we did nothing to bring the latter two COVID restrictions on ourselves, whereas a person who chooses to have three children would have chosen to bring the restriction of sterilization on themselves.

So mandatory sterilization after three children (1) is a lesser infringement on personal liberty than what we have endured in the lockdowns, and (2) unlike the lockdowns it has a net positive benefit/harm ration for society: increasing wealth, happiness, and good outcomes in life for your first three children; and improving the environment for all species and reducing the financial burden on everyone else in society.

References

1. Kolbert, Elizabeth. *The Sixth Extinction*. New York: Henry Holt and Company, 2014.

2. Wagner, DL. 2020. Insect Declines in the Anthropocene. *Annual Review of Entomology* 65:457–80. https://doi.org/10.1146/annurev-ento-011019-025151

3. Foley JA DeFries R et al. 2005. Global Consequences of Land Use. *Science* 309:570-574. Https://doi.org/10.1126/science.1111772

4. Tree, Isabella. *Wilding: Returning Nature to Our Farm*. 2018. New York: New York Review of Books.

5. Action Against Hunger. https://www.actionagainsthunger.org/world-hunger-facts-statistics

6. Daily, Gretchen C.; Ehrlich, Anne H.; Ehrlich, Paul R. 1994. Optimum Human Population Size. *Population and Environment*. 15 (6): 469–475. https://doi.org/10.1007/BF02211719

Chapter 49

Climate Change

I would regard climate change, or global warming, as the second most important problem facing humanity. Habitat loss and extinctions are the first, as noted in the previous chapter.

Neither habitat loss and extinctions nor global warming are likely to actually cause the extinction of our species. But both will make the planet less hospitable for humans and result in a decrease in our numbers and decrease in our wealth and quality of life. They both will greatly affect future generations of humans. In 200 years, humans will care very much what we did to stop habitat loss and stop global warming. They will care much less what we did to decrease wealth inequalities, fight racism, or end police abuses. If we have not dealt with those latter problems, they can deal with them then. But if we have not dealt with habitat loss, extinctions, and global warming, they will have limited, if any, options for dealing with them then.

Here let us brainstorm what steps we can take to fight global warming, regardless of seeming political feasibility, economic cost, or extent of infringement on personal liberty.

We are often told what steps we can take as individuals to fight global warming. Those steps include things like take public transportation, drive a more fuel efficient car, bike or walk instead of driving, don't fly or fly less, eat a vegetarian diet, eat local instead of food flown from across the world, live in a smaller house, insulate your house, turn off the lights, conserve water, recycle.

Almost never does any one say, have fewer or no children. But here is a graph that I created from the data in Wynes et al. (1) and Murtaugh et al. (2) of the relative amount of carbon reduction from the commonly suggested personal actions to reduce CO_2 emissions.

Approximate CO₂ Emissions Reduced Per Year

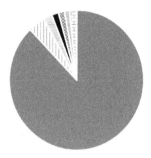

- ■ Have one fewer child   ⁞ Live car free
- ≣ Avoid one flight   ■ Purchase green energy
- ⊠ Use hybrid car   ▩ Eat a plant-based diet
- ⊤ Everything else

Having one fewer child has about 7 times greater effect on the CO_2 emissions you are responsible for than all other possible interventions put together. (By the way, purchasing carbon offsets has zero effect. We cannot buy our way out of this.)

However, the subject of overpopulation and the suggestion we have an ethical responsibility to reduce our procreation is such a toxic subject that the authors of this paper (Wynes et al.) summarized their calculations and results as recommending four actions: have one fewer child, live car free, take one fewer flight per year, and eat a plant-based diet. Is that the way you would summarize this graph? Does it look like four actions stand out as having a larger impact than the rest? Or does it look like one action stands out?

This means if you compare the lives of

- o   person A, who has just one child and otherwise is the biggest environmental pig ever: voted for Trump, drives a Hummer, owns a private plane, eats tons of meat, leaves every light on in his house constantly, never recycles, lives in a large house, etc., with
- o   person B, who thinks of herself as a hippie, always votes Democratic (except occasionally for the Green

party), is a vegetarian, turns off her lights, recycles, bikes to work, owns a Prius with a bumper stick that says "live simply that others may simply live", etc., but had two children with her husband,

person A has lived the more environmentally virtuous life.

From an environmental perspective, almost the only thing that matters is how many children you have. That is true for your contributions to global warming and CO_2 emissions. It is even more true for your contributions to habitat loss and extinctions. So to the question of what you can do personally to help protect the environment and reduce global warming, the answer is have no children or one child.

Therefore, my proposed policies to reduce global warming start with the proposed policies to reduce population growth in Chapter 48.

The second best, or maybe the first best, thing we could do is to set aside 50% of land of each habitat to nature for exclusive use of other species, as discussed in Chapter 48. Natural habitat sequesters far more carbon than cropland or urban land, so converting 50% of our land back to nature will serve to remove a huge amount of carbon from the atmosphere. It will also tend to force us to reduce our population.

But reducing our population will take generations and converting half our land back to nature will take time and not be a complete fix. And global warming will raise the temperatures past the point of permanent alteration of our ecosystems within 20 years, if the momentum from what we have already done will not take us past that point even if we stopped emissions completely today. So we need faster fixes.

I think we will have to deliberately engineer the climate to reduce temperatures. The possible strategies are reviewed in References (3-5).

One strategy is to fly thousands of planes in the upper atmosphere to disperse sulfates that form droplets and screen out a fraction of sunlight.

Another is to send a fleet of ships into the oceans with spouts to draw seawater and shoot seawater into the atmosphere, where the droplets will evaporate, leaving salt that will seed condensation to create more clouds, which will filter out more sunlight.

A third strategy is to break up high altitude cirrus clouds by injecting ice nuclei, such as bismuth triiodide, into areas where they form. High altitude cirrus clouds trap outgoing longwave radiation (basically heat), so the effect would be to increase outgoing longwave radiation. The problem of global warming is that CO_2 traps longwave radiation, such as infrared radiation, and that traps heat. So this approach aims to negate that by *increasing* escape of longwave radiation from our atmosphere.

A fourth strategy is to fertilize the oceans, or specific areas of the oceans, with iron, which will promote growth of photosynthetic algae, which will capture carbon in their biomass. This has the benefit that it actually draws CO_2 out of the atmosphere, so it reverses the problem. It also pulls dissolved CO_2 from the oceans, which helps solve the problem of acidification of the oceans that arises from increased CO_2 in the atmosphere, which becomes increased dissolved CO_2 and carbonic acid and bicarbonate in the ocean.

A fifth possibility that has been proposed is to put one enormous mirror or thousands of small mirrors into space between the earth and the sun. "The mirror or mirrors would orbit at Lagrange point L1, a gravitationally stable point between the Earth and the sun that's about four times the distance from the Earth to the moon. The mirrors would barely be visible from Earth and would block just 1 percent to 2 percent of the sun's light." (Reference 5). It sounds cool, but it is apparently probably too expensive to be feasible.

It is also proposed to have a fleet of machines—and it would have to be a lot, like on the order of the size of the world's current fleet of cars and machines that burn oil—directly removing CO_2 from the atmosphere and trapping it with pressure underground or in some other way sequestering it. I am skeptical it could work. By the laws of thermodynamics and entropy, it would cost a great deal more energy to remove dispersed CO_2 from the atmosphere and concentrate it or purify it than the energy you got when you burned carbon fuels to produce the CO_2, which converted carbon from a concentrated form to a dilute form. So it is certainly far better to stop burning it than to burn it now on the theory that later we will use solar energy or some form of renewable energy to remove it from the atmosphere.

I would fertilize the oceans with iron right now. By removing CO_2, that would partially reverse global warming as well as ocean acidification. None of the other solutions address ocean acidification, and removing CO_2 from the atmosphere is the best way to reverse global warming since the other solutions involving reducing sunlight would leave in place some relative warming of the poles relative to the tropics.

Beyond that, we probably should start with the first three options above to reduce sunlight. Ultimately, though, we are stuck with living with a good portion of the global warming and its effects. The rise in CO_2 in the atmosphere is probably permanent, and nature will find a new equilibrium for that.

Besides those solutions we should:

- Tax carbon.
- Stop entirely government subsidies for oil, coal, and natural gas.
- Increase greatly subsidies for solar and wind power.
- Convert entirely to solar and wind power for electricity generation within 20 years, if not 10 years.
- Use solar power for space and water heating (or solar- or wind-generated hydrogen or methanol).
- Convert to hydrogen- or methanol-powered cars, buses, trains, and planes, and produce the hydrogen or methanol with electricity generated by renewable energy or otherwise with solar energy.

The first three of those steps could be taken immediately and would cost nothing compared to what we are doing now and would benefit our economy. The fourth would be largely a result of the first three policies and I think could be done in 10 years if we were committed. As to the fifth, using solar power for space and water heating is basically just putting black surfaces in the sunlight, so the technology is simple.

The last point you have probably heard little of. Electric battery cars seem to be the direction of the future. But the batteries take a half hour or more to recharge and have limited range, so they seem like a poor replacement for liquid fuel transportation. Hydrogen has the highest energy content to weight ratio. That is why NASA uses it for rocket fuel. Hydrogen-powered cars, buses, and even planes exist, and some Japanese car makers are still betting on hydrogen cars over electric cars.

Hydrogen can be made from water with electrolysis without any pollution if the electricity is made from solar or wind.

The only problem with hydrogen is it is a gas at normal temperatures and pressures, so it takes up a lot of space, or it has to be stored pressurized in heavy, mental containers.* There may be technical solutions developed to solve that storage problem. But one alternative is methanol. Methanol has the advantage that it is a liquid. Methanol can be made from hydrogen and CO_2, although at the cost of some energy.

Hydrogen can be converted to electricity by fuel cells, where it com-

---

* Maybe that is not such a large problem, since the same problem exists for natural gas, and we have natural-gas-powered buses and cars. But mostly natural gas is used for heating and in stationary sources. It does not work as well in vehicles.

bines with oxygen to directly produce electricity without combustion. That is more energetically efficient than burning hydrogen to power an internal combustion engine. Methanol can also be fuel for a fuel cell, though not as easily and efficiently as hydrogen.

So if it were up to me, I would focus on development of an energy system that uses hydrogen or methanol as the primary fuel to store energy.

One obvious step: Ban Cryptocurrencies and Blockchain Exchange

Cryptocurrencies, such as Bitcoin, and a new art fad called non-fungible tokens or NFTs, are examples of blockchain technology. Each transaction paid for with Bitcoin is compiled into a 'block' that requires a computationally demanding proof-of-ownership in order to allow everyone involved to be anonymous to each other but still have a verifiable transaction. This uses enormous amounts of computer power and electricity. It is estimated that the electricity use from cryptocurrencies resulted in emissions of 33.5 million metric tons of CO_2 in 2018 (Reference 6). The carbon emissions from cryptocurrencies are larger than the entire carbon emissions of Argentina, and, alone, without including any emissions from any other source, could raise global temperatures by 2°C by 2040 (References 6, 7). As far as I can see, the only purpose of cryptocurrencies in particular is that they allow anonymous financial transactions, which allows drug dealers and other criminals to launder their money and allows them and others to evade taxes. Blockchain technology is also used for non-fungible tokens (NFTs), which are holographic works of art whose ownership is tracked by the same technology. Their purpose is just that some consider them "cool" (ironic in that they heat the planet).

These have no legitimate purpose. They just help criminals do better financially and evade detection. On the "benefit" ledger, we have "helps criminals profit and evade detection and evade taxes." On the harm ledger, we have "helps criminals profit and evade detection and evade taxes and contributes massively to global warming." What to do? Gee, this is a tough call how to regulate that. Here's an idea: How about we just ban it?

So my proposal is to make it a crime for a U.S. resident or citizen anywhere in the world to conduct any transaction using blockchain technology and to have any account or asset that uses blockchain technology or to operate a computer server that has a blockchain account, and make it a crime for anyone anywhere in the world to operate a computer server that has a blockchain account for even one U.S. national person and or that tracks a transaction of even one U.S. national person or for anyone anywhere in the world to buy or sell any asset with a U.S.-based person via blockchain technology.

References

1. Wynes S and Nicholas KA. 2017 The climate mitigation gap: education and government recommendations miss the most effective individual actions *Environ. Res. Lett.* **12** 074024

2. Murtaugh PA and Schlax MG. 2009. Reproduction and the carbon legacies of individuals. *Global Environmental Change* 19:14-20. https://doi.org/10.1016/j.gloenvcha.2008.10.007

3. Reynolds, JL 2019. Solar geoengineering to reduce climate change: a review of governance proposals. *Proc. Roy. Soc. A.* 475:20190255. https://doi.org/10.1098/rspa.2019.0255

4. Timperley, Jocelyn. Sept. 24, 2020. China Dialogue. "How to stop global warming? The most controversial solutions explained." https://chinadialogue.net/en/climate/geoengineering-how-to-stop-global-warming-most-controversial-solutions-explained/

5. Kaufman, Rachel. Aug. 8, 2012. "Could Space Mirrors Stop Global Warming?" *Live Science.* https://www.livescience.com/22202-space-mirrors-global-warming.html Accessed April 21, 2021.

6. Li, Tiffany C.. March 15, 2021. "Bitcoins, NFTs and other crypto-fads are destroying our planet." *MSNBC.* https://www.msnbc.com/opinion/bitcoin-nfts-other-crypto-fads-are-destroying-our-planet-n1261139

7. Mora C, Rollins RL, et al. 2018. Bitoin emissions alone could push global warming above 2°C. *Nature Climate Change* 8:924-936. https://doi.org/10.1038541558-018-0321-8

Chapter 50

Depression and Unhappiness. Proposals If Happiness Were Our Goal

I do not regard depression as really mental illness. It is just extreme unhappiness.

The primary goal of our government, after ensuring the environment is protected for other species and humans, should be per capita domestic happiness, or maximal happiness and, more importantly, minimal unhappiness or depression. We are failing miserably at that. Western industrial societies have the highest levels of depression of any societies that have ever existed. Here are some facts about depression:

- Hunter-gatherer societies such as the !Kung San (the exclamation mark designates a click in their language) in southern Africa have almost no depression.
- The World Health Organization reports that overall prevalence of mental illness is 27 percent lower in low-to-middle income countries than in high-income countries (Reference 1).
- The Amish in the U.S. have depression rates less than half that of the rest of the U.S. population (References 2, 3).
- In high income countries, depression is 39 percent higher in urban settings than in rural settings (References 4, 5).
- The COVID lockdowns caused moderate-to-severe depression in the U.S. to go from 8.5% of the adult population pre-COVID to 27.8% during the lockdowns in the spring of 2020 (Chapter 5).

I view depression as primarily caused by loneliness and a feeling of lack of connection with other people. All of those factors above point to that conclusion. Hunter-gatherers have no depression because they live in bands of fewer than 200 people and they therefore know pretty well literally every person they encounter in their life. Nobody is a stranger. You live your whole life with people you grew up with and a large fraction of them are relatives. So you are stuck with each other and you better be nice to each other and get along.

The Amish, poorer nations, and rural areas in rich nations in the world today have the same characteristics, to a lesser extent. People are less likely to move away from where they were born, more likely to live with or near relatives, and generally know a larger fraction of the people they encounter each day.

The Amish and hunter-gatherers are also more stable societies. For hunter-gatherers especially, life essentially does not change over the course of your life. You do not need to find new skills and retrain for a new career because your old job no longer exists because of changes to the economy or technology. You do not need to learn the intricacies of a new word processing program or spreadsheet program or cell phone or TV provider every year. Once you learn what you need to live, that knowledge applies for the rest of your life. That is no longer true for us. That pace of change adds a large stress to our lives and contributes to our unhappiness and depression.

Fast pace of life equates to stress and makes us unhappy. Feeling there is not enough time to get done everything you have to get done does not promote happiness. And that explains the differences above also. Life is slower for hunter-gatherers and traditional societies like the Amish than it is for us. It is also somewhat slower in poorer nations than richer. And it is slower in rural areas than urban areas. Studies have shown people in urban areas literally walk faster and talk on the phone faster than people in rural areas.

So depression is caused basically by loneliness and fought by increasing your interactions, especially face-to-face interactions, with people who care about you and, even more importantly, with people you care about. That is, I have found that perhaps the best way to fight my tendency to depression is to get out of myself and focus on people and things I care about instead of on myself—in other words, to give love, instead of worrying about receiving it.

If depression is primarily caused by the lack of positive social interaction with people who care about us, the COVID lockdowns were perfectly designed to maximize depression, and that is the effect they had: Prevent face-to-face interaction with our social support systems as much as possible by closing schools, houses of worship, restaurants and bars, and health clubs. Require people to work from home so they do not interact socially with coworkers. To the extent you cannot prevent face-to-face interaction, mandate people wear masks. This accomplishes a few goals: It makes it harder to recognize people, much harder to send and receive non-verbal communication, which is the majority of our communication, and harder to see whether someone is smiling. It also neatly provides a reminder (as if we needed one) that we are in a "crisis" and that this is the worst year of our lives. In fact, that is purported as a benefit of mask mandates. I do not think it is a benefit.

Another goal mask wearing accomplishes is to divide us from each other. We are taught the message that anyone resistant to wearing a mask—who is, in fact, just trying to live his life the way he always has and the way he was raised—is a terrible, ignorant person who is trying to kill you.[*]

You literally could not have designed policies more perfectly to maximize depression. And indeed, those policies managed to take the society with the highest depression rate in human history and triple that depression rate.

So what would I propose to reduce depression and maximize happiness?

Forbid mask wearing.

Actually, I guess I would allow people to wear masks if they want to, in the interest of personal liberty, but I would teach the data that shows mask wearing has little or no effect on the spread of COVID or other infectious diseases—and teach that we want to see your beautiful face! It would not be terrible if we actually forbade mask wearing, and that would certainly cut depression and therefore cut suicides and have a positive effect on average happiness levels.

Do the opposite of every policy of the lockdowns:
Go to church more, not less.
Go out to restaurants with friends more, not less.
Shake hands and hug more, not less.
Get married and have a big wedding.
If a loved one dies, have a funeral and invite everyone to it.
Meet in person more, not less.

---

[*] I mean it when I say these were the goals of the mask mandates and the other mandates of the lockdowns. We have seen that they had probably no effect at all on the number of COVID deaths; but they tripled depression and divided us from one another and increased hatred and blaming of each other. Either the architects of these policies were completely incompetent, or the depression and the division and hatred of each other were the real goals.

Work together with your colleagues if possible, not isolated at home.

Go to a health club more, not less.

Travel more, not less.

Mandate everyone wear a name tag in public.

I'm serious. This was famously proposed by Kramer in an episode of *Seinfeld*.

It does not have to be your full name. It can be your first name only, your full name, or a nickname, or a joke or non-name if you do not want to play along. If you want to be addressed as Mr. Smith or Ms. Smith or Mrs. Smith instead of by your first name, you could put it that way on your name tag, and that might be a good signal to others of how you want to be addressed.

I am serious about mandating this. Maybe even have a one dollar fine if you are caught in public without your name tag.

People could add additional information of "I want to meet people. Please approach me." Or "Please leave me alone. I do not want to talk today."

This would be great for me because I am terrible about remembering names. It would also make it easier to strike up conversations with strangers and promote that, which promotes forming new friendships.

A name-tag mandate would be actually a smaller infringement on personal liberty than a mask mandate, in that masks are uncomfortable and make it harder to breathe, whereas name tags are not. Moreover, if you do not want to reveal your identity you can use a joke name or non-name.

A name tag mandate would increase happiness, rather than decreasing it, as the mask mandate does.

Shut down the internet for 24 hours every Sunday. No e-mail, no web browsing.

This would slow our lives. It might promote talking to each other and social interaction. There is no question it would increase happiness. The major downside is Mark Zuckerberg would make less money. Boo hoo.

Forbid transmission of television signals for 24 hours on Wednesdays.

Similar to the internet ban. Would force us to get off of screens and do something better for ours bodies, minds, and spirit, like talking to someone, reading a book, playing tennis, going for a walk, or gardening. I'm not proposing it for the same day as the internet ban because (1) we have NFL games on Sundays!, and (2) it would be too much of a shock to forbid all visual entertainment on the same day.

Forbid wearing ear buds or ear phones in public on Wednesdays.

Would make it easier to approach people and have a conversation. I am not suggesting we do it every day since I suppose people have a right to isolate themselves if they want, but we can nudge them out of it one day per week.

Mandate everyone go outside for a walk of at least 15 minutes between 2:00 and 3:00 in the afternoon, and mandate businesses allow workers a break of at least 15 minutes in this time frame to take the walk.

Walking is the best exercise there is, and almost everyone can do it. Both exercise and being outdoors are great for our moods. This would have a significant positive effect on happiness. And by requiring everyone to take their walk outside at about the same time, everyone will be there, you can strike up conversations with people, you can meet your neighbors, you can make new friends. All of those factors of the exercise, being outside, and increased socialization would promote happiness.

The only drawback is maybe in urban areas if everyone has to be outside in that hour it may be too crowded, especially in downtowns. So practically you might have to make allowances and let people take their walk at another time and just encourage, but not mandate, a specific hour.

The reason for specifying a specific hour is to promote social interaction, and also to promote compliance. If we just say, "Take a walk sometime," people may not comply, and there will not be much greater opportunity to meet people. But if we say it has to be 2:00 to 3:00 in the afternoon, you will have a greater chance to meet people and you can notice if a neighbor or coworker is never walking at that time.

You can be exempted with a note from your doctor saying you cannot walk. Otherwise, I encourage people to narc on your neighbor. Call the government and say, "Hey, I have not seen my neighbor Tim walking in two days. Please send him a ticket for $20." (That's a joke. Sort of.)

This would actually be very akin to the custom of a siesta in the Spanish-speaking world, except ours would be more active with a walk.

Mandate dog ownership.

OK, I'm not serious about this one. You know yourself, and if you do not want to own a dog, maybe owning a dog would not make you happier. But for most people, owning a dog is just about the easiest way to get happier. Cats also, but to a lesser extent.

But I would encourage dog or cat ownership and inform people of the research that people who own dogs, and to a lesser extent cats, are happier than the petless people. So if the goal is happiness, get a dog.

I would also require apartments to accept tenants with dogs or cats (maybe not snakes though) with no penalties or restrictions.

References:

1. Kessler, RC, Aguilar-Gaxiola S, et al. 2009. The global burden of mental disorders: An update from the WHO World Mental Health (WMH) Surveys, *Epidemiol Psichiatr Soc.* 18(1): 23–33.

2. Lambert, K. G. 2006. Rising rates of depression in today's society: Consideration of the roles of effort-based rewards and enhanced resilience in day-to-day functioning. *Neuroscience & Biobehavioral Reviews* 30(4), 497-510.

3. Furman, R., & Bender, K. 2003. The social problem of depression: a multi-theoretical analysis. *Journal of Sociology and Social Welfare* 30(3), 123-137.

4. Peen J, Schoevers RA, Beekman AT, Dekker J. 2010. The current status of urban-rural differences in psychiatric disorders. *Acta Psychiatr Scand.* 121(2):84-93. https://doi.org/10.1111/j.1600-0447.2009.01438.x

5. Haseltine, Eric. 2016. "Amish Asthma Rates Offer Clues to Preventing Mental Illness." *Psychology Today.* https://www.psychologytoday.com/us/blog/long-fuse-big-bang/201612/amish-asthma-rates-offer-clues-preventing-mental-illness

Chapter 51

Proposals for Other Problems

Income Inequality and Inequality of Opportunity

I   Progressive taxation is fine and a good thing. But first, we should try to insure the market tends toward equal incomes, meaning higher incomes for lower and middle class working people by the force of the market, rather than by government mandate.

Wages respond to supply and demand, just like everything else. When the population declines, which is to say the number of workers declines, wages for lower class workers go up. Employers have to compete for unskilled or less skilled labor, and they compete by raising wages.

The Black Death in the Middle Ages resulted in a decrease in the population, and wages went up dramatically (Reference 1). It was the best event in history for peasants and lower class people—if you were not one of the people who died.

When the Mariel Boatlift occurred in 1980, resulting in 125,000 Cubans emigrating to Florida, wages in Miami dropped precipitously. That is supply and demand. There were more workers, so the wages for workers fell.

Research shows people in smaller generations have higher average wages than people in larger generations. If you come of age and enter the workforce in a small generation, there are fewer people competing for entry level jobs, so you are more likely to get a job and employers have to pay entry level jobs more. And the interesting thing is, those higher wages are not a one-time thing that occurs only in your first few years in the workforce; they persist for the entire careers of people in smaller generations. The same is true of people who enter the workforce in a good economy versus a bad economy. Those entering work in a good economy make a higher starting wage, and people's wages tend to go up a fairly fixed percentage as they progress through their careers, so that higher starting wage persists for the entire working life of those fortunate enough to enter the workforce during good economic times. (Incidentally, that is one of the crimes we have committed against young people, especially those who graduated from college or high school and entered the workforce in 2020. We deliberately crushed the economy, ruining their job prospects and incomes at the start of their careers, and that misfortune will continue to harm their wages for their entire careers.)

So the best thing we can do to reduce income inequality and raise the wages of low income workers is to decrease population and especially to decrease immigration. Contrary to what the media would have you believe, immigrants *do* compete with Americans for jobs and lower the wages of American workers, especially lower income workers. That is the reason business loves immigration—it decreases what it has to pay for labor. That is not true just for unskilled labor but also for skilled labor. The tech industry is bound and determined to bring in as many Indian software engineers as possible, or outsource the work to India, in order to cut wages for American software engineers. Why do you think the U.S. medical community requires that to practice medicine in the U.S. you have to have attended a residency program in the U.S.? It is not because German- and Canadian-educated doctors are incompetent. It is to reduce the number of physicians in the U.S. and thereby keep physician pay high. That is part of the reason any industry has licensing requirements—to restrict entry into the job to keep wages high.

Likewise, foreign trade or importing goods and services without any tariffs on them decreases U.S. wages because it makes U.S. workers compete with the other 7 billion people on earth for jobs, instead of just with Americans, and most of those people are willing to work for less than Americans.

On the immigration point, sometimes people argue we have a moral obligation to admit immigrants because we should love everyone equally and it is bigotry or bias to favor Americans over foreigners. No. It is perfectly ethical to favor your family over non-family. It is not immoral or favoritism to pay for your child's college education and not distribute that money equally among every college student in the U.S. We all favor our family over non-family and friends over strangers. If we have a job to hand out, and our child or friend wants the job, if they are reasonably well qualified, we give it to them. We do not feel obligated to search for someone who may be slightly better qualified. Likewise, it is perfectly appropriate, and I would argue more ethical, to care more for your own countrymen over foreigners. I would argue it is more ethical to give a job to an American than to search the world over and give it to an immigrant who might be marginally more qualified and bring the immigrant into our country. Love your family over non-family, friends over strangers, and countrymen over foreigners.*

So to equalize income in the U.S.:

1. Increase trade barriers and decrease trade with the rest of the world, so more products are made in the U.S. and more services are performed in the U.S., and wages can rise by not having to compete so much with lower paid foreign labor in foreign countries.

2. Decrease immigration. I would allow zero legal or illegal immigration except our fair share of humanitarian refugees and all spouses of U.S. citizens. But even if you don't go that far, decreasing immigration by any amount increases U.S. wages at all levels, especially at lower income levels.

3. Decrease the birth rate in the U.S. In addition to decreasing immigration, decreasing the birth rate also tends to decrease population, and that increases wages and improves income equality. For my proposals on how to decrease the birth rate, see Chapter 47.

Racism

Tax Billionaires for Reparations Payments to Native Americans and Black Descendants of Slaves.

There are obviously plenty of other things that can and should be done to fight racism, but this is a proposal I have not heard others make.

Native Americans and Blacks who are descendants of slaves have suffered far more discrimination than other groups and are where we should focus our efforts. Native Americans lived here and we stole their land from them and then committed cultural genocide against them. Slaves were brought here against their will and then worked without pay and tortured and killed with impunity. Then, after slavery ended, we did not treat them much better for about 100 years.

Other groups, such as Hispanics, Asians, and Blacks who are immigrants from Africa or the descendants of voluntary immigrants from Africa, are in a different category. I do not believe any of those groups have suffered nearly as much discrimination, and furthermore they

---

* I am aware that economists argue that immigration and free trade do not affect wages. To do so, they have to construct elaborate arguments that by some magic the law of supply and demand applies in every other area of economics but not in the labor market. I choose to believe the data and the basic logic that the law of supply and demand applies to labor.

came here voluntarily.

We have about 800 billionaires in the U.S. and they hold $4.3 trillion in wealth. We could have a 100% wealth tax on wealth above $1 billion and raise more than $3.3 trillion from that group, and they would not even feel it. They would still have $1 billion each, which seems plenty to me.

According to the U.S. Census Bureau, 13.4% of the U.S. population is Black or African American alone, 1.3% is American Indian or Alaska Native alone, and 2.8% are two or more races present. That adds up to 17.5% of our 328 million people, or 57.4 million. If we taxed wealth over $1 billion at 100% and divided that $3.3 trillion among the 57.4 million Blacks and Native Americans, it would be $57,491 per person. If you gave it only to the adults, it would be something like $75,000 per person. That would be a start on reparations. It is not sufficient; but it would be something.

The benefit to harm ratio of this would be something like 70,000 to 1. The payment to each of the 57 million Blacks and Native Americans probably is as much or more of a benefit to that person as the loss of billions is a harm to one of the 800 billionaires when he is still left with $1 billion.

This proposal addresses one of the arguments against reparations or one of the arguments why reparations are politically difficult, which is that whites today do not feel like they are racist and do not feel they are responsible for slavery that occurred more than 150 years ago, so they do not want to take an economic hit to pay for reparations. By taxing billionaires, it is only 800 people taking an economic hit, and they can handle it without any pain.

Instead of a 100% one-time tax I would make it a 25% annual tax on wealth over $1 billion, on top of their income tax obligations. A 25% tax would allow them to borrow against their holdings to pay the tax and sell their holdings in an orderly way. I would anticipate after five years or so there would not be much wealth over a billion left to tax; but if there is, great, we can continue to make smaller annual reparations payments.

One could also change this proposal by, instead of using the $3.3 trillion for reparations to Blacks and Native Americans, hand it out to everyone. That would result in about $10,000 per person, or maybe $13,000 per person if you only paid adults. But I would propose using the money for reparations.

Diabetes and Excessive Sugar Consumption

Ban sale of soda pop, both with sugar and with artificial sweeteners.

I am convinced that stuff is every bit as bad for your health as cigarettes, and worse for your mood and mental health. When you drink one, you get a quick sugar high and dopamine hit, but that is followed by a trough of greater magnitude than the peak. And my recollection is that studies suggest soda with artificial sweeteners is about as bad as the sugared stuff for raising weight and diabetes risk, although I have not looked into it for this book. So I would ban both sugary soda and soda with artificial sweeteners.

I don't actually feel strongly about this and probably would not actually want to ban the sale of pop. But if we really intend to promote health and promote duration of life, banning soda pop would have far greater positive effect and be a smaller infringement on our liberty than a mask mandate, let alone stay-at-home orders or closing churches and every gathering place.

Suicides and Drug and Alcohol Abuse Deaths

Here my proposals would be the same as those to reduce depression (Chapter 49). If you reduce depression, people will be less likely to kill themselves and less likely to abuse drugs and alcohol.

I would note, though, that reinstating prohibition of alcohol sales and possession would decrease alcohol abuse and probably have a net positive effect on our health. I would still oppose it as infringing our liberty and because most of us can drink responsibly and alcohol can increase our happiness in loosening inhibitions at social gatherings. But reinstating prohibition would be a much more sensible and less destructive policy than the COVID lockdowns were (as would literally almost anything you could propose short of genocide or a pointless and destructive war quite a bit worse than Vietnam). It probably would extend average life expectancy and at least arguably improve average quality of life and would be a smaller infringement on our liberties than the lockdowns have been.

Police Violence
Fire bad cops

My solution to police misconduct is simply to fire bad cops. Making them attend yet another seminar on diversity and not being a racist is not going to change anything. You improve the cops simply by weeding out the bad ones. If you keep firing the bad ones, pretty soon you don't have many bad ones. Occasionally you make a mistake and hire a bad cop, but you figure it out soon and fire him or her. And the culture changes. As cops figure out that they will be fired for misbehavior, they start behaving better.

It is almost impossible to fire a cop, at least in Minnesota and it seems everywhere, and the reason is mostly mandatory arbitration. Some police officer beats a 15-year-old black kid for no reason, and the city tries to fire him, and it goes to arbitration, and the arbitrator says, basically, "Well, he didn't kill the kid. And there was another cop in the state two years ago who beat a black kid for no reason, and the city there did not fire him. So you cannot fire this one." Those were pretty much the facts when Richfield, Minnesota, tried to fire Officer Nate Kinsey in 2015 after he was captured on video striking a Somali-American teen in the head. Officer Kinsey had also previously been disciplined for excessive use of force. The city of Richfield tried to fire him. An arbitrator overturned his dismissal. Richfield appealed all the way to the state supreme court, which upheld the arbitrator's decision.

Similarly, the Minneapolis *StarTribune* on April 3, 2021, front page, reported that in 2016 in Minneapolis "two officers were caught on camera punching a handcuffed and apparently intoxicated man. Both were fired but won their job back through arbitration."

Any of us working in the private sector can be fired for any reason or no reason, so most of us do not see why police officers cannot be fired, it seems, unless they are actually convicted (not just charged) with a crime at least as serious as manslaughter.

I assumed police unions were the source of the problem, that they had negotiated these mandatory arbitration clauses into their contracts. But it turns out in Minnesota at least that state law *requires* arbitration before you can fire any public employee. So even if you could get the police union to agree to remove the mandatory arbitration, you could not do it. State law has to change. And, embarrassingly for me as a Democrat, Democrats in our state legislature refused to change that law even after George Floyd was murdered by the Minneapolis police and we had international protests and rioting. Republicans wanted to change that law, but they wanted to remove arbitration for all public employees, not just police, and Democrats opposed that. Personally, I don't care much one way or the other whether teachers or other public employees can be fired more easily, although I would generally oppose that change probably, but it is essential that we be able to fire cops without arbitration and well worth giving it up for all public employees if that is the only way to get rid of arbitration for police.

I also think Democrats did not really even want to remove mandatory arbitration for police, even if Republicans had offered to keep it for all other public employees. Democrats never pushed for that or made an issue of it. They seemed to just want the issue to go away as soon as possible with no publicity. And Republicans were not acting in any better faith. They did not really care whether police could be fired without arbitration; what they cared about was being able to fire teachers and all public employees, and they were using the George Floyd killing as an excuse to achieve that goal and maybe embarrass Democrats for opposing the proposal.

In every city, I would give the mayor, the city council, and the police chief each independent authority to fire any police officer for basically any reason, except because the police officer opposed you politically or some other clearly wrongful reason. If an officer is fired for a wrongful reason he can sue for damages and maybe to get his job back. But he does not get to keep his job and collect pay while the case is heard. And he has to have been fired for a truly wrongful reason. He cannot argue that "there was some other cop who did something just as bad and was not fired, so you cannot fire me."

References:

1. Henry George, *Progress and Poverty; An Inquiry into the Cause of Industrial Depressions and of Increase of Want with Increase of Wealth, The Remedy.* Garden City, NY: Doubleday, Page, & Co. 1912. Pages 132-133.

Part 8

Chapter 52

Conclusion

It is not a matter of legitimate disagreement whether the lockdowns were a mistake. It is not a matter of legitimate disagreement whether an approach of no mandatory restrictions at all, but just educating people on their risk from COVID and on what modifications to their behavior would reduce that risk and then letting them decide for themselves whether and how to modify their behavior, would have been a better approach than lockdowns. Lockdowns have no advantage at all. If you think life is better than death, a long life is better than a shorter life, happiness is better than depression, more money is better than less, education is better than ignorance, child abuse and domestic abuse are bad things, and more personal freedom is better than less, then you agree the lockdowns were a mistake.

Why did we do it? Why did we turn this molehill of COVID-19 into a mountain that justified sacrificing our happiness, our liberty, and the interests of our children for a over year in a futile attempt to reduce deaths from a natural viral upper respiratory tract infection moderately more deadly than the flu?

I think a large part is a desire for our lives to have meaning, to be part of a great cause and great struggle, and to be together with everyone in our society in that cause. We live these wealthy, lazy lives, playing video games and watching entertainment on demand, and we are not asked to make any sacrifices for a cause greater than ourselves. We are jealous of previous generations that marched for civil rights and in some cases were killed fighting for civil rights in the 50's and 60's and that fought totalitarianism and evil in World War II. Their lives had meaning; ours too often it seems do not.

So I think when our leaders called on us to sacrifice for a cause greater than ourselves, to prevent COVID deaths, we were eager to accept the challenge. The problem was, it was a stupid cause. It is a natural cause of death that almost exclusively strikes the sick elderly near death anyway. And it is not that much deadlier than the flu. And our sacrifices had no effect on COVID deaths anyway, but caused enormous needless suffering in depression and deaths due to suicide and drug overdose that resulted in vastly more lost time of life than COVID deaths prevented and vastly more lost time of life than COVID itself. And we imposed enormous sacrifices on our children for no purpose and no benefit to them, or to anyone else for that matter, and without their consent.

The irony is, we have a cause that demands our sacrifices and united common effort. In fact, <u>it is the greatest challenge humanity has ever faced</u>, a much greater cause and challenge than even the civil rights movement or defeating the Nazis. That cause is saving the earth from us for the benefit of future generations of humans and for the benefit of every species of life other than us, and actually for our own benefit too. In particular, we have two crises: the first and greater is mass extinction caused mostly by habitat loss, and the second is global warming caused by greenhouse gas emissions. Extinction is irrevocable. We will never get these species back. Global warming is mostly irrevocable too. Even if you do not care about other species, mass extinctions and global warming will make humanity far poorer and will reduce human numbers by at least 80%. Those are worse consequences than we ever faced in World War II or even with slavery and legalized racial discrimination. And the problems of Naziism and civil rights, if they were not solved at one time, could still be solved later. Extinction is irrevocable. It cannot be solved later.

So I would call us to abandon our misguided sacrifices and mission to fight COVID-19 and take up what is actually the greatest challenge ever facing humanity in our 100,000 year history, which happens to face us right now. (Or really the two greatest challenges, if you separate extinctions and global warming.) If we want meaning in our lives and to face a great challenge, we are the most blessed generations ever. Let's grab on to that meaning and rise up to that challenge.

Acknowledgement

As with my first book, *Ending War in Our Lifetime*, the person I want to thank is my good friend Horst Loeblich, for his encouragement, editorial suggestions, and support.

About the Author

Hugh McTavish is the founder and Executive Director of COVID Sanity (COVID-Sanity.org). He is a Ph.D. biochemist and immunologist and also a patent attorney. He has authored 18 refereed scientific journal articles and is the inventor on 21 U.S. patents. He has started two pharmaceutical companies off of his own inventions—IGF Oncology, LLC, for a targeted drug for cancer, and Squarex, LLC, for a treatment that prevents cold sores or oral herpes virus outbreaks. The cancer drug invention came as an outgrowth of his having cancer. It was an improvement on the drugs and treatment he received as a cancer patient. The cold sore treatment he invented in order to treat his own frequent cold sores and originally tested on himself. Dr. McTavish's previous books are *Ending War in Our Lifetime: A Concrete, Realistic Plan* and *Wild Plants of the Minneapolis/St. Paul Area: A Field Guide to Trees, Shrubs, and Wildflowers*. He lives near St. Paul, Minnesota.

Made in the USA
Monee, IL
24 September 2021